# Bending Genre

# Bending Genre

## Essays on Creative Nonfiction

Edited by
Margot Singer
and
Nicole Walker

Bloomsbury Academic
An imprint of Bloomsbury Publishing Inc

B L O O M S B U R Y
NEW YORK • LONDON • OXFORD • NEW DELHI • SYDNEY

**Bloomsbury Academic**
An imprint of Bloomsbury Publishing Inc

| 1385 Broadway | 50 Bedford Square |
|---|---|
| New York | London |
| NY 10018 | WC1B 3DP |
| USA | UK |

www.bloomsbury.com

**BLOOMSBURY and the Diana logo are trademarks of Bloomsbury Publishing Plc**

First published in 2013
Reprinted 2013, 2014, 2015, 2016

**Library of Congress Cataloging-in-Publication Data**
Bending genre : essays on creative nonfiction / edited by Margot Singer and
Nicole Walker.
pages cm
Includes bibliographical references and index.
ISBN 978-1-4411-8065-0 (hardcover : alk. paper) — ISBN 978-1-4411-2329-9
(pbk. : alk. paper) 1. Creative nonfiction–Authorship. 2. Essay–Authorship.
I. Singer, Margot. II. Walker, Nicole.
PN145.B4285 2013
808.02–dc23

| ISBN: HB: | 978-1-4411-8065-0 |
|---|---|
| PB: | 978-1-4411-2329-9 |
| ePDF: | 978-1-4411-9526-5 |
| ePub: | 978-1-4411-1725-0 |

Typeset by Newgen Imaging Systems Pvt Ltd, Chennai, India
Printed and bound in the United States of America

# Contents

Part III   Unconventions

# Acknowledgments

The following essays first appeared in other publications (at times with different titles and/or in different form): "It Is What It Is," by Eula Biss, in the *Seneca Review*; "On the EEO Genre Sheet," by Jenny Boully, in *1913*; Robin Hemley, "Study Questions for the Essay at Hand: A Speculative Essay" in *Ninth Letter*; Wayne Koestenbaum, "Play-Doh Fun Factory Poetics" in *Salmagundi*; "Split Tone," by Lee Martin in *Brevity*; "Hermes Goes to College," by Michael Martone, in *upstreet*; "Ostrakons at Amphipolis, Postcards from Chicago: Thucydides and the Invention and Deployment of Lyric History," by Michael Martone, in *Ascent*; "Lions and Tigers and Bears, Oh My!: Courage and Creative Nonfiction," by Brenda Miller, in the *Writer's Chronicle*; "Why Some Hybrids Work and Other Don't," by Lia Purpura, in *DIAGRAM*; "42 Tattoos," by David Shields, in the *Village Voice*; "On Convention," by Margot Singer, in the *Writer's Chronicle*.

# Introduction

## Margot Singer and Nicole Walker

*An artistic movement, albeit an organic and as-yet-unstated one, is forming. What are its key components? . . . Randomness, openness to accident and serendipity, spontaneity; artistic risk, emotional urgency and intensity, reader/viewer participation; an overly literal tone, as if a reporter were viewing a strange culture; plasticity of form, pointillism; criticism as autobiography; self-reflexivity, self-ethnography, anthropological autobiography; a blurring (to the point of invisibility) of any distinction between fiction and nonfiction: the lure and blur of the real.*[1]

With these words David Shields throws down the gauntlet in *Reality Hunger: A Manifesto*. The novel is dead, Shields claims. Bored by the artifice of fiction, writers are "smuggling . . . larger and larger chunks of 'reality' into their work."[2] The burgeoning literary genre of creative nonfiction—including lyric and personal essays, narrative journalism and memoir—stands at the vanguard of this movement. Hybrid, innovative, and unconventional, creative nonfiction is the preeminent expression of the blurry reality of our times.

The blurriness of the lines between the genres, of course, has provoked much anxiety and debate. How much "creative" license can nonfiction writers take? Is it permissible to create composite characters, consolidate events, or reconstruct details that have been forgotten or can't be known? Can you alter the facts to protect the innocent—or to improve the rhythm of a sentence or intensify the drama of a scene? Hardly a year goes by without a fresh scandal over a phony memoir by a fraudster like Margaret Seltzer or James Frey. Essayists and fact-checkers face off.

Unfortunately, the fracas over the *ethics* of nonfiction has sidelined important questions of literary *form*—and these are the questions that motivate this book. We all know that something crucial happens to how we read a story when we understand that its events really occurred, that the people and places described really exist. There's no question that there's a special intimacy that comes from recognizing the voice of an essay or memoir as the author's, from listening to that author think and wonder, reminisce, confess, reflect. But what distinguishes creative nonfiction as a genre, we propose, is not *only* the truth-value of the writing. It's the ways in which the raw material of "reality" is transformed into literary art.

Literature has long encompassed a broader field than poetry and fiction. The art of what we now call "creative nonfiction" stretches back to the confessions of St Augustine, the letters of Lucius Seneca, the aphorisms of Francis Bacon, the meditations of Samuel Johnson and Michel de Montaigne. Its antecedents include Plutarch's consolations, Kenko's "Essays in Idleness," Jorge Luis Borges' lectures, Virginia Woolf's reveries, the "nonfiction novels" of Truman Capote and Norman Mailer, the "new journalism" of Joan Didion, Tom Wolfe, and Gay Talese. Since the memoir heyday of the 1990s, creative nonfiction has emerged as the most vital and innovative area on the contemporary American literary scene. Even as literary fiction and poetry are increasingly marginalized, best-selling authors such as Dave Eggers, Nick Flynn, and Susan Orlean are pushing the memoir in poetic, self-reflexive directions and roaming far from the journalistic beaten path. From Sei Shōnagon's 1,000-year-old lists to the loosely linked fragments of Maggie Nelson's *Bluets*, creative nonfiction continues to break new ground.

It is perhaps surprising, given its long history and popularity, that creative nonfiction has garnered such scant attention from literary scholars, critics, and theorists. Early efforts by John Hellmann, Eric Heyne, Barbara Lounsbery, Chris Anderson, and others in the 1980s and 1990s have not led to sustained scholarship in this field.[3] While recent work in autobiography/ life writing studies and narratology has made important interdisciplinary contributions to our understanding of the function and meaning of storytelling, from a literary/critical perspective, creative nonfiction remains virtually unexplored.

As writers and teachers of creative nonfiction, we think it's time to move beyond the tired arguments over truth-telling toward a more sophisticated conversation about this protean genre's possibilities and forms. In formal terms, how does creative nonfiction work? In what ways does it splice together elements of other genres to create a hybrid—and what elements are uniquely its own? What do we make of essays that take on structures typically found in poetry, reference books, music, or interactive games? What meanings are made when essays are built from fragments or assembled with the associative logic of collage? How do nonfiction writers negotiate narrative time, white space, lyric compression, exposition, metaphor, and point of view? In short: what distinguishes creative nonfiction from other kinds of literary prose?

In 2007 we invited fellow writers David Shields and Nick Flynn to join us in presenting a panel on genre-bending creative nonfiction for the Association of Writers and Writing Programs (AWP) conference in Atlanta. In the years since then, we have continued the conversation, exploring creative nonfiction's hybridism, structures, and techniques. This book is the result. Our contributors are experienced teachers and writers at the cutting edge of creative nonfiction. Their essays not only push our thinking, but also model the innovative forms of writing they discuss. They speak to us as writers in terms that we hope will inspire, provoke, and engage.

Creative nonfiction is commonly defined as fact-based writing that uses the techniques of fiction to bring its stories to life. As Lee Gutkind has put it: "Ultimately, the primary goal of the creative nonfiction writer is to communicate information, just like a reporter, but to shape it in a way that reads like fiction."[4] Creative nonfiction certainly shares with fiction the elements of detail, image, description, dialogue, and scene. Like fiction, creative nonfiction strives to "show, not tell," to appeal not just to readers' intellects but to their hearts and senses, to put the reader "there." Yet Gutkind's definition seems too limited. Surely the goal of creative nonfiction is not just to "communicate information," but also to bring the reader on a journey of discovery as we explore our selves and our experience of the world. And what about the wide range of essays whose emphasis is on idea rather than story, on meditation rather than reportage? What about creative nonfiction that feels more like poetry than fiction, relying on lyric compression rather than narrative to achieve its aims?

We organize our textbooks and courses into tidy generic categories, but literary genres are notoriously difficult to theorize or define. We think of genres as fixed and clearly bounded when in fact transgression is the norm. Indeed, we would argue that there is no such thing as *non*-hybrid genre. Certainly poems typically have line breaks and prose does not and plays are primarily made of dialogue. But the categories are not mutually exclusive. Prose, like drama, is grounded in dialogue and scene. Poems can be narrative; essays can be lyric; novels can be written in verse. Novels and stories may in general rely more heavily on narrative, essays on exposition, poetry on the lyric, and plays on dramatization, but ultimately narration and exposition and lyricism and dramatization are *rhetorical modes* employed by every literary genre.[5] To say as Gutkind does that creative nonfiction uses the techniques of fiction may be a description, but it is not a definition. It doesn't tell us anything about what makes creative nonfiction unique. Creative nonfiction is fact-based by definition, yes. But, as readers, we distinguish one genre from another on the basis of formal conventions, not content. For example, the conventions of journalism (third person voice, neutral tone, "inverted pyramid" structure, etc.) signal that a piece of writing is "true," objective, grounded in reported facts. By contrast, a poem (with its line breaks, lyrical language, emphasis on image, etc.) may well be as fact-based as any historical or newspaper account, and yet we still don't read it as "nonfiction." Memoirs may read like novels, as Gutkind says, but novels read like memoirs, too. Indeed, since its earliest days, the novel has created verisimilitude by appropriating nonfiction's forms (think of Aphra Behn and Samuel Richardson's epistolary novels, or Daniel Defoe's faux autobiography, *Robinson Crusoe*). Too often we confuse form with substance as a result. As the Israeli writer Amos Oz told the *New Yorker's* David Remnick in a 2004 interview, "James Joyce took the trouble, if I am not mistaken, to measure the precise distance from Bloom's basement entrance to the street above. In *Ulysses*, it is exact, and yet it is called fiction. But when a journalist writes, 'A cloud of uncertainty hovers' . . . this is called fact!"[6] To writers like Oz, all narrative is "real."

Genres, in sum, are not fixed categories with clear-cut boundaries, but constellations of rhetorical modes and formal structures grounded in varying degrees of fact. Genres are rooted in convention. They are also shape-shifters, in a continual state of flux. As Tzvetan Todorov has put it: "A new genre is always the transformation of one of several old genres: by inversion, by displacement, by combination."[7] In Part I of *Bending Genre*, we argue that creative nonfiction does not simply borrow elements from fiction and poetry, but bends and recombines them to make a hybrid that perpetually troubles and transcends generic bounds. According to the *Oxford English Dictionary*, the word "hybrid" in its original usage referred to the crossbreeding of domesticated pigs with wild boar. In literature, too, hybridization infuses wild energy into familiar forms. The hybrid is transgressive, polyvalent, queer. The hybrid challenges categories and assumptions, exposing the underlying conventions of representation that often seem so "natural" we hardly notice them at all.

Part II of *Bending Genre* moves from a discussion of the meaning and implications of hybridity to an examination of innovative structure in creative nonfiction. Here we consider how essays make meaning through various narrative and non-narrative forms. What happens when we abandon the linear structure of story for branching tangents, digressions, and associative leaps? We examine the strange cases of essays that take the (fictional) shape of a concrete (nonfictional) form, such as a list, an outline, a contributor's note, a computer game, a map, a Tweet. We look at how essays manipulate time, image, and language to represent emotionally charged events. We explore how the essay, like a musical theme and variations, circles and probes, varies its rhythm, modulates from major to minor key.

Part III of *Bending Genre* considers how creative nonfiction both breaks and builds on literary conventions to create its own, new forms. In this section, we probe these "unconventions," including the use of first versus third person narration in nonfiction, questions of appropriation, the literary qualities of exposition, the meanings created by fragmentation and white space, the paradoxical operation of metaphor. We explore how essays toggle between research and reflection and make imaginative leaps. Far more than mere stylistic devices, these "unconventions" give writers of creative nonfiction fresh approaches to their material, new ways to help the reader see the world anew.

As readers, we tend to take realistic narrative for granted. We treat as "natural" the linear chronology of story, the way time is dilated or compressed, the artifice of dialogue (so different from recorded speech), the highly selective filtering and reordering of the infinite details of the world. But rather than creating a transparent window onto reality, unconventional nonfiction tends to highlight the slipperiness of representation. It raises fundamental questions about the nature of memory and storytelling, "reality" and "truth." To these innovators, writing about the self, reporting facts, and telling stories becomes an exercise in existentialism, ontology, and epistemology. What differentiates these contemporary philosophers from Wittgenstein, Kant, and Hegel, though, is that their philosophies are told through compelling narratives and lyric prose.

Each contributor to this book brings a distinct approach and writerly personality. Some of the essays are analytical and theoretical; they mark the first substantive attempts to create a poetics of creative nonfiction. Other essays take a more playful or innovative form, modeling the very techniques and approaches they explore. Our essays offer a wide variety of perspectives on the historical trajectory of innovative nonfiction, reflections on the challenges of writing across generic categories, and meditations on nonfiction's wide-ranging possibilities and genre-bending forms. All of our contributors are acclaimed writers of innovative creative nonfiction; most have published widely in other genres as well. They also bring deep experience teaching creative writing at leading colleges and universities.

*Bending Genre* stands at the beginning of what we hope will eventually become a substantial body of critical essays by and for writers of creative nonfiction. It is meant to serve as a guide and inspiration for teachers, students, scholars, writers, and the many others interested in creative nonfiction as a literary art. We believe it offers a useful companion to more traditional textbooks and anthologies, a way of opening new options to students and writers, and a starting point for continuing discussions of creative nonfiction's many innovative forms.

What does it mean to "bend genre"? Is it true, as Walter Benjamin famously said, that "all great works of literature either dissolve a genre or invent one"?[8] Or, as Ben Marcus hopes, that "once upon a time there will be readers who won't care what imaginative writing is called and will read it for its passion, its force of intellect, and its formal originality"?[9] Of course, once the novel was truly "novel" too. Even today, works like *Tristram Shandy* and *Moby Dick* still feel radically innovative and new. Will blurry, hybrid lyric essays and collage memoirs hold up equally well over time? From the beginning, the project of literature has always been an attempt to "re-present" reality through language, to capture the essential truth of our experience of life in words. As writers across and between all genres, we continue to try.

## Notes

1   David Shields, *Reality Hunger: A Manifesto* (New York: Knopf, 2010), 5.
2   Ibid., 3.
3   See John Hellmann, *Fables of Fact: The New Journalism as New Fiction* (Champaign: University of Illinois Press, 1981); Eric Heyne, "Toward a Theory of Literary Nonfiction," *Modern Fiction Studies* 33.3 (1987): 479–90; Barbara Lounsberry, *The Art of Fact: Contemporary Artists of Nonfiction* (Westport, CT: Greenwood Press, 1990); Chris Anderson, ed., *Literary Nonfiction: Theory, Criticism, Pedagogy* (Carbondale: Southern Illinois University Press, 1998).
4   Lee Gutkind, ed., *The Best Creative Nonfiction*. Vol. 1 (New York: Norton, 2007), xi.
5   On rhetorical modes vs genres, see Robert Scholes, Carl H. Klaus, Nancy R. Comley, and Michael Silverman, eds, *Elements of Literature*, 4th ed. (New York: Oxford University Press, 1991), xxx. See also Gérard Genette, *The Architext*, trans. Jane E. Lewin (Berkeley: U. C. Berkeley, 1992), on the distinction between literary structures (such as novels or stories) and linguistic structures (such as narrative or exposition).
6   Amos Oz, quoted in David Remnick, "The Spirit Level," *New Yorker,* November 8, 2004, www.newyorker.com/archive/2004/11/08/041108fa_fact.

7 Tzvetan Todorov, "The Origins of Genres," *New Literary History* 8, no. 1 (Autumn 1976): 161.

8 Walter Benjamin, "On The Image of Proust," in *Walter Benjamin: Selected Writings, Vol. 2: Part I: 1927–1930,* ed. Michael W. Jennings, Howard Eiland, and Gary Smith (Boston: Belknap Press, 2006), 237.

9 Ben Marcus, "The Genre Artist," *The Believer,* July 2003, www.believermag. com/issues/200307/?read=article_marcus.

Part I

# Hybrids

At first it seemed like nonfiction eked out its existence from the bare scrap metal left behind by poetry and fiction. A queer blend, a magnetic encounter where the positive charge of poetry met the narrative charge of fiction. But at some point, the relationship becomes its own thing—a marriage—an entity unto itself. Now the marriage deserves a little understanding, a little therapy, a little ceremony of its own. Now the couple, not the individuals, gets invited to parties, hosts wine tastings, goes driving in the country. Now, when the marriage walks in to the room, no one comments on what the people were before, but the way this marriage has sustained so much, so long.

# 1

# Why Some Hybrids Work and Others Don't

## Lia Purpura

The chili-chocolate gelato didn't work because the chili numbed my mouth, as did the cold—and all that activity canceled out the chocolate.

Cockapoos and Labradoodles work well for owners, but they really hack off the breeders whose business is promoting and maintaining singularity. I'm sure the dogs are nice (and really, what's not to like in Labs and Poodles and big-eyed Spaniels) but for me, they don't work because the names are dumb and make perfectly dignified animals sound like toys. Of course, we, who have a Standard Poodle, also irk breeders since we refused to have her tail docked and she has no haircut to speak of. Most people assume she's a Labradoodle. I can see it's hard to be a breeder.

The wild orange trim on the staid, dark red house down the street could've worked, but then my neighbor went and used a different orange on the door and now everything clashes. The problem here is consistency— not the wild-domestic hybrid itself. For example, satyrs work—one end is all thoughtful and conversant, the other, all animal-action. I'm not sure exactly how they work. Nymphs would know best. But I do know, in a satyr, the wild part stays wild, the cultivated part stays cultivated. Satyrs are complicated but consistent. Friends, your best, most redemptive love won't change a satyr.

One can buy a hanging indoor/outdoor fixture to serve as either a porch light or living room light, and if you're undecided, need both, need one temporarily then that's a good idea. But the halogen office lamp used on the porch, as a porch light—that doesn't work. Many things work in new contexts, but not if their initial purpose dominates. Then porches go makeshifty; then they start looking like scrappy undergrad rentals.

The fig tree in our yard is a hybrid gesture, a combo of Mediterranean botany and Mid-Atlantic desire. (That it was given to us by our Greek friend, Constantine, who's a Japanese historian, is even better.) The tree didn't work for two years, but we kept at it, pruning and watering and mulching, because we liked the leaves so much—they were so (we couldn't help it)

*Biblical*, and then lo! on the third year the tree took and produced seven good figs. Sometimes a hybrid gesture takes a long time to root.

Chocolate-covered potato chips worked for me, but not for my friend who likes both chocolate and chips a lot, but couldn't see them together and so didn't even try one. "They don't look right," she said, "the chip is deformed by the chocolate." I felt the chip was *re*formed, brought back from the edge of way-too-salty, by the good and loving hand of dark chocolate. "It looks like tree lichen," she said. "It tastes like perfect union," I said. "You have no idea what you're missing." My friend is not an "opposites attract" type. Nor does she fancy the synaesthetic swooning of Nabokov, on whose prose I regularly gorge.

I'm pretty sure that celebrating Christmas and Hanukkah together in the same house doesn't really work out. Same with Easter and Passover, though they both share a lamb. Holidays are micro-climates; they greet you at the door and waft and settle. Balsam and ham. Latkes and candle-smoke. Rituals are jealous entities: the Hanukkah bush, the tree decorated with dreidels—they seem sad and deflated when made to sit nicely next to each other and conjure small talk.

This morning, the ad in the *Baltimore Sun*, for the latest ritzy harbor-side restaurant read: "Max's: A New Tradition." Well, no. That doesn't work. Tradition, I thought, had something to do with time.

Mules—the offspring of a male donkey and a female horse—don't "work" in one sense. Neither do hinnies (offspring of a female donkey and male horse). I mean they don't reproduce. But they are real characters. In other words, some hybrid gestures produce singular things. One-time-onlies. Anomalies that are stubborn and ornery. That know their own mind. It might be better to simply enjoy them. At a distance. No use teaching them as "models."

Zebras *look* like hybrids—the offspring of one white and one black horse-like animal—but aren't. The debate rages on (are they black with white stripes, or white with black stripes?), but either way, they're just exactly what you see: a black-and-white beast. Beware the assumed hybrid. In other words, some people are amused to find they write a thing called "the lyric essay" when all along they were just doing what felt natural, simply asserting the sum total of who they are as writers. That no two zebras have the same *pattern* of stripes—now *that's* more interesting, by far.

Starbucks offers a mass of senseless hybrid gestures. Just to start, there's the tyrannical and embarrassing naming system you have to comply with, or risk irritating your barista. Why "tall" and then "grande"? Why "crème" and then "wet" or "dry"? Why "double" and not "doppio?" What's with the random Italianate leanings? Then there's the "you call it/ have it your way" culture that allows for such excesses and hybrid disasters of taste as the "iced decaf, triple grande, no whip soy, five pump, Mocha-mint."

Here's a scene: I am just out of college and back home in New York, working all day, and writing at night, and it's causing the usual problems. I am in a starkly beautiful sushi bar, eating my one weekly piece of uni, and drinking my half-price Miller Light, slowly. It's the roaring, late-80s and one of those baby millionaires sits down next to me and we get to talking. "I'm going to retire at thirty and write a novel," he tells me. He tells me he has "so many ideas." I was tired and righteous and broke. I said something like "nice dream, bub, but if you're not doing it *now*, if you don't *need* to do it, it's not gonna happen." I meant, some things have to be there at the outset. I meant—though I wouldn't have said it this way at the time—"You have no drive to hybridize! If you *needed* to write, you'd be, right now, a banker-poet. An insurance guy-novelist. A waiter-playwright. That hyphen would be a little table where you set your work, nightly. A little bridge you crossed, after dinner, to far realms, and crossed back again, in the morning."

If hybrids *fail* because they produce dumb, goofy names, as noted earlier, they *succeed* when they offer new, sonorous ones. The *pluot*, a hybrid of plum and apricot is lovely (Ah! hints of "plié" and "Roualt"). The *tangelo's* great (bite in and there's "Tango" and "Angelo" waiting). Not the *papple*, a too-hard, slightly mealy crossing of pear and apple, with the unfortunate echoes of "nipple" and "pimple" and "pap." Not the *peacotum*, a peach/apricot/plum hybrid, with its echoes of "cotyledon." Though it might have been worse. The peacotum's early developer wanted to name the fruit after the nice, soft fuzz it retained, scientifically known as "pubescence" which would have given us—I'm serious now, this was the guy's plan—the pube-plum. The best thing at the farmer's market in Baltimore: the apples. Apples are, a priori, hybrids—or graftings, to be precise. Adam and Eve on one side, the power to keep doctors away on the other. My favorites, the Stayman-Winesap and Jonagold, have names that *work*. They indicate fruits that take their essential qualities seriously. They want you to believe in them—not laugh at them. The wine descriptions on the little tags at Well's Discount Liquors in Baltimore are fantastic, and the impulse there, to present taste as an essentially hybridized experience, to be accurate by way of complexity, is right on: snow and shale, squid and wolf, rose and lichen . . . forgive me . . . A.R. Ammons slipped in here, that master of hybrid states of being.

Hybrid tenses work because they help us bend time. Consider the neat and quick gesture the future perfect allows: "By next year/I will have done X." Such projection and back-tracking rolled into one. I also love the similar veering I undergo when reading certain poems of Marvin Bell that take place in what he calls the "posthumous present."

The hybrid word "ginormous" works and doesn't. Officially, it's in the new Webster's. Aurally, it's euphonious (whereas the other option, as I figure it—enormant—sounds like a sci-fi bug. And the even more messed up enormgi is weirdly bacterial). But I don't use the word "ginormous"—it doesn't work for me, because I'm not 13 and in junior high.

Hybrid times of day and night work, *and* have much spiffier names than "day" or "night." On one end there's "day-break," "dawn," "aurora." On the other, "twilight," "gloaming," "crepuscular." Such is the poetry of the liminal dark.

The hybrid car, Prius, works, though not without all kinds of battery problems I hear and some longer-term issues of toxic disposal. And also it sidesteps the issue of over-consumption, when rationing is likely what we need to do, now and forever. That's pretty radical. Rationing's un-American. And as of yet, hybrid cars don't have industry backing or any real government muscle behind them. Then again, there are also no accredited MFA programs offering degrees in the prose poem. Thankfully, for the clever, rogue prose poem. Institutionalizing hybrids is complicated.

In a recent letter from my novelist friend Kent Meyers, I was instructed about the wonders of hybrid corn varieties, whose purposes include increased yield, rootworm and corn borer resistance, early ripening and alkaline soil compatibility. And of the hybrids of his youth, how fondly he recalled the legendary XL-45, the gold standard hybrid for corn farmers in Morgan, MN. Is it any wonder that he's just completed his own hybrid, a novel-in-stories (whose title is, by the way, "Twisted Tree")?

So hybrids respond to need, and thus are vital and heightened forms of attention. Consider the split vision and special alertness of the sad kid laughing along with the rest but secretly monitoring jolly, drunk Dad for the first signs of meanness. Or the cop on a date, on line at the movies—scanning for trouble, mentally noting, annoying his girlfriend who claims he can't ever relax. Or those of us who have trained ourselves to hold one conversation while monitoring a few others at nearby tables in restaurants.

In her memoir *Seeing Through Places*, Mary Gordon writes of her mother's reverence, her love, really, for the priests in their life, and of the priests' mutual deep regard for her mother. One might be tempted to call such love "stunted," "unrequited," or "sad." Or, one might call up the term "passionate restraint." That's a hard one . . . love is, whose origins are mysterious, whose success requires odd and challenging integrations, whose future is always surprising.

# 2

# Queering the Essay

## David Lazar

*Let me be known all at once for a queer Fellow.*
                              Richard Steele, *The Spectator*, No. 474

Genre and gender are indissolubly linked, etymologically intertwined. Clearly the two words emerge from an intertwined root system that speaks to typologies, distinctions, styles—and they are almost homonyms, fraternal sound twins. Turn to genre in the dictionary, and you will be pointed to gender. Early uses of genre cited in the OED refer to distinguishing types of people; the first cited, interestingly, by Lady Morgan, says, "But what is the genre of character . . . which, if in true keeping to life and manners, should not be found to resemble any body?" (1818). How queer, that one of the first uses of genre suggests a person who is impossible to characterize. Genre is a category after all. So is gender. And the gender category difficult to characterize by normative standards is queer. The genre category difficult or impossible to characterize, the essay, is also queer. The essay is the queer genre.

The words have further etymological complexities when one considers that gender can be translated into *genre* in French, *genero* in Spanish, and *genere* in Italian—the Latin stem form of *genus*, kind. The Greek root of *gen* means to produce which gives us genesis, oxygen, gene.

In Leviticus, God says, Thou shalt not let thy cattle gender with a diverse kind; thou shall not sow thy field with a mingled seed. We can imagine the result, a genre of hybrid calves, or worse yet, queer cattle mingling all over the place. They wouldn't know what to call them.

The history of genre has evolved through Western literature as a story of creating distinctions, discrete categories for the most part, and subdivision. Poetry, Fiction, and Drama with their various subgeneric extensions, period demarcations, stylistic innovations: Romantic Poetry, The Epistolary Novel, Kitchen Sink Drama, ad infinitum. But until now, one of our major genres, The Essay, has resisted classification. Has resisted *gentrification*. To read through the history of essays on the essay is to a large and fascinating extent to see practitioners of the form struggling to articulate what the form is and refusing to keep the form stable, refusing to narrow its sense of possible performative and formal dimensions, frequently inverting commonly accepted conventions (idling is good and natural, sensibility and self-awareness are virtues, intense attention to the self leads to an enlarged perspective, eros is located profoundly in friendship). Nancy Mairs, Rachel Blau DuPlessis, and others have suggested a feminine affinity for the essay, feminizing Montaigne along the way, which is quite a trick when one considers how excessively women are discounted in Montaigne's overt discourse. But Rachel Blau DuPlessis suggests in "*f* words: An Essay on the Essay" that the openness, distrust of systems, skepticism, and transgressive nature of the form are reasons "why the essay has been summed up by the term feminine."[1] And in "Essaying the Feminine: from Montaigne to Kristeva," Nancy Mairs finds qualities in the "Montaignesque" essay that break or escape phallocentric discourse.[2] At the end of "On Some Verses of Virgil," Montaigne does say, shockingly, that "except for education and habit, the difference [between the sexes] is not great."[3]

I'd go a step further and suggest that the essay as a genre doesn't just resist classic gender binaries, but in many ways queers them. I'll put the statement out of the rhetorical closet: the essay *is* a queer genre. What do I mean? I mean this in a most specific way. In the way that queer theory defines queer as a continuing instability in gender relations that undermines the traditional binary of gender, replacing it with indeterminate, transgressive desires. The desire of the essay is to transgress genre.

Queer and essay are both problematic, escapable, changeable terms. Both imply a resistance and transgression, definitional defiance. But there is also more. For example, Judith Butler's sense of performativity and gender and its importance to the constitution of gender through reiteration speaks to the operation of persona in the essay. Much has been written about persona, but we know this: it is never fully controlled or calibrated; it is subversive, and always has been, because, like gender performance, it "is the kind of effect that resists calculation" at least to some extent.[4]

The most memorable essays are formally labile and so stretch our sense of what essays might be. All essays think, come to ideas, create lasting images, seem to have some association with their personae. The elasticity of persona itself is part of the essay's queerness. I mean this in both a metaphorical sense and as it speaks to gender. Look at the queerness at the heart of the essay: Woolf and Baldwin, Rodriguez and Fisher, Barthes, Lamb.

The essay is not and has never been genre normative; this is essential to the nature of the essay. Calling the essay "lyrical" or even "personal" seems to me to be putting a generic leash on it, domesticating it under the guise of setting the essay onto some untrammeled ground. However, for 430 years the (not so) simple noun "essay" has allowed us to resist the normalizing impulses that govern other genres, and led to Pascal and Sebald and M. F. K. Fisher. What is queer about the essay is its resistance to stability, categories—even the one I'm advancing in this essay. The best theories of the essay—Lukács, Adorno, Montaigne, Emerson, DuPlessis—turn in on themselves, lose argumentative coherence in the direction of passionate, expansive thinking about the essay. Essays about the essay tend to be transgressively shapely, if we think shapely and circuitous are lively and harmonious concepts, as I do.

Réda Bensmaïa, perhaps the most compelling contemporary critic of the essay, writes in *The Barthes Effect* that:

> Among all the terms that relate to the literary genres, the word Essay is certainly the one that has given rise to the most confusion in the history of literature; since Montaigne used the term to describe his writings, "essay" has served to designate works that are so diverse from a formal point of view, and so heterogeneous from a thematic point of view, that it has become practically impossible to subsume a single, definitive type of text under this term.[5]

Bensmaïa goes on to note, and pay attention to the language, that until recently, the genre of the essay, "A unique case in the annals of literature," "is the only literary genre to have resisted integration . . . in the taxonomy of genres."[6] The language and connection to gender seem clear enough. The essay has been the queer gender, borrowing from, at times parodying other forms, constantly creating new unstable ones, but never—queerly—fully taxonomized, defined, institutionally appropriated.

Perhaps until now.

John Frow speaks of genre as a form of symbolic action.[7] If this is the case, what have essayists enacted, symbolically spoken, by writing essays? What has it meant, "to essay"? Has this question ever really been asked, other than formally? I would argue that to essay has frequently been a generically queer behavior, writing this form that resists and undermines other categories. It is also a form that asks for secrets to be exposed, feelings to be explored, memory to be reconsidered, and gender roles to be stretched (think of the end of "Some Verses of Virgil"), for outlandish, strange, unsympathetic or merely whimsical ideas to emerge as we adapt or adopt personae, and extend the reach of our empathetic imagination.

Bensmaïa argues that the essay, "born practically and aesthetically with Montaigne . . . still had to be born theoretically [unlike other genres] . . . above all with Roland Barthes, this genre judged 'unclassifiable' for a long time was finally able to make its 'theoretical entrance' into the history of literature and the theory of literary genres."[8] As theory, the essay also retains its essence as a fragmentary book of the self. Clearly, with Barthes as the theoretical impresario, the queerness of the genre, the way it signifies its refusals, its openness, its difference, becomes both obvious and, to Bensmaïa, approaches a kind of generically canonical status. If this is true, it may ironically undermine the essay's queerness over time and also exactly explain why the taxonomy of essays is going on now. The essay, queerly, has always existed ahistorically. The development of "new" forms like the lyric essay is an attempt to usher the essay into a more conventional evolutionary pattern, with the lyric essay as the postmodern phase of the form. The irony is that it makes the essay seem more taxonomically like other forms of literature, and therefore less queer, less resistant to typologies, and also that it may appropriate the form into the more conventional genres, like poetry. Of course, essays have always indulged in hybrid behavior, transgendered.

Are essayists queer? Yes, or they have been, I'd argue, because along with the great motto of the essay, Montaigne's "Que sais-je" (which carries with it the duality of inflection: what do *I* know, and what I *know*), I've always thought the other great line that speaks to the heart of the essay (and perhaps I'm giving myself away as an essayist, but I believe this is reflected in the prismatically digressive attentiveness of the essay voice) comes in fiction, in Henry James's *The Art of Fiction*, when he urges us to, "Try and be one of the people on whom nothing is lost."[9] Essays embody sensibility and a sense of self (think of Hazlitt's "On Gusto"), and the feeling, embodied in style, of the essayist's difference from everyone else, even when speaking of common things. I wish James had written expansive essays, in addition to the prefaces of the New York edition. In his famous letter to Henry Adams, he writes, "I am that queer monster, an obstinate finality, an inexhaustible sensibility."[10]

Perhaps there is an element of queer desire in this very subject for me, my desire to be a queer essayist marking my sense of the genre itself, spilling over, if you will. But perhaps again this is my point. I want to betray my motives, want my sensibility to color the world I'm seeing, and the literary world I inhabit, and I want to lose nothing in trying to be aware of how this coloration is taking shape, even in its potential excessiveness.

In the case of Charles Lamb, we see an extreme version of the essay's queerness most vividly, as Lamb, struggling with the intensity of his discourse, the sensibility of self-protective nostalgia in his self-maternalizing, ends up offering a series of resistances to masculinity, both directly, and through ironic self-degradation: he is "beneath manhood," refers to "my infirmity," his "mental twist," the "symptom of some sickly discourse," all addressed to the male reader ("a busy man, perchance"), to whom he both seems somewhat embarrassed and threatens to "retire, *impenetrable* [my italics] to ridicule, under the phantom cloud of Elia." Time itself is feminized: the old year's "skirts" and the new year's birth.¹¹

Perhaps one of the reasons Lamb has been singled out as "dear" and "saintly" as what I think are unconscious cognates for queerness is not simply because readers have given him grief points, and responded to his whimsy, but have subconsciously *allowed* him a resistance to conventional emotional valences they might have found excessive in most male writers, writers working in genres that were, perhaps, less performative. I think this reaches an apotheosis in Lamb in his essay "New Year's Eve."

Whether the essay will become less queer the more it becomes typed, subcategorized, postmodernized, or avail itself of some continuing inner "heresy," to invoke Lukács, is up for grabs. I worry about the essay's domestication, a false sense of formal radicalization. Merely breaking up paragraphs or adding poetry to essays (Cowley did that in the mid-seventeenth century) doesn't make an essay queer or politically resistant once that becomes one of the old bag of essay tricks that all beginning essayists must practice to construct barricades to the paragraph, within whose contours, Lamb, Woolf, Baldwin, Montaigne, wrote such wild, fascinating, queer words.

Essays on the essay never pin the essay down. A queer theoretical essay wouldn't even want to. But it's worth noting that the essay has always been a site of resistance, a place where things have happened rhetorically as well as formally that haven't happened elsewhere. Sir William Temple, anyone?

## Notes

1  Rachel Blau DuPlessis, "*f* words: An Essay on the Essay," *American Literature* 68, no. 1 (March 1996): 33, www.jstor.org/pss/2927538.

2  Nancy Mairs, "Essaying the Feminine: From Montaigne to Kristeva," in *Voice Lessons: On Becoming a (Woman) Writer* (Boston: Beacon Press, 1997), 71–87.

3 Michel de Montaigne, "On Some Verses of Virgil," in *The Essays of Michael Lord of Montaigne*, 1580, 1897. Trans. John Florio, 1603. World's Classics edition. Vol. 3 (London: Frowde, 1904), 284.

4 Judith Butler, "Critically Queer," *GLQ: A Journal of Gay and Lesbian Studies* 1, no. 1 (1993): 25.

5 Réda Bensmaïa, *The Barthes Effect: The Essay as Reflective Text* (Minneapolis: University of Minnesota Press, 1987), 95.

6 Ibid., 129.

7 John Frow, *Genre: The New Critical Idiom* (Abingdon: Routledge, 2005), 2, 13, 154.

8 Bensmaïa, 99.

9 Henry James, "The Art of Fiction," published in *Longman's Magazine*, September 1884. In *Henry James: Literary Criticism*. Vol. 1 (New York: Library of America, 1984), 53.

10 James to Henry Adams, March 21, 1914, in *The Selected Letters of Henry James*, ed. Leon Edel (New York: Farrar, Straus and Giroux, 1955), 174.

11 Charles Lamb, "New Year's Eve," in *Elia and the Last Essays of Elia*, ed. E. V. Lucas (London: Methuen & Co, 1903).

# 3

# Don't Let Those Damn Genres
# Cross You Ever Again!

Lawrence Sutin

While I was trying to decide what to say about crossing genres—which I like to do and enjoy reading others do—I had a weirdly literal dream. There was an outsized railroad semaphore flashing the warning "Do Not Cross" as I approached on foot. On the other side of the tracks stood a group of writers, some of whom I knew in waking life, such as Michael Martone, and others only through author photographs, such as Jenny Boully, whose book I had recently taught. I took a look to the left and to the right. No train. I ran across the tracks. It was no big deal to any of them that they or I had crossed, and I said to one of them, the poet and prose-shortist Mary Ruefle, that all of us, meaning all of humanity, had been doing this our whole lives, crossing boundaries of all kinds, and it was never going to end. She nodded and we started walking and I don't remember in the dream having an idea where we were going. I don't remember in waking life having an idea about that either.

Now is not a more fertile time for cross-genre writing than any other time. It has always happened. When it draws attention, it is often due to the challenge it poses to literary labeling. In the crimping way that we are sometimes influenced by names of periods, many of us alive today are aware that something called modernism supposedly died, oh, maybe 60 years ago, and something called postmodernism has been around since and needs to die, as it keeps falsely insisting that there is nowhere new left to go. What has kept PoMo on life support is the terminological difficulty of moving on from a figment that styles itself as having already happened in a vague post-future.

A term I occasionally use in my head to the fascination with cross-genre explorations: "transliminal"—recurrent crossings from one distinctive state of consciousness to another. In the transliminal epoch in which I hereby declare that we are all living it is a delight to cross genres so as to underscore the everyday crossings that everyone makes from sleeping to waking, private to public, culture to culture, talking to listening, paper to screen, paying attention to not, sobriety to excess to silence, history to fantasy to memory to dream, all the while in and out of love and hate and certainty and utter incomprehension.

Here are some crossover ancestors to whom I am grateful.

Bashō, who in *Narrow Roads to the Deep North* employed the distinctive perspectives of prose and haiku and demonstrated how such combinations excel in balancing and harmonizing inner and outer realities in the course of a journey both physical and spiritual.

Dante, who in *La Vita Nuova* merged criticism, memoir, and poetry to reveal implicitly how he came to be the poet capable, after years of love sonneteering, to cast the Divine Comedy with his lady love Beatrice at the side of God in the heights of Heaven.

Virginia Woolf, who in *Orlando* combined the conventions of mainstream romance and time-traveling fantasy to explore the then forbidden terrain of bisexuality in a manner that both hearkened back to Shakespeare and anticipated the more fluid concepts of sexual identity of the present day. Woolf created special illustrations for the book to portray the male and female forms of her protagonist.

William Blake, the greatest of all cross-genre artists, whose masterwork in this regard, *The Marriage of Heaven and Hell*, forged together visual engravings, poetry, and prose into one of the most profound portrayals of the human psyche ever created.

Dostoevsky, who in the 1870s, in his periodical *A Writer's Diary*, merged political journalism, literary essays, memoir slices, and short stories into an amalgam that readers accepted because of the brilliance and passion of the author. These days we call what Dostoevsky did blogging.

Sir John Mandeville, the sixteenth-century author of *The Travels*, a book that is often disparaged as the work of a charlatan. But Mandeville wove together the geographical and zoological conceptions of his day, added ample doses of myth and juicy rumors, and produced a book that offered a rare vision of humanity viewed whole. Mandeville was a model of honesty and fairness. As he bluntly admonished his readers: "Let the man who will, believe it; and leave him alone who will not."[1]

The French prose poets from Baudelaire to Mallarmé to Max Jacob to René Daumal to René Char and Jean Follain, all of whom combined to establish that the boundary line between poetry and prose is indiscernible when the artist's intention is sufficiently focused. As Mallarmé put it ever so simply and truly: "Every time there is effort towards style, there is versification."[2]

Zora Neale Hurston, author of *Tell My Horse*, who went beyond her formal training in anthropology to combine a meticulous observation of and personal response to the vodou cultures and practices of Jamaica and Haiti. Hurston's ear for the speech-patterns of her informants, her eye for their movements and their passions, remain models for cross-genre explorers of the planet.

Robert Walser and Jorge Luis Borges, both of whom decisively blurred, in their respective ways—the lyric and the laconic—the boundary line between the story and the essay such that it has been exceedingly difficult ever since to keep writers from jumping back and forth between them as they will.

Tom Phillips, author of *A Humument: A Treated Victorian Novel*, who extended the cut-up method proposed in the 1950s by William Burroughs to the thoroughgoing alteration—linguistic and visual—of an existing book by means of language cross-outs and insertions, collage and other imagistic impositions, so as to create a radically new text. A contemporary American writer who has brilliantly taken up this method to create what she calls "erasure books" containing "new poetic texts," is the aforementioned-in-the-dream Mary Ruefle. Thanks to Mary's example, I'm doing erasure books myself these days, a wonderful crossing.

Ludwig Wittgenstein, the philosopher and prose poet who would have, I think, vehemently disclaimed the latter title. Wittgenstein gave a portion of his inheritance to two poets, Rainer Maria Rilke and Georg Trakl, whose work he valued but could not, he claimed, understand. I believe, however, that he understood them well enough. What is of the essence in Wittgenstein is his passion for unfettered precision and playful daring in every sentence.

All of these homages having been paid, what is there left for us to do in the Age of Transliminality? Oh, all sorts of things, everything really. On my own personal list of possibilities that I would like to do or see there are these three:

One: the ever-increasing mutation of point-of-view so that several could be portrayed in even a single sentence that would be through sheer precision of perspective and detail remain nicely clear for the reader willing to enter the text.

Two: a work that flows seamlessly between poetry and prose and back again, with the sense that the two forms have become lovers.

Three: fact-based studies of all kinds rescued from the monopoly of academic purview. Dispassionate does not mean unbiased or intelligent. These new cross-genre studies, which are in fact already appearing, with the works Suzanne Antonetta as a stellar example, employ the roaming personal consciousness of the author as a means of more deeply exploring the subject in question.

I would like to close with a brief and perhaps unnecessary comment on truth telling. As I have done the bulk of my writing in the oxymoronically named genre of "creative nonfiction"—a mathematics professor of my acquaintance burst out laughing when he first heard the term—I am often asked about falsification in memoirs. I reply, first, that there are liars in every profession and, second, that writers, like visual artists, have discovered and our discovering myriad means to create telling and beautiful human portraits. Our inner lives, with their fantasies and self-deceits, are as much a part of memoir subject-matter as the confirmable facts of date and place.

Truth is malleable, but thankfully, it is also breakable, so that we can know a liar and catch them at it when they fabricate lives and perspectives for the purpose of ensnaring the empathy and interest of readers. Having said that, I say to all writers of integrity—use every method at your disposal to astonish me, and genre boundaries be damned. As chaos theory teaches us, there is apparent chaos, then apparent pattern, then apparent chaos again, and the cycle continues infinitely so far as we know. So with genres and their crossings.

## Notes

1   John Mandeville, *The Travels of Sir John Mandeville*, trans. C. W. R. D. Mosely (New York: Penguin, 1984), 144.
2   Stephane Mallarmé, 1891 interview with Jules Huret, published in Huret, *Enquête sur l'évolution littéraire* (Paris: Fasquelle, 1913), 58.

# 4

# Genre-Queer: Notes Against Generic Binaries

## Kazim Ali

2.

If writing is a way of thinking, the poem itself offers the best form of structure. It invents its own rules under the making. Neither line, nor form, nor diction or syntax is taken for granted by the writer. It is an anarchic piece of text that lives between boundaries.

This quality of the poem can be taken into prose.

And fiction, the novel, the essay, memoir and critical writing—they do not look on the page like what they contain inside.

(A house must have a kitchen, for example.)

Forms of prose have somewhat calcified.

What poetry—in its queerness of structure, language, intents, and appearance—can offer to prose is *life*, the same thing that queer life has always—throughout all cultures, ancient and modern—offered to heteronormativity. Drag anyone?

Remember the kiss between Kitty and Laura, the 1950s suburban housewives in Michael Cunningham's *The Hours*: "You didn't mind, Kitty?" asks queer Laura in desperation. "Mind what?" Kitty asks in wide-eyed and brutal denial.

Similarly, in prose, innocuous as the kiss between conspirators against the norm—Kitty's body after all, in a certain fashion, is as queer as Laura's: she is unable to have children. Thus unable to achieve the paragon of heterosexual bliss, she succumbs to Laura's kiss.

So, is the queering of genres just as similar a trick? A way for queer writers (poets) to join the Mainstream of prose, the way queer citizens stage their battle for equality and civil rights around the institutions of the military and marriage, both instruments of imperial state power and political and familial inheritance?

Or can it be political enough to bring the resources of poetry into prose, to allow new structures for the mind in its thinking?

Kimiko Hahn. Bhanu Kapil. Harryette Mullen.

Eleni Sikélianòs, *The California Poem.*

Laura Moriarty describes a reading by Norma Cole of her work *Scout.* Norma had recently had a stroke. Moriarty, a dear friend of Cole's and whose book *A Tonalist* is dedicated to Cole, describes the stroke in one single deadly sentence: "They found her on the floor." She goes on to describe the reading: Cole, having newly learned to speak, chose words intentionally difficult to pronounce. When she reads "violets," Moriarty hears its differently: "Violence, I hear, thinking how physical thinking is, how the body (how life itself) makes its own violence, how sometimes things don't change as quickly as we would like, how sometimes they change at the speed of (blood or) light."[1]

The text is a body because it is made of the flesh and breath and blood of a writer. The "mind" which declares intention is a collection of senses, sense-responses, and memories. Chemically it is invented in the brain. Thought *is* matter.

Work resists binaries between thought (theory) and action (creative work).

Can the poem extend theory? When Moriarty writes "(blood or)" she makes a case for thinking two things at once, or in other words anything that *could* happen *does* happen. It's not literary theory but actual science.

So perhaps the genre-defying writer is a queer one, who understands gender and genre derive from the same classifying, categorizing impulse—the impulse not to invent but to consume, commodify, *own*. Said another way, genre and gender are both *reading* practices, resulting from "authorial intention"—the author's desire to bracket and frame the text, control (or contribute to the control of) how the text is received, read, "understood."

Riki Wilchins writes, "Gender is a system of meanings and symbols—and the rules, privileges and punishments pertaining to their use—for power and sexuality: masculinity and femininity, strength and vulnerability, action and passivity, dominance and weakness."[2] I like that she equates the categories of gender directly to power and its various expressions. The question of genre is not aesthetic. Certain kinds of writing (bodies) are valued *more*, are promoted and supported and legitimized and that the kinds of writing that are undervalued or marginalized are precisely those which undermine (in both their form and content) traditional power structures and traditional ways of thinking.

But gendered bodies and genred writing as a matter of course simplify, reduce complexities, essentialize and "normalize." Wilchins goes on to say, "In popular thought, men and women are considered examples of 'real' genders and drag, transsexuals, and butch/femme couples are considered copies" but then declares, "all gender is a reuse of familiar stereotypes according to the rules for their use. All gender is drag."[3]

Transgender and transgenre space transgresses all requirements of civilization: that we—*as* texts—must be read and have fixed meanings. Tiresias' seven years as a woman are invisible to us. The myths do not speak of it.

Like books in print culture, we are meant to stay between our *covers*.

In one version of the myth, no longer extant, Tiresias stays on in Thebes as a woman, Jocasta lives on and Oedipus, blinded, wanders alone in the wilderness. Ursule Molinaro, genre-bender extraordinaire, wrote it as *Power Dreamers*.

What if genre, like gender, is fluid, *constructed*: by the publisher, critic, reader, *even writer*.

Can a writer determine so strongly how a work is seen or positioned?

Morton Feldman called such "the anxiety of the artist." And maintained a zone of anarchy must exist in the first place for the work to be created.

What is music: Cage, who uncaged silence and made noise into art.

What is painting: Ono, who first exhibited paintings along with their instructions and then dispensed with the paintings and exhibited only the instructions.

Regarding *Bright Felon* and *The Disappearance of Seth*: two texts written simultaneously, with the same voice, each moving nonlinearly with the sentence as the unit of transition rather than the paragraph. Both in prose, one fiction and the other autobiography.

To take genre itself as a form of drag.

That is to say, to read *Bright Felon* as "memoir" means with all the attention on how memory makes or fakes meaning. To read it as "poems" means language and structure become more important. To read it as "fiction" or as "essays" means what?

To read Carole Maso as "fiction" rather than "prose poetry" means the silence and staccato of the sentences can be read as erotic, or in the case of *Ava*, the disappearing sentences and awareness are read as her dementia and eventual death.

So why then, besides ease for library cataloguers or bookstore clerks or publishers' representatives, is Maso's book *Ava* considered a "novel," her *Aureole* considered "short stories," and her *Beauty is Convulsive* considered "prose poems"? Don't ask Maso the question—why should she know any more definitively than you?

Scalapino doing drag in her "novels"—fluid run of poetic thought unfolding in nonspatial, nonlinear decahedral shapes, flow-winged and flowing.

And what then do we do with the lyrical western landscapes of Willa Cather, Cormac McCarthy, or John Steinbeck, embedded as those "prose poems" are within the form of novels? Trans-genre or genre-queer?

They are in a fashion "queer spaces," Steinbeck's alternating chapters of lyric, kept tidily apart from the main narrative of the book, separated as a border zone. Cather has a harder time handling it—her poetry suffuses the book, interrupts it—in the case of *My Ántonia*, fatally wounds the narrative drive and in *Death Comes for the Archbishop* renders it functionally obsolete. What was perhaps initially meant as a colonizing story ends up as a fabulous failure.

Reading the beautiful train-wreck of narrative in the progression of Cather's novels as they travel west from New York City is like reading the chain of Marguerite Duras novels that began with *The Ravishing of Lol Stein*, and continues with *The Vice-Consul* and ends with *L'Amour*, the last novel she wrote for 13 years—a period of time in which she concentrated on filmmaking and short prose works including *The Malady of Death*.

These books take place mostly in the liminal space of beaches, the ocean roaring just beyond, its sound mirroring the savage wailing of the madwoman—or in the case of *L'Amour* by which time the madwoman and Lol V. Stein herself have conflated into the body of one woman (i.e. Lol's madness is no longer represented externally) the wailing is contrasted to the deadly silence and speechlessness of the protagonists.

First Lol's story is told and then Anne-Marie's (in *The Vice-Consul*); in *L'Amour* both women appear, both themselves but not themselves. Duras retells the story two more times as the films *La Femme du Gange* and *India Song*. What does she intend by retelling the narrative over and over again? By the time she tells the "true" story "as it happened" in *The Lover*, no critic or reader knows quite what to make of it. Duras herself insisted that *The Lover* was not a memoir or an autobiography but a novel.

So upset by the way the novel was being adapted to film she wrote the book one more time—as *The North China Lover*—intended, as a more cinematic version of the events of the earlier book, to be a treatment for a film as yet unmade.

At the close of *The North China Lover* a body falls overboard on the voyage from Saigon to Paris. It is ambiguous whether or not this body was Paulo who we know from *The Lover* does not survive to return to France.

In *Je Nathanaël* Nathalie Stephens talks through the body of Nathanaël, the shadow half of Nathalie, the other gendered soul, the essay in the novel, the novel in the poem. What fell overboard in *The North China Lover* is the earlier version, the nonfiction in the volume *The Lover*.

In Nathalie's case Nathanaël himself is the text, a fuckable text: "Who wants Nathanaël? I do I do. Only he doesn't exist . . . I have only seen him from behind in a painting and not a very good one at that."[4]

The genre-queer text can be seen only from behind? Perhaps it means we can encounter it as writers not as "readers." "What is a fuckable text?" Stephens asks. We can't cruise the text like we were going to pick it up and take it home; we have to be the ones lingering in flattering light, waiting to be seduced. Do you have the patience for it? It's Barthes' dream, the dream of the writer-centered text the one that gives pure *jouissance.*

And once you've experienced the bliss of the disorienting text you have a hard time going back to novels and essays that draw from nineteenth- and eighteenth-century models. You get drunk on the real possibilities of what shapes language can make. The space between literature and life, lingers, is a wound of perception.

Maso, in *Break Every Rule*, takes up the woundedness of language—she sets out to create a new form for thought, one that can hold both eros and death, in books like *Ava* and *Aureole*.

Fragments bring silence in, the erotic moment (*Aureole*).

Not the exploding of narrative but a nonlinear lifting out of discrete moments.

After all (in Woolf's *Mrs. Dalloway*) "he looked over the edge of the sofa and into the sea."

Like Septimus who has lost his ability to remain in one fixed place in time (and so travels back years to the war and across hundreds of miles to the trenches), Leslie Scalapino's fiction dissolves all boundaries and concepts of the "present moment" as discrete and "whole" in its "fragmentariness." She brings thoughts together as threads. Experience is frayed. All things are in the mind and how the mind travels, especially hers!

Remember the first time you saw Maya Deren's film *Meditation in Violence*. The dancer Chao-Li Chi is inside a small room of an apartment but with one leap in the air he lands on a roof-top patio. It takes some time and repeated viewings for you to realize that at a certain point Deren started looping the film backwards. Chi's moments were so graceful and contained in themselves you didn't even notice.

We transition through genred spaces, but when we accept that texts like bodies can be genre-queer then the possibilities for both interpretation and artistic creation are boundless.

If we want to think about genre like gender it means we are thinking of the book as a body. In this case maybe Duras' chain of novels are like Cylons from the newly reimagined *Battlestar Galactica*, each book the same essence downloaded into a new corporeal form. The Cylons are, after all, perfectly "queer": ageless, eternally beautiful. Their primary obsession is to learn to procreate; they are willing to exchange their immortality and embrace death in order to do so.

That other human-created artificial life from, the Creature of Frankenstein, is similarly obsessed with finding a mate. His obsession with sexuality is mirrored by his obsession with textuality. He carries Frankenstein's journal in his pocket wherever he goes and at the end of the book he leave notes for Frankenstein, even carved into the very stones of the earth. Frankenstein and the Creature both are held in the arms of text—Robert Walton's letters to his sister Margaret.

If the monstrous and queer seem always obsessed with textuality, is it true they always seem to work against conventional memes of gender and genre? The queer seeks always to understand itself, but why? Is it because in the heteronormative world of patriarchy, economic marriage and inheritance we must use language and forms of thought ("genres") in order to construct ourselves at all?

In the novel *Dracula*, the primary dramatic action is one of *categorization*; the vampire hunters keep meticulous records, collect newspaper clippings, interview transcripts, journals, all in order to *understand* what Dracula *is*. At a climactic moment in the novel Dracula breaks into the house and kills Lucy and then destroys all the original diaries, Seward's dictophone cylinders, all of it, in the fire.

But the story of the novel is the victory of technology over mystery: the vampire hunters still have records because Mina has been transcribing all of their findings on her new typewriter. Though the original material is burned, the typescript remains and it is this that receives primacy: "We ask none to believe us," declares van Helsing in a statement worthy of the turn of the century about to occur. "We need no proofs." The simulacra have *become* real or at very least, good enough to be.

Later of course, racing against time on the mountainous Transylvanian roads, the vampire hunters are able to beat the Count to his castle only because that original slayer, Mina, has memorized the timetables of the trains.

1.

But in any case a poem is not a question of memorizing time-tables (mastering form and meter) nor is a novel a question of structure or classical outlined form.

Writing is—Duras knew it, Scalapino and Cather did too, and Maso—part eros, part riot. Anne Carson pointed out that eros is inherent in the distance between two bodies (between a writer and her subject, for example), but riot, the province of Bacchus, generally involves having your head torn off. By your mother.

If you know what your text is "about" you are probably in trouble already.

When I began as a writer I was deeply involved in multiple creative practices, writing earnest narrative poetry in adopted personas and little fractured prose pieces I had no name for—essays that evaporated and novels without characters in which nothing happened.

Throughout my college years I had two poets whispering in my ear—one a post-structural critic named Helen Elam and the other a performance artist named Judy Johnson. By day I was lectured about the (crystal-clear to me at the time) connection between a Volvo and Derrida and at night I recited poetry while being menaced by a woman in a gorilla suit.

In this way I learned early and quickly that there is no separation between theory and art, that ideas are everything we have, and that art in these ideas becomes physical. As gender can only restrain the primal spiritual and sexual energy of the body into boxes so too genre does to literature.

If Charles Olson is right and the central fact of America is "SPACE," then what are those spaces, one piled on top of another, each with secret other names, scrubbed clean to make the fiction of "AMERICA." It may be that an American writer has the *need*—no question of desire—to write into these vexed spaces with the only techniques available: a fragmentation of narrative and multiplicity of lyric selves.

In other words: *is* language adequate to define experience?

To say nothing (yet) of: Empire.

Not only new language and new characters, or new forms for the novel (thank you Fanny Howe, thank you David Mitchell. Thank you Stein, Duras, Maso, Nin, Cather, Stoker, and Moriarty) but we actually need a new brain, new *shapes* for thought.

We've always already done this in poetry. A knowledge of poetic form now applied to the novel, the essay, the memoir. And genre (in the writing of Nathalie/Nathanaël) not so much evaporates—meaning is still in the air somewhere—as *disappears*.

And who *is* Willa Cather, who once wore a man's suit and called herself "William Cather," in the midst of all this? Landscape in Cather *is* gendered while the people—with a handful of exceptions—seem mostly to move *against* traditional gendered norms (Alexandra, Father Latour, Thea, Jim, and so on).

Maso: "If writing is language and language is desire . . . if syntax reflects states of desire . . . then why when we write, when we make shapes on paper, why then does it so often look like the traditional, straight models, why does our longing look for example like John Updike's longing . . . in the formal assumptions: what a story is, a paragraph, a character . . .?"[5]

Writing is a way of thinking. Maso here dreams of that space for desire, for lust, for love.

Not an explosion of narrative but a new way of narration. As Maso says, she wants to "figure out how to go on after the intensity of the moment . . .

to compose a life afterwards, how to conjure back a world worth living in, a world which might recall, embrace the momentary, glowing, obliterating, archetypal."[6]

3.

The first publisher I submitted my book *Bright Felon* to suggested I condense radically and reshape the material into poems.

The first publisher I submitted my novel *The Disappearance of Seth* to suggested I reframe the book as an essay or meditation on the monument, specifically in this case, the 9/11 memorial.

But even to move from one form of writing to another is not transgressive in the purest sense—you are still stuck in a sense of separation between genres, as in gender binaries.

So I am not talking here about "cross-genre" or "mixed-genre" books which utilize both prose and poetry, or utilize techniques or qualities from each to make the work—examples might include *The Collected Works of Billy the Kid* by Michael Ondaatje, Louise Glück's *Meadowlands,* Anne Carson's *The Beauty of the Husband,* Jean Toomer's *Cane,* or Theresa Cha's *Dictée,* all books I admire very much.

Rather I mean those books whose genre is unto themselves, whose whole texts live with bodies ungenred as genderqueer bodies, take their own gender unto themselves, neither accepting one category nor another.

Books are bodies in a form. Maso wants to know how do you (in fiction) go on beyond climax—it means sexually of course, but the heart of the question (especially in Maso) is not sex but death. How do you go on beyond death. A question also asked (and answered) by Mark Doty (not known as an experimental writer really) in his most genre-queer book *Still Life with Oysters and Lemon*—part memoir, part art criticism, part prose-poetry, all rapture.

Is any book (let's ask Nathanaël) a completed whole—of "novel" or of poems or of fiction or essays or any other category—or is it really mainly a series of related gestures?

(Note: read one of Darwish's prose books here: *Journal of an Ordinary Grief, Memory for Forgetfulness,* and *In the Presence of Absence.* Thank god these are finally all three translated into English. Palestinian literature, as a genre, arrives late on American shores. And most of Darwish's books arrive on American shores after Darwish himself, who came for necessary heart surgery, which he did not survive.)

Darwish, that whirling dervish of form, wrote prose as poetry and never wanted to know the difference. "My homeland is not a suitcase," he declared in an early political poem, asserting the right of the Palestinian people to recognition of their sovereignty on their own land and denying it would be so easy to pack up and move across the new border into a neighboring state. But years later, after decades of wandering through the world—Moscow, Beirut, Cairo, Tunis, Paris—he would glumly amend the line in recognition of his actual lived life: "My homeland is a suitcase."

Cather, William, or Willa, whichever you like, seems always to return her rebels to the homeland social order. Her characters work themselves up to a moment of overturning the power structure and then oddly, and in somewhat deadly intent, swerve: first in *O Pioneers!* Alexandra visits Shimerda in prison to apologize to him; then of course there is the fabulously sudden disappearance and then odd reappearance of Antonia in the novel which bears her name; and of course the actual titularly promised death of the Archbishop, simultaneously a haunting evocation of the landscape as free and eternal from human consideration and the narrative of religious, political, and racial empire.

What is literature anyway but a dream of thought into language? It is an act of love-making, of translation, of making the body (text) move.

Genre defends itself, creates a literature for the reader to not be a writer anymore. In other words, eat what's on your plate, it might (or might not) be good for you.

But to use one's own body. To dance—as the feel-good slogan goes—as though no one is watching. What is your movement vocabulary? How does poetic form live in your own awareness, own body, own language? So you might not know what poem, novel or essay you can make but what *writing* can make of you.

Genre, like gender, is not so much passé as it is *boring*. The future holds more and the possibilities poetic languages offer us for increasing human perception are not merely for the promise of pleasure but of planetary importance.

## Notes

1 Laura Moriarty, *A Tonalist* (Callicoon, NY: Nightboat Books, 2010), 60.

2 Riki Wilchins, "A Certain Kind of Freedom: Power and the Truth of Bodies—Four Essays on Gender," in *Genderqueer: Voices from Beyond the Sexual Binary,* ed. Joan Nestle, Riki Wilchins, and Clare Howell (New York: Alyson Books, 2002), 25.

3 Ibid., 28.

4 Nathalie Stephens, *Je Nathanaël* (Toronto: BookThug, 2006), 49.

5 Carole Maso, *Break Every Rule* (Berkeley: Counterpoint Press, 2000), 157.

6 Ibid., 23.

# On the EEO Genre Sheet

Jenny Boully

## On interviewing

A few years ago, when I was on the job market, I was asked repeatedly to define nonfiction. I knew I could venture into one of two courses: I could give the traditional textbook definition, or I could say what I really felt. If I said what I really felt, then I knew that I wouldn't get a campus visit; I wouldn't get the job. If I gave the textbook definition, it would make the interviewers feel as if I was on their side, that I was a safe candidate, that I would be someone that the Chair and Dean approved of. Because I have a natural inclination to be rebellious, I always chose to go the road of the untraditional. The interviews then became centered less on my qualifications and more on my transgressions. Some interviewers felt that I was misguided, that I needed counseling. You see, they aimed to tame me, and it became their goal to do that before the next candidate arrived. It wasn't about what I could offer, but rather about what they could fix.

I still ask myself, quite seriously, why is it that fiction is allowed to borrow from nonfiction, but nonfiction is not allowed to borrow from fiction? And, seriously, I really want to know.

## On former students

One of my goals as a teacher of nonfiction is to totally destroy every held belief that a student has about essays and nonfiction. Essays are my thing. Essaying is very much my thing. I expect my students to essay. I expect them to essay fiercely and obsessively. I want to see, truly, what new thing they will unleash into the universe. One student wrote quite beautifully. She wrote so poetically, but what she wrote wasn't verse. It was essaying; it was essayistic; it was an essay. Many of my students did this over the years, but this one student did it quickly and passionately. I met her later, randomly, on a street corner in the West Village. She said that she was depressed; her new teacher wouldn't let her write; her new teacher told her that she was writing poetry and the class wasn't a poetry class. She asked her teacher if a prose poem could be nonfiction and the teacher said no. I told her, why don't you, quite discreetly, slip her a copy of Pope's "Essay on Man"? That, if anything, should give her a mind fuck, you know.

When I went home at night, I realized that *I* was depressed. I kept thinking about my former student and all her talent being pushed on the curb by a teacher who could have been in the room interviewing me, asking me what my definition of nonfiction was.

## On being mixed

Once, when I was 22, I worked in the mall in Roanoke, Virginia. I worked at several stores in the mall. I needed the money. I could go from part-time shift to part-time shift and not even have to leave the mall. One day, on break, a local came up to me and asked me if I was "mixed."

## On being mixed two

So, it seems that I am mixed. I am quite mixed. I am more mixed than many, many people I know. My father is half Cherokee, half white man. We've never known where his white ancestors came from; he became a ward of the state when he was 8, and so much of his history was lost. My mother is Thai, but she has curly hair, as do I, which leads me to think that there must be something else lurking in there.

In terms of what I write, it seems that my writing too is also mixed. I am sometimes called a poet, sometimes an essayist, sometimes a lyric essayist, sometimes a prose poet. My second book was published under the guise of fiction/poetry/essay.

I find these categorizations odd: I have never felt anything other than whole.

It seems to me that the inability to accept a mixed piece of writing is akin to literary racism. I think of the Equal Employment Opportunity (EEO) data sheets. Choose the genre that you feel most accurately describes you.

## Please be X, Y, or Z

I want to know, seriously, why what is often "other" ends up being labeled as poetry. I think it's like something forcing me to check the white box or the Native American box or the Asian box. Which of these most accurately describes me? Does this mean to myself or to other people? Other people who meet me for the first time always ask me if I'm Spanish. When they ask me where I'm from, I always say Texas. So that confirms for them that I'm definitely of Hispanic descent. I never say that I am from Thailand. I was born there, but I can't say I'm from there. From, to me, denotes a forming of awareness and identity and memory. Most of these happened for me in Texas.

When I was younger and when I dated, my dates were always very uneasy about asking me about my ethnicity. You could see it in their hesitating restaurant decisions, their waiting to see if I'd order in a language other than English if I'm taken to an ethnic restaurant. And then always, inevitably, I'll be asked if I'm Spanish. When I say no, they are, always, invariably disappointed. The two biggest disappointed dates: the Spanish analyst who worked for the government and the boy who had just broken up with his Spanish girlfriend—I don't know what he was hoping to find in me.

## Poetry as refuge

A refuge is where unwanted animals go. It is also where some of my submissions to journals end up. Some intern or graduate student has dropped my submission into the poetry pile; in a way, that person has made it possible for my submission to live. It would not have lived in the nonfiction pile. There, it would have starved to death, or it would have been eaten alive. Once, I got a rejection slip from a nonfiction editor saying, "I'm not sure how to take this. I don't know what this is." That particular journal was solely a nonfiction journal; my submission, therefore, had nowhere else to go.

## On the EEO genre sheet

I'm not sure which genre I would select. I guess, being who I am and doing the type of work I do, I would have to choose many. Do I choose "other" (if the option is even there) and fill it in (if there's even a fill-in space there)? Isn't having to choose, being forced to choose, also essentially racist: being told that there simply isn't an easy category for you: you just don't fit in; you destroy the natural order of things. The term "other" also immediately connotes an agenda: if you don't fit into one of our predetermined categories, well, then, you aren't playing the game correctly. You are an other. You will always be an other. You will get thrown into a slush pile marked "origin unknown."

## Coda

And so, in the literary world, I find that I spend a lot of time trying to keep anyone from getting disappointed in me.

I may look like an essay, but I don't act like one. I may look like prose, but I don't speak like it. Or, conversely, I may move like an poem, but I don't look like one.

Do I bend genre? Or does genre bend me? I think it's the latter. I have always been the same person: I have always been made up of three things. My birth may be fictional; I may be from poetry; I might now be living in essays. I cannot see these three things as separate parts of my identity; rather, they form to make one entity. I may be the product of fiction, nonfiction, and poetry, but they too come together to form one entity. To be told to choose is to be told that you disrupt the neat notion of where things belong, that you don't belong.

# 6

# Ill-Fit the World

## T Clutch Fleischmann

In her essay collection *Everybody's Autonomy*, Juliana Spahr explores the ways that avant-garde texts (meaning, reader-centered, genre-bending, experimental and shifting and odd) encourage the participation of the reader and invite a sort of liberating community. The world she sees in these texts approaches a transformative and challenging anarchy, where the reader is expected to cross borders and to explore her own limits while participating in the meaning of the text. In addition, as Spahr sees it, "avant-garde forms are not at all divorced from cultural concerns, but are actually often used to critique dominant cultures."[1] In this sense, she rejects the notion that the avant-garde is the home of rich white men, carrying out a tradition of intellectual posturing and play that began ages ago. Instead, she sees the history of marginalized[2] people innovating and radicalizing texts, aesthetics and structure and politics all performing interdependent functions.

This is, of course, an old and available history, even if it is one people typically refuse to acknowledge. Take, for instance, Margaret C. Anderson editing *The Little Review* (in an editor's note from 1916: "Revolution *is* Art. You want free people just as you want the Venus that was modeled by the sea. . . . All my inadequate stammerings about Emma Goldman have been to show her as the artist she is"[3]), a journal which regularly included women modernists, only to have the men end up in anthologies, leaving generation after generation to find Mina Loy on their own. Or the constant "borrowing" of techniques from non-white cultures in order to innovate white literature. Likewise, the diverse ways that art by marginalized people eludes and upends dominant aesthetics have been mapped in a long critical history, whether looking at bebop, at Joyelle McSweeney's and Johannes Göransson's theories of disabled texts, or at countless other examples. This essay takes these realities as a given, even if they are not always taken as such by others. Instead of trying to prove the connection between innovative writing and people on the margin, then, I'm interested in taking the line of thought I first heard clearly articulated in *Everybody's Autonomy* and applying it to the innovative (or lyric, or experimental, of bent and bending) essay. Going a step further, it seems that the defining qualities of the genre seem to be inherent to the type of liberating and anarchic reading that Spahr identifies.

An aside on terminology: as often as not, Deborah Tall is given credit for the term "lyric essay." In her essay "Terrible Perfection," discussing her relationship as a woman to the canon of literature, Tall says that she has "been inspired and consoled over the years by the voices of many women, but also by the voices of men on the margin—the poor, exiled, oppressed— those who, even if they made the canon, ill-fit their world in some revealing way."[4] Tall's description of people who "ill-fit their world" seems especially powerful to me, the ill-fitting becoming an action and a revelatory power. The word "lyric" also has some useful history behind it. Linda Gregerson, describing lyric poetry, claims that "impediment produced the lyric voice,"[5] that something had to keep the poet away from the lover in order for lyricism to come into being. If the essayist has a love, it is her topic, and Gregerson's logic holds there, too. But, even so, maybe there's something more interesting (more essayistic) in a clustering of terms, in redefining what we talk about by talking about it. Lyric essay, bent essay, hybrid essay: all both stabilize and occlude something that might be useful.

While Spahr and many other critics have given attention to avant-garde and genre-bending writing in general, the fact that some of these essays maintain a stance *as essay* is important. There is something about the essay as a genre that we're holding onto rather than adapting the terminology of docupoetics, of prose poetry, of non-genred writing. It seems useful, then, to have an understanding of what a traditional essay does. Ken James, in his insightful introduction to Samuel Delaney's *Longer Views*, calls the type of essay for which Montaigne is known "meditations in which the sovereign self is the authoritative ground for analytical inquiry,"[6] which seems about right to me.

Of course, there's a lot about that type of essay that does not sit comfortably. There's the sense of a "sovereign" self, as though the individual could or should exist free of the influence of the other individuals. "Sovereign" also implies a power dynamic, claiming the "authoritative ground" on which truths can be declared. This is not troubling because of postmodern concerns regarding the slipperiness of meaning and the constructed nature of truth, exactly. Rather, it is troubling because it presents the "I" of the essay as someone who all alone can enter the world, equipped with analytical tools and committed to bringing some truth back to the reader, no impediment allowed between herself and her topic. "This is how it is, and here is my proof," this type of essayist seems to say. These sovereign essays preclude many of the concerns central to Spahr's inquiry: that writing, much like what she says of Lyn Hejinian's foundational *My Life*, "points to how the question of the personal is responsible to the larger question of the collective;" that we must find a way "to be both autonomous and related;" that it is ultimately "more productive to see this writing as a dialogue that negotiates between these positions of pluralist inclusion and respectful, categorical separation."[7] Put another way, the traditional essay as James describes it is interested in convincing us of the truth (the biography, the research, the reality of a place where the writer does not live) rather than in exploring some truths together.

But that authoritative tendency is not inherent to the essay, and the formal qualities of (genre-)bending essays challenge any sense of authoritarianism on the writer's part. Take, to start, truth, the foundation on which the genre is arguably built, and the focus of much handwringing over and criticism of lyric essays. There are two political realities tied to truth to which the essay as a form is obligated to respond. The first is that authoritative fact, both historically and today, has been used to silence and exclude significant numbers of people, whether forcing immigrants to lie in order to stay alive and safe or perpetuating the idea that transgender people are lying when we assert our own identities and bodies (to give only two examples). The second is that the process of asserting individual truths, of "speaking your truth," has been a powerful social and political tool in the modern world. These are realities to which the essay is always responding, not by discounting truth, but by acknowledging and embracing the power of truths, by using the shifting, hidden, exposed, and expansive truths of the margin as collective tools to help us better understand the world, rather than lifting up a blunt instrument meant to convince others that our own experience is the right experience.

Kevin Young's *The Grey Album*, for one, offers an insightful account of black literature and art responding to and subverting authoritative truth. Young recounts the necessity and power of what he calls storying, "both a tradition and a form" in which "the fabric of black life has often meant its very fabrication, making a way out of no way, and making it up as you go along."[8] Whether looking at slaves forging papers in order to reach freedom, at Alice Walker pretending to be Zora Neale Hurston's niece in *In Search of Our Mothers' Gardens*, or at Danger Mouse's mash-up of Jay-Z and the Beatles, Young reveals storying not as a type of lying, but as its own literary technique, its own truths made alongside the reality that authoritative truth is violent, oppressive, and silencing. It's no surprise that one of the greatest and earliest writers of the contemporary essay, James Baldwin, gets considerable attention from Young, with Baldwin's references to Bessie Smith in his own essays providing an example of successful storying. It's also important that, while storying and the traditions charted by Young are unique to black culture in the United States, bent truths in a broader sense are a common tool in the art of marginalized people. Gertrude Stein can write Alice B. Toklas's autobiography, sliding a queer life into everyone's hands; Leslie Marmon Silko's *Storyteller* places together family photographs, myth, and prose that blur any distinction between fiction and fact; and Lauren Slater's *Lying* is a "slippery, impish, playful, exasperating text, shaped, if it could be, like a question mark."[9]

None of these are examples of the writer lying, which is one reason that the bent essay—the essay that Acts Up and steps outside of the line it was supposed to stand behind—might still be called essay rather than something else. To claim truth as collective and problematized and challenging, like Stein and Young and so many others have, is to move toward the type of literature Spahr champions. What better technique than storying, than the embrace of nonfacts, to meet Spahr's description of writing as "a dialogue that negotiates between these positions of pluralist inclusion and respectful, categorical separation?"[10] What better ground than the essay to challenge ourselves to acknowledge all these truths, holding them in our head together, maybe moving somewhere new? Hybridizing forms, combining "fiction" with "nonfiction," does not simply create a form with qualities of both, but instead results in a mode in which neither exists on familiar terms, where we're asked to conceive notions of truth with new criteria and from new ideologies. Adhering to authoritative ideas of truth, as many essayists want to do, either misreads or ignores those essays operating out of different traditions.

Running parallel to these questions of truth are the spatial and visual qualities of bent essays ("Why all the white space?"), the urge to include images, blanks, topography, odd indents, and constellations of text. These, too, can be understood not simply as a dismantling of the authoritative text (there is not only a lack of thesis-body-conclusion, of conventional rhetoric, of memoir-like narrative, there's sometimes a lack of text, here). Rather, we are given accumulations of image, emotion, lie, truth, lyricism, language, dirt, and emptiness that operate out of their own, self-defined rubrics and accomplish unique means. Claudia Rankine's *Don't Let Me Be Lonely*, a contemporary masterpiece of the lyric essay, is a clear example. It begins in half-page blocks of text, Rankine slipping between first person and second person, residing in the space where other and self are not comfortably delineated (after recounting her grandmother's death, the next block begins, "Or one begins asking oneself the same question differently.

Am I dead?"[11]). As the book accumulates, images including medical scans of a friend's breast, stills from movies, and the repeating motif of a fuzzy television all hold space. These images do not serve as the core medium of a fact-proving diagram, but as several of many accumulating realities, all with their polyvalence, the little invisible lines going in all directions. A fuzzy television does not break up the idea of a traditional essay, but unexpectedly creates beauty and community within the sense of broken connections and troubled intimacy that a traditional essay, in its authoritarian sovereignty, often has trouble performing.

Again, in my reluctance to view these formal techniques as simply disrupting the authoritative essay, I do still want to insist that these *are* essays. *Don't Let Me Be Lonely* is fundamentally, in topic and in genre, about the experience of the self (Rankine's self) in the world. It explores the loneliness that comes with living in society, that insistence on the self (our self and the selves of others) as both autonomous and obliged to community. And by combining text and image in unconventional ways, it does not simply enact this disjunction between individual and society, but rather works for new combinations and analogues of meaning that strive to create and reveal our interconnectedness. It's similar to what happens in Barthes *A Lover's Discourse* (echoed in Jenny Boully's *The Body*, in Anne Carson's *Nox*), where the topic is understood not by a clear narrative and rhetoric of fact, but by an acoustic collage of definitions, personal history, philosophy, culture, and subjectivity in order to address, in Barthes' words, "the following consideration: that the lover's discourse is today *of an extreme solitude.* This discourse is spoken, perhaps, by thousands of subjects (who knows?), but warranted by no one."[12] Thalia Field's *Bird Lovers, Backyard*, Fanny Howe's *Glasstown: Where Something Got Broken*, Bhanu Kapil's *Schizophrene*—these read to me firmly as essays, just ones where the permeable, accountable self is one of several grounds for inquiry (to twist a phrase).

The last formal quality I'll mention (although there are certainly many more that could be touched on) is that resistance of the permeable essay to explain itself, to define its terms in a way that holds the audience's hand. In the case of authoritative essays, that explaining is often the main function, the informative mode driving it forward. The memoir genre,[13] for one, typically takes as its primary task the duty to inform others about the writer's lived experience. And the informative role works nicely, there, married to the experiences of (in many cases) marginalized people, serving some sort of liberating function in that the traditionally silenced experiences are spoken, and those from privileged positions take the time to hear those experiences.

This process is one of the foundations of contemporary feminism, and certainly, that's a foundation much too strong to discount.

There's a common belief, however, particularly in anarchist critiques, that no one should ever be obligated to "explain" her difference. The assumption that a marginalized person should feel the duty to define, contextualize, or rationalize her own life to someone else is suspect (although certainly fine when she chooses to do so). The bent essay engages more with this understanding than with the (also wonderful, also important) tradition of consciousness raising circles. In essays such as Theresa Hak Kyung Cha's *Dictée*,[14] for one, the focus is on using inventive language and form not to communicate experiences of colonization and domination (among other topics), but in order to engage with the world and the language in which those experiences are born and create instead new worlds, new languages; in Spahr's words, "that Cha pursues and presents not simply a critique of colonization on the level of content, but that she also writes her work so as to decolonize reading." Were Cha engaging with the traditional, authoritative sense of essay and memoir, her work would document its images and quotes, translate its languages, and actively move toward a cohesive narrative with which the reader could walk away. Instead, we are given a writer who thankfully and generously refuses to give us that experience, preferring disjunction and other techniques to create an essay in which the reader, by accepting unexpected turns, will walk away challenged to continue her engagement, to stay permeable and stay involved in the inquiry.

Poet Amy King, in describing queer poetry, offers a description that can be applied here as well. It is enthusiastic enough to quote at length:

> The focus shifts from who is what stable identity to an energetic movement, from the secure footing of "what is" to the risk and broadcast of hope in the one constant we know: that there is no there there, there is only now and then now, there is no permanence, and that knowledge encourages the exploration of what now really is beyond the false fences of security, of a center, a normal, for higher dreams and greater privileges that can be shared between us, among us, in our constant becoming, however fleeting, however impossible, for in the end, should it ever get here, the impossible of the *What Else* is the only thing worth pursuing.[15]

In *Dictée*, like in King's queer poetics, the role of knowledge is not so much to inform, but to *encourage exploration*, especially when that exploration leads us further into the place we call the margins. The genre-bending essay is not discrediting truth or knowledge, but using them (as with all of its formal qualities) for new purposes, obligating us to enter literary, social, and political grounds with which we may be unfamiliar. It is here where, as Gloria Anzaldúa describes it in her preface to *Borderlands*, "the space between two individuals shrinks with intimacy."[16]

\*

I have a sentimental connection to *Borderlands* worth mentioning. I encountered it for the first time at 20 or so while studying literature as an undergraduate. Although I was happily enough reading my way through the canon of the twentieth century in the classroom, I found *Borderlands* not in an academic context, but through a social group. I was at the time establishing my identity as a queer feminist, and I found a group of friends eager to share our own experiences with one another and equally as eager to learn about each other's experiences with gender, with race, with different bodies and histories and addictions. We stayed up into the evenings together, arguing and listening. This is a familiar story—many of us have been there.

In this group, there were a few transformative books we were passing back and forth, among them *Borderlands* and *Gender Outlaw* and a few others that strike me now as distinctly and powerfully essays operating in the modes I've been describing (the same mode, maybe, as the late night conversations). Although I previously would have called myself a poet, it was in seeing Kate Bornstein and Gloria Anzaldúa perform a bending and permeable essay that I fell into the form. I was excited about these books, for their content as well as their formal qualities. My friends and I talked about them in sustained, exacting detail, and I slowly found myself preferring to read and write essays.

Yet, while these texts were foundational and formative for me and many others, I rarely (if ever) see them discussed when we look at the contemporary essay as form. They instead seem to stay in the subgenres of feminism and cultural studies. All of this is to assert one last time that it would be a dangerous mistake to ignore the history and the potential of the bent essay as a liberating as well as an artistic tool. Of all the functions of art, what is more exciting than the possibility that we might, through participation, understand ourselves and the world more deeply (and what more intimately an aspect of beauty)? The essay as genre has always been intrinsically tied to this project. But to rigidly hold the genre now to the notion that exploring the world involves authoritarian truth, straightforward lucidity, and linear thought is to ignore the shaken and shifting complexities of life. Further, to exclude from the conversation that link between marginalized people and genre-bending essays is to exclude so much of the rich history of the genre. Certainly, the hybrid essay can operate in ways that are not explicitly political, and many of the indelible qualities of the essays discussed above have at most a loose, associative link to the politics and experiences of marginalization, just as there are plenty of writers creating bent essays from dominant or un-marginalized experiences (there's no need to list them here, you can find them elsewhere easily enough). But that is irrelevant to the fact that the essay as genre has been and continues to be a rare tool in creating fresh types of reading experiences and powerful, challenging methods for ill-fitting the world.

In her introduction to *I'll Drown My Book: Conceptual Writing by Women*, Laynie Browne reminds us that "it is often at the stage of anthologizing that numbers start to shift so that women are not adequately represented."[17] The hybrid essay has reached the point where it is becoming a point of focused study; it would be incredibly disappointing to watch it go the same route so many other genres have gone, tied only to an already established literary history rather than used to expand our understanding of literature, contemporary and past. The full potential of the form lies in texts that challenge, in not shying away from the anarchic realities of truth and self and community, and in celebrating the breadth of a genre that seems to expand more quickly than its expansion can be noted. The metaphors of marginality and white space, of unspoken truth and elision, of disjunction and community are all readily available (just as the fact that genre and gender share an etymology always remains conveniently obvious). In *Times Square Red, Times Square Blue*, Samuel Delaney celebrates the now-shuttered porn theaters of Times Square and the social contact they encouraged. His description of the relationships he formed there could serve also to describe the type of relationships that are made possible by a permeable essay: "You learned something about these people (though not necessarily their name, or where they lived, or what their job or income was) . . . The relationships were not (necessarily) consecutive. They braided. They interwove. They were simultaneous."[18] Whatever our own limitations, this seems a good direction to go.

## Notes

1  Julianna Spahr, *Everybody's Autonomy: Connective Reading and Collective Identity* (Tuscaloosa: University of Alabama Press, 2001), 87.
2  I use the term "marginalized" here not to emphasize the process of oppression or exclusion, but rather to point to spaces outside of dominant cultures in which other literacies thrive.

3   Margaret C. Anderson, "A Real Magazine," *The Little Review* III, no. 5 (August 1916).

4   Deborah Tall, "Terrible Perfection: In the Face of Tradition," in *Where We Stand: Women Poets on Literary Tradition*, ed. Sharon Bryan (New York: Norton, 1993), 189.

5   Linda Gregerson, "Rhetorical Contract in the Erotic Poem," in *Radiant Lyre: Essays on Lyric Poetry*, ed. David Baker and Ann Townsend (St. Paul: Graywolf Press, 2007), 45.

6   Ken James, "Introduction" to *Longer Views: Extended Essays*, by Samuel R. Delaney (Middletown, CT: Wesleyan University Press, 1996), xxxvi. Importantly, James argues that both Delaney and Montaigne actually worked in very different modes than this authoritarian model.

7   Spahr, 71–2.

8   Kevin Young, *The Grey Album: On the Blackness of Blackness* (St. Paul: Graywolf Press, 2012), 17.

9   Lauren Slater, *Lying* (New York: Penguin, 2001), 221.

10  Spahr, 72.

11  Claudia Rankine, *Don't Let Me Be Lonely: An American Lyric* (St. Paul: Graywolf Press, 2004), 7.

12  Roland Barthes, *A Lover's Discourse: Fragments*, trans. Richard Howard (New York: Hill and Wang, 1979), 1.

13  Spahr offers an overview of critiques of the autobiography genre's "bourgeois authorial self" through innovations by Stein and others: 34–5, 68–9, 75–7 etc.

14  The entirety of Spahr's discussion of *Dictée* informs my thinking here and is much more valuable than my shorthand version. Likewise, *Dictée* itself seems to me to be an essential essay in the contemporary tradition, and certainly deserves much more sustained attention than I am giving it.

15  Amy King, "The *What Else* of Queer Poetry," *Free Verse: A Journal of Contemporary Poetry and Poetics* (Winter 2009): <http://english.chass. ncsu.edu/freeverse/Archives/Winter_2009/prose/A_King.html>

16  Gloria Anzaldúa, *Borderlands/La Frontera*, 2nd ed. (San Francisco: Aunt Lute Books, 1999), 19.

17  Laynie Browne, "A Conceptual Assemblage: An Introduction," in *I'll Drown My Book: Conceptual Writing by Women*, ed. Caroline Bergvall, Laynie Browne, Teresa Carmody, and Vanessa Place (Los Angeles: Les Figues Press, 2012), 14.

18  Samuel R. Delaney, *Times Square Red, Times Square Blue* (New York: New York University Press, 2001), 57.

# 7

# Hermes Goes to College

Michael Martone

## The first thing

The very first thing the baby Hermes does is steal the cattle of Apollo his brother. Apollo figures it out, confronts his baby brother, the little thief, in his crib. Hermes hasn't even learned to speak yet, to walk. The first thing he has to do is steal the sacred cattle of his brother Apollo, who figures it out and is about to extract terrible godly retribution for the transgression when Hermes offers up to his brother the second thing he does after he is born. He gives his older brother a little something he has been monkeying with while in the crib. He gives his brother the lyre—tortoise shell and horn and leather straps and string—so that all-seeing Apollo is charmed, calms down, can compose his great Apollonian art.

## Confused on purpose

Robert Scholes, in his little book *Elements of Fiction*, roots out that both fact and fiction derive from the Latin "to do" or "to make." A fact—the real thing—is a thing done. In fact, fact has no reality once it is done. It has no existence, is unreal. It leaves instead an abundance of residue, evidence, traces, the fact of its once having been done. A fiction, on the other hand, is a thing made and once it is made it comes into existence. It has a reality. It can be sensed, stored, savored even. Fictions in this way are realer than facts whose evidence of the facts' doneness—letters, say, or reports, newspaper dispatches, diaries, etc.—can all be faked. The truth is for a very long time we have been operating as if fact and fiction were steady and distinct categories when in fact . . . And all that evidence of fact—the material of the real—can be faked, of course. We are really always already quite confused anyway.

## The genre of genre

I am worried that we don't worry enough about the subliminal influences of the institutions in which we find ourselves housed, colleges and universities, which for me seem to be diabolic engines for sorting, categorizing, defining. If you think about it, the kind of writing my writing students are most engaged in is criticism, specifically the critique of fellow students' creative writing. The institution is a critical institution and insists we act critically. We want to think of such influence as benign, but it is not. We have adapted our writing, this writing, to the academic model, to the critical turn of mind. It must be seen as serious, empirical, enlightened. Even now in this essay, in this collection of essays that is interested in blurring the lines of genre, we still must use words like genre. We are interested in the confusion of genre, the borrowing of technique between the genres, the tension that exists as one genre rubs up against the other. But still we are quite conscious and quite ready to admit to the easy use of "genre" altogether. We worry the categories of fact and fiction. Nonfiction and fiction. Prose and poetry. What we don't worry well enough is the category of category, the genre of *genre*.

## The art of inconvenience

To invoke "literary" or "genre" is to create a frame where something can be made safe. It is a kind of precinct, a ghetto, even. Writers in America seem to have voluntarily committed themselves to some kind of reservation—the university—and assigned their work to very controlled publishing venues—the literary journal, the little mag, the peer-reviewed periodical. Now there are many very nice, tasteful, serious literary journals, etc., but I can't help thinking that one thing these publishing venues are signaling the world is this: this this, this published this, is harmless, tamed, framed, controlled. And that this fiction, this nonfiction, this art, is not really a part of your life, dear reader. This is a zoo you can visit. I like art in its natural habitat, in the wild. Or if it is in the journals, it is acting like a bug, a germ, resistant to the antibiotic. Art that doesn't know its place. Art out of place. Art that disrupts convention, corrupts expectations. I like the notion of defamiliarization, of attempting to open up received notions and categories to wonder or to, at least, satire. I like art that appears in settings not thought to be artistic, not sanctioned precincts of appreciation. At the crosswalks and the crossroads. Contested spaces. Outside the warehouses of the galleries and the tasteful storage sheds of the literary journal. The prank and the stunt. Art that is inconvenient, that disrupts, that by its nature corrupts, degrades, disturbs boundaries instead of politely sharing, tweaking, or bending them. Art not generically generic genre.

## Meet John Smith

I attended a massive state university where it was a widely held belief that each student there was no more than a number. So with only a made-up social security number we created a student, John Smith, and registered him by means of then current IBM punch cards acquired at the field house registration. Tuition was cheap, then, and everyone in my dorm, whose population was larger than most towns of the state, chipped in a buck or two. We enrolled him in large lecture classes—someone from the dorm was taking the class and shared the notes with the one who took the exam as John Smith. He was a C student. He did not attend the commencement held at the huge stadium and is now on the rolls of the alumni association where he still receives the magazine at the P. O. Box we opened for him and maintain in Oolitic, Indiana. Sure, I realize with advanced software, heightened anxiety of identity theft and terrorist breeches of security, and the cost of college now actually an arm and a leg instead of 20 bucks a semester hour, such a stunt would be impossible today. Or maybe not—one could hack the system virtually now and not have to worry about anything physical at all, but that is a thought for another day.

## A warning warning

Today I teach at a massive state university where the regulation of vehicular and pedestrian traffic captures our attention. There is a sign, a giant yellow diamond warning, that pictures the international symbol of a human walking. You know these signs alerting you to a crosswalk, and you probably know the ongoing editing of the sign, its evolving story. One day you discover a sketched-on undulating hula-hoop ovaling the waist of the stick figure. That then is erased by the DOT. Then circles are stenciled to the feet, roller skates, that are, in a day or two, painted back over. A halo or horns added to the head. Or trailing lines indicating speed or sweat or blood or comic nerves, the shakes. A cast and a sling appear and are expunged. A red reflective button nose. Wings and goggles. And all the time the maintenance crews come back to set it all back in order. The warning sign must merely warn, while art, on the other hand, warns against such maintenance.

## Reader's World

All through college I worked for a bookstore called, really, Reader's World, and Reader's World like most bookstores divided its floor of product into categories of genre—the wall of fiction with its subdivisions of western, sci-fi, lit, and romance, and the expanse of nonfiction breaking into such groups as gardening and home repair, biography, war, psychology and therapy, self-help and how-tos, true crime and nature, travel and religion. Here is a secret of what I learned in Reader's World. Readers are not generic in the usual sense. That is to say their cognitive maps organizing information do not correspond with the one in the store or the one in the university for that matter. The primal division for my customers was not fiction and nonfiction but story and not story. Real or not, factual or not. These were questions, certainly, but not of primary importance. Consider that the Reader's World I worked in was located in a shopping center called Canterbury Green, the boxes of the various stores gussied up in fake timber and wattle and asbestos tile that was meant to look like thatch. Consider too that while I worked at Reader's World I shelved a brand new magazine called *People* and I remember trying to figure out where to place it on the rack on the spectrum from the tabloids, enjoying their first flush of upwardly mobile success, to *Time* and *Newsweek*. The customers seemed to live comfortably in this in-between state. And the conflation of fact and fiction—one I think today is even more pronounced—was collapsing from both ends of the range. Books popular while I worked at Reader's World included *Ragtime* by Doctorow, a fictional animation of history, Mailer's *The Executioner's Song*, reportage expanded by fictional devices, Toomer's *Cane* and Hong Kingston's *Woman Warrior*, a book so blatantly both fiction and non and about the very subject of genre as to make it unclassifiable. And, in fact, we spent the summer moving our copies of *Woman Warrior* from one area of the store to another and then leaving copies, a few copies of the title, in each of several sections, salting the whole store.

## Stealing things in

I have my students in both my fiction and nonfiction classes make books and distribute them as part of the semester's project. Book is a category that is in decay here. I have had a student write a story in the form of a police report, and he filed it as a police report at the police headquarters. Another student wrote a sequence of prose poems on the subject of meat. Her book, bound in blood red wrappers with a bone white spiral spine, she then took to the Winn Dixie to have shrink-wrapped on a Styrofoam tray by the butcher there. And still another hand-printed his story, about a character who uses a 30-foot strip of sized cloth to floss his GI tract, on a 30-foot strip of sized cloth. But most do books that look like books, keeping Kinko's busy with standard staple folds and cardstock covers. I point out to them, as they have to distribute their books as well, that libraries and bookstores have elaborate apparati to prevent you from stealing a book out of their stacks but they have nothing to guard against you stealing your work into the bookstore or the library. And that's what they do, shelving their own work or leaving it to be shelved, allowing the librarian to affix the catalog number, enter it into inventory.

## Hermes clueless

So after reading this essay, we go back to our cribs. Do we go back there knowing more? Do we return having learned something or other? I'd like to think we have come here to unlearn. That's not to say "forget," but to return in a state of not-knowing. Once the contraption of tortoise shell and horn and leather strings fell into the hands of Apollo he knew what to do with the lyre. Open up a music department and study the heck out of the thing till it reveals its secrets—its bone, its horn, its leather. Hermes had no idea what his hands created save maybe an improvised distraction, the sleight of hand, of a thief. He's the artist, clueless, making something new out of those old received categories of bone and horn and skin, out of those old scraps and odds and ends something new in the world. Make things. Steal them into the world.

# 8

# Headiness

Karen Brennan

Boundaries & the thrill of violating them would not exist were it not for each tidy box of genre, complete with rules for the performance of each.

Imagine a squarish container inside of which a little creature resides. & here is the creature creeping toward the lid & here is the creature pushing the lid open & sniffing the air. Other creatures, better behaved, remain inside their boxes, lids fastened. They do their thing. They never tire of their "thing" which they perform repeatedly & excellently. We shall leave them there.

This creature, however, our little creature (or creation)—I think of it as a tiny, multi-headed serpent—with her curious nose, slithers out of her enclosure & what does she encounter? More enclosures, boxes inside of boxes? Or does she encounter the sky—as limit?

There is a specific *physical* restlessness that motivates the genre-bender. We feel it in our muscles. As ennui. As torpor. A type of pain. Truly *bent*, as in perverse, she inclines herself—to fit there. Or flees.

Thus what we call "hybrid" writing or writing that merges genres or steals a thing to use elsewhere with another (mixing & matching, collaging, assembling)—poetry with prose, fiction with nonfiction & all permutations in between & beyond, including literary criticism with poetry or history. Or nonfiction. Fiction with whatever we can imagine—science, cooking, carpentry, TV crime, photography, painting, jazz, gardening . . .

& as for our Greek referents, forget the Centaur & the mermaid, lovely as they are, perfect as they may be for our present discussion. I would rather resurrect the Hydra, a slippery metaphor for the trouble we make, we hybriders—the water serpent with poisonous breath & many heads, like our tiny box-escaping replica above. For each decapitation Hydra grew two more heads, a proliferation of heads or headiness, which in any era—Greek or modern—is a threat. Also she was the guardian of the Underworld. Heady with power.

The opposer, therefore, of order & state. A Dionysian force (to stick with the Greeks) chaotic, bacchanalian, we who bend genre are falling-down drunk, giddy with the freedom to do what we want. Suddenly. (Or deluded.)

The monological law. One head per body type-of-thing. Or: genre as capital: rewarded for our obedient containment. One reward: safety. Another few: recognition, power.

Think also of "queerness." Early feminist theory word-play: genre & gender. Always a link to behavior, the norm, the status quo, conservatism. & so to venture away is to defy nature, for some—

My own hybrid proclivities are maybe a form of ADHD. Just now, I ventured into nature—to my garden to check the yellow flower plant I planted yesterday. Too shallow. I unearthed it, scooped out two more shovelfuls, the edge of the shovel digging unpleasantly into my flip-flop, than replanted. Very pleased with myself. Meanwhile my coffee was boiling over in the Bialetti &—

thinking also about today's email which announces a rally in front of Bank of America to protest—

—& remembering, because how can I not, groups of us for years congregating in the living room of my 3rd Avenue house in Salt Lake City back before I fancied it up, then sold it—there is Margot & Nicole & Pam & Jeff & Derek & Katherine &, further back, Wendy & Kate & Julie & Lynn & Matt & Shira—

—& Rebecca & Steve & Matthew & Rae—to protest. We dragged in the chairs from the dining room, sat on pillows in front of the fireplace, sprawled on the rug. & there we routinely dismantled the icons of our trade: point of view, dramatic structure, character, voice . . .

We made artists' books, We threw images into our fiction. We threw fiction into our poems. We wrote fake nonfiction & true fiction & poetry sprinkled with prose & pictures & music & thinking . . .

To be honest, it was *they* not *we*. I looked on, amazed most of the time, that a smatter of simple suggestions could generate such riches. Such excitement. For how long had we been confined? It felt like forever.

Virginia Woolf. "*I* is only a convenient term for somebody who has no real being," she writes in *A Room of One's Own*, already interrogating that vexed lynchpin of patriarchal culture, identity.[1] You in your place, me in mine, which is leftover Renaissance thinking when we believed that the earth was the center of the universe all the way down to the divine right of kings & extending to our fathers presiding meanly over the dinner table.

I am suggesting that at the root of the genre *minder* (nemesis of the *bender*) is an old-fashioned belief in entitlement. What better justification for Bank of America's perfidious practices, the subtext being a fierce (& greedy) attachment to the status quo?

Be yourself, they used to tell us, an instruction that always baffled me because who in the world might that be? I was a disappointment to my father who had a different kind of girl in mind. More glamorous, less rancorous. I hated high heels, forgot to brush my hair, couldn't seem to keep my voice down.

In my own living room I am quieter, fascinated. We are *Creative Writing Course Number 701, Section 2*, a creature with many heads. Some of us further out on a limb than others. How do you fashion yourself in relation to your culture? Region? History?

(Myself, a former Catholic & so always inclined to break the rules. In boarding school I pranked—rang the forbidden bell in the tower & the nuns came scurrying out. Excited, oppositional, thrilled by the looks that saddled certain faces as a result of my aberrancies. *You did what?* Baffled, repelled. It was all very funny to me.)

Problem: how to get at the depths, beyond the sly clutches of words & boxes of words assembled in orderly categories we call genre? How to avoid being caught & stunned in another doomed category? How to give shape to the wildness & still keep moving (changing) if only to honor the moving, changing momentum of the natural world? The thinking, breathing world, but also the world on top of that one—movies & shopping malls &—

*Just keep taking it all in*, say the Zen masters. *Be mindful of it all.*

Mostly we read for pleasure, in Roland Barthes' sense.[2] We get cozy, turn pages, disappear into a text as into another world. What's wrong with that?

The Text of Bliss, for Barthes, is a higher form of reading/writing. We struggle with such a text; it irritates us in its—what?—refusal to play by the rules. Refusal to let us disappear into that other world, forget ourselves . . . oh how we want to dream . . . We could argue that such a text is too real—hyper-mimetic. It keeps us in the here & now, no escape

which the Zen master would approve of.

(But, says me, suspicious of Any Dogma, in this case, is one lopped off head replaced by two others, doubly grimacing . . .??)

(I am using my metaphors against each other or to be honest they have escaped their signifying containers, they are spilling over the edges—vehicle and tenor alike are intermingling, queering themselves silly . . .)

Because I think sometimes with irritation why can't we disappear into another comfortable world?

My garden offers a similar irritation. Why can't it just be itself without me? Lovely & lush as is the wont of any garden, my dreaming spot? The garden of our imaginations, the garden of our past books, the garden here & now, its lack of oomph, needing a little more yellow over there & some blue in a pot & a lacy froth of leaves pirouetting under the Mesquite; perhaps a fountain of prose to mingle with all that fragmented lyricism . . . why must I attend & attend?

Here is Beverley Nichols, famous gardener, exquisite proser:

> I wish that Our Rose would divert her energy exclusively to the kitchen garden. I have never yet eaten asparagus from a pinholder, but I am willing to try.[3]

Guy Davenport, unearthing the complexities of the still life in *Objects on a Table*, an essay collection I adore & return to for inspiration, digs deep, reading through layers of appropriation, associations miraculously blooming from other associations, becoming strange & beautifully far-fetched, heads abounding, proliferating . . .

On van Gogh:

So the still life is a permutation of a theme, with variant and more literal symbols (as how not from a painter who reads the Goncourt, Zola, and de Maupassant?). We can go further and note than *onion* is the same word as *union* by etymology, and this holds in Dutch as in English. The onions, then, functioning as analogues of the redeeming pear, are also apple and pear together, subsuming all the objects in the painting into the one complex symbol.[4]

Or Coleridge, digressing from his discussion of "myriad-minded" Shakespeare:

The organic form, on the other hand, is innate; it shapes as it develops, itself from within, and the fullness of its development is one and the same with the perfection of its outward form. Such as the life is, such is the form. Nature, the prime genial artist, inexhaustible in diverse powers, is equally inexhaustible in forms.[5]

& Derrida chiming in:

The 'tower of Babel' does not figure merely the irreducible multiplicity of tongues; it exhibits an incompletion, the impossibility of finishing, of totalizing, of saturating, of completing something on the order of edification, architectural construction, system and architectonics.[6]

My garden in twilight is full of shadows. The Mesquite branches stretch darkly across an expanse of pebbles, flanked by a small mountain of bougainvillea, & the hibiscus I planted two days ago, already covered with the sexy mouths of orange blooms. Into this wild array I can throw anything—more verbena or a trowel planted upright & decorated with a green rubber hose.

In my living room, the Living Room of my past, with the green walls, the Victorian fireplace (1896), the window overlooking snow or spring, a mimosa tree, either stark & ice-rimed or a-glow with tiny pink blossoms with fringed tails, more like insects than . . .

In my living room we honor the fragmentary, the undogmatic, the revolutionary, each other
    including whatever we can whatever we want whatever is around like dinner on the fly . . .
        & so

our tiny hydra, having sprung from her box, wanders aimlessly, exhibiting incompletion, the impossibility of finishing, two heads (or tongues or idioms) emerging to replace each one lost . . . inexhaustibility in all directions: inexhaustibly she beholds, she subsumes . . . she whose identity is always shifting, like our minds. & so the possibilities are endless, heady (she collages herself, she appropriates herself). But do we wish to encourage her to divert her energy to our kitchen garden? We do.

## Notes

1   Virginia Woolf, *A Room of One's Own* (London: Harcourt, 1929), 3.
2   Roland Barthes, *The Pleasure of the Text*, trans. Richard Miller (New York: Farrar, Straus and Giroux, 1975), 3–5.
3   Beverley Nichols, *Garden Open Today* (New York: Dutton, 1963), 126.
4   Guy Davenport, "Apple and Pear," in *Objects on a Table: Harmonious Disarray in Art and Literature* (Berkeley: Counterpoint, 1998), 78.
5   Samuel Taylor Coleridge, *Essays and Lectures on Shakespeare* (New York: Dutton, 1937), 47.
6   Jacques Derrida, "Des Tours de Babel," in *A Derrida Reader: Between the Blinds*, ed. Peggy Kamuf (New York: Columbia University Press, 1991), 246.

# 9

# Propositions; Provocations: Inventions

Mary Cappello

## I. Definitional terrain: theory

**A bestiary**

There's a difference between cultivating a sensibility and leaving a creative writing workshop with a bag of tricks. If we only have time for short bursts, I grant you this box of pebbles. You may: (1) throw them like dice; (2) perform a shell game with them; (3) worry one in particular and see what it conjures; (4) line them up and create a Zen garden from them, with or without a water feature.

On good days, I think of creative nonfiction as a vehicle for what object relations theorists call "the unthought known," or as an egress from or easement into what Noam Chomsky calls the unspoken framework for thinkable thought.

I write creative nonfiction because while many may ask how I'm feeling, no one asks how I'm thinking.

Creative nonfiction releases language from its vehicular, indexical, instrumental, referential mode. It takes nothing for granted, and may be the most "meta-" of all nonfiction forms.

Creative nonfiction invents its reader, for anything worth writing is written for the audience that does not yet exist.

Creative nonfiction exceeds training and its regulatory paths, its bracing wheels. It gives back, and it surpasses; it out-strips what you were taught; it ventures the harder thing, knowing all the while, it could fail. It approaches its subject as an enigma that it hopes to realize rather than to solve.

Give us this day our daily genre: a shift in life should incite a shift in practice. Try eating dinner followed by breakfast, and then, at day's end, lunch.

Creative nonfiction appreciates the power of prepositions. Instead of writing *about*, as in, "what is your book about?," it writes *from*. Or nearby, toward, under, around, through, and so on. Rather than mean, it does. It animates. A process and a set of relations more than any Thing. I wrote a book from breast cancer. I wrote an essay against the sublime. Writing about supposes that writers merely supply adjectives to life understood as noun (or predetermined, waiting in the wings, Thing). But we know that literature is of the world and creates its own worlds; performs more than reflects; moves. Creative nonfiction is anything but mimetic.

Creative nonfiction wants to put forms of wandering, exploration, and play back into the plodding unfolding of each day and of each form, of each life.

The operative distinctions are "transform" rather than "transcribe," and "apposite" rather than "opposite." Creative nonfiction remakes rather than reports. Like poetry, it relies on novel appositions that make exquisite demands: opposition cancels, apposition makes apparent; opposition negates, apposition fosters and opens. Why not call it poetry then? Because of the way it enjoins and calls upon a *witness*, but also an interloper, and eavesdropper: placing oneself where one is not supposed to be.

Start simply by identifying key words and see where they lead: "adjudicate"—a legal word. What might the Law have to do with genre? "Code"—a relative of "codify" and "codex" (an early type of book), or, a safe in need of cracking. "Mark of belonging": who knew that genre cared about insides and outsides, outlaws and in-laws, securities and insecurities. "Classificatory vertigines"—I don't recognize this last word any more than you do, but I love how it takes an adjective ("vertiginous") and makes the idea of genre into a dizzying, newly coined, noun. Genre: a container. Genre: an abyss, into which we must abandon hope if we dare enter it. The words appear in "The Law of Genre" by Jacques Derrida, and all I'm doing is playing in its fields rather than treat "theory" as a bugbear best avoided.[1]

"Literary hybrid" does not really do justice to creative nonfiction, though I'm as likely as the next person to fall back on such a phrase. Does creative nonfiction really *mix* forms and genres, or does it move between forms, investigate interstices, eke out formal un-intelligibilities? The word "hybrid" usually conjures the unthreatening beauty of a prize-winning rose. One that doesn't quake or quiver in the wind (a literary cyborg?). It's not an "Oh rose thou art sick" type of rose: no room for sick forms—but only reparative ones. It fails to accommodate creative nonfiction's manipulations of time and tone (its music or rhythms); its shift of vantage point (its purposeful attention to a margin rather than a center); its testing of a limit and willingness to spill (a sax played beyond the instrument). On the other hand, hybrid *could* suggest a politics if we let it.

Hybrid: the new form made possible when areas of thought and of experience sequestered in life are allowed to share a space in art.

Hybrid: a broaching of impurity that results in something exquisite.

### An argument

The best thing "creative nonfiction" did as a category was to incite a definitional crisis around the genre of nonfiction; the worst thing it did was to extract that quality that is essential to our being alive—"creative"— and use it as an empty signifier. "Creative" as a descriptor almost always promulgates a falsehood: that some people are creative and others not; that some acts are creative and others not. Excising an implicit characteristic of life from life and then using it as an adjective renders the life grotesque. It's for this reason that I prefer the phrase "Literary Nonfiction" to "Creative Nonfiction," though each category is differently problematic, and both can be proved to be equally useless. (For yet another critique of writing produced under the aegis of "creativity," see Kenneth Goldsmith's provocative collection of essays, *Uncreative Writing.*[2]) What would happen if we dispensed both with "creative nonfiction" and "literary nonfiction," and instead gave each new instantiation of our nonfictive forays the name most suited to the terms of its experimentation? Mnemic collage. Detour. "Ritual in Transfigured Time." Cabinet of Curiosity.

## II. For the love of it: Practice

### Lessons

At the end of the first day of an undergraduate class that was an "Introduction to the Major" (English), a student came up to me and said: "I know I'm going to love this class because you think a lot like me. You think 'outside the box.'" I had to explain to him that he would not do well in the class if he was interested in "thinking outside the box"; nor was I interested in "thinking outside the box," a phrase I find utterly meaningless. Of course, I could also have said, if we think alike, doesn't that contradict our thinking outside the box? What we'd be doing this semester, I explained, was attempting to—lovingly, assiduously—describe the contours of the box; to get to know the box; to find a language for the box so that we might, in the course, not of a semester, but of a lifetime, find a way to remake the box, or create a box inside the box. Liberal Humanism has given boxes a bad name, hoping to set our sights on that flailingly empty outside-the-box place of false freedom all the while maintaining the box as producer of meanings we never learned to author.

Translating an imperative into an endlessly unfolding version of itself can allow student writers to get a feel for time, space, discourse, and tone. Like playing scales at different tempos, a student of creative nonfiction can practice reorienting sentences in this way, and thus become cognizant of writing as compositional range. Here are three examples of what I mean:

> "Eat a gummy bear."/Draw a morsel of rubbery sugar molded in the form of a miniaturized Pooh species to your mouth and deposit accordingly so as to enable swallowing.
>
> "Sew the button on."/Bring the plastic disk shaped like a pie and perforated to the face of cloth while drawing cotton laced through a needle into and out of each perforation.
>
> "Tell me something nice."/Bring your lips together while pushing sound through them from the box lodged in your throat in order to articulate and transmit a rosy sentiment full of cheer and maybe praise as to what makes me lovable.

Assignments are only worthwhile if they can help make a student of this genre feel she is being sent on a type of Mission Impossible. Otherwise, I prefer to give my students "incitements." Getting a feel for the octaves and keys inside of sentences is one thing; learning to experiment with form is another.

Francis Picabia was pursing the "problem of the vibrant line." Gertrude Stein was in the habit of improvising on the white keys only, in the evenings. Photographer Sophie Calle, feeling lost in her own city of Paris, began following people and photographing aspects of their points of arrival. She also took a job as a maid in a hotel, eavesdropped on tenants and later photographed their belongings. Glenn Gould used to sit in busy cafes and listen, not to what people were saying, but to the collective cadences that he heard in the sea of voices there, then compose a piece of music out of this. I ask my students to devise an experiment that they spend at least two weeks carrying out before translating their results into a piece of writing. But this is just one of many ways in which we interpret and pursue "experiments" and "the experimental" in the course of a semester. We do a lot of thinking together about what exactly would be entailed in *inventing* a form (rather than treating form as arbitrary or writing in a formal void); reappropriating a form; and, plumbing the depths of an antiquated, forgotten or lost form.

Once when I was asked to become a blogger for a website devoted to all things Italian, I invited people to theorize, compose, and invent short forms with me instead. I thought I'd counter the logorrhea of the digital age with a literary short form called "cicchetti," which are late afternoon snacks imbibed with prosecco served in tiny glasses called "ombre" (clouds) in parts of Northern Italy. Literary cicchetti would be intimate, for the moment. They'd be unnamed pleasures or flights of fancy. Neither meals in themselves, nor preludes to a meal, cicchetti would have something anticipatory about them and yet not be equivalent to antipasto. Needing nothing more or less, pitched to receive the divinations that spring from a break in the day, cicchetti would be longer and mellower than coffee breaks. Cicchetti: relative to Italian traditions of sleeping or at least drowsing, resting, meditating, or having sex after noon, the time at which people in other parts of the world and in other cultures are drinking tea, ingesting stimulants, and hoping to wake themselves up.

Snacks have political dimensions, and why not?—they are the stuff meant to meet the unmet needs of regularly imbibed meals, but their very existence bespeaks degrees of bourgeois comfort and excess. One cicchetti collaborator, Mikhail Epstein, helped me to think about this since his own work with the (collective) short form was the effect of material conditions and an expediency. In 1980s Moscow, he had cofounded the Laboratory of Contemporary Culture, a group of thinkers from a range of disciplines who met in order to produce improvisations on the trivia of everyday life. Time was of the essence and so was the production of a counter-discourse, so they wrote all together on the spot on topics they agreed upon then and there for 1 hour. The idea, in Epstein's words, was to produce "a metaphysical assault on everyday things," and from the short pieces that emerged to produce micro-encyclopediae of the quotidian, the mundane, and the daily. Improvisers were also invited to "become specialists in alternative, virtual or non-existent disciplines."[3] Epstein continued this tradition after emigrating to the United States but with much less frequency and intensity.

Context is everything, and there is no form without an attendant politics even if its conditions of possibility are not apparent at the time. This is why I suggest we start out at least with a degree of compositional self-consciousness. At the height of the AIDS crisis, I was moved to create a two-part invention in prose, or what I called a "discursive double portrait." Though the phrase may sound heady and abstract, it aims to unlock sentience and presence. Discursive autobiography requires that my students and I begin by studying the difference between language and discourse—that is, discourse is plural and relational; language is singular. Discourse allows for a panoply of linguistic effects over and against mere representation. Discourse makes subjects of us all; language teases us into believing that the "I" in our sentences and our selves are self-same. Discourse implicates our relationship to language in a whole host of practices, institutions, and systems of power; language enjoys a purity apart, untouched by the systems it maintains and supports. I can attach nearly any adjective to discourse and find language working in particular ways therein: try, literary; racist; popular; familial; nationalist; communal; cancer; or, Facebook for starters.

To compose discursively requires that we turn in the direction of the discourses that have made us who we are rather than start from a place of what we think "happened" to us in the course of our lives. Rather than start with un-mediated experience, the charge is to identify any number of discourses that shaped us but that have gone un-tapped, from prayers and recipes to parental injunctions; from refrains in storybooks to AA mottoes; from birth certificates to tests, from drills and songs to pledges of allegiance.

My own discursive experiment was an attempt to write a *Three Lives* for the contemporary moment, and I started by studying other triptychs by queer writers following Gertrude Stein, like Hilton Als (*The Women*) and David Plante (*Difficult Women: A Memoir of Three*). I wanted to make a portrait of a gay friend of mine who was HIV-positive, but I also hoped to write a portrait of our friendship. My choices weren't arbitrary: for one thing, in an age beset by loss, I didn't want to lose my friend to the forms that were available for telling our lives at the time: to the vortex of sentimentality, the flat trap of obituary, the stationary enclosure of eulogy. I sought to write a living history rather than an elegy to the dying or the dead. I was also moved by philosopher Michel Foucault's formulation about the bases of homophobia in "Friendship as a Way of Life."[4] People's hatred of queers wasn't a response to what they perceived as aberrant sexual acts, he explained, but a reflex against the threat that homosexuality produces new forms of friendship, makes new forms of love possible, even restructures the meaning of kinship. What form could I invent that could be true to the dimensions of a friendship between a gay man and a lesbian?

Coincidence and available prescience always helps me along, and in the course of my writing, I found myself within earshot of one of Bach's famous "two-part inventions." The call and response of the piano's left hand and right, the meetings, cross-hatchings, and simultaneous individuating vectors that make the two part invention so mobile and beautiful seemed perfect for the double portrait I hoped to create. Could language do what this music for piano was capable of? That was my charge. I made a collage of appositional discourses in which my friend and I figured: for example, leading phrases like "he dreamt," "she dreamt," "he believes," "she believes," or imagined personal ads suitable to each of us, and I held these traces together with a separate ribbon that ran like both an interruptive and returning through-line made up of the sights I had glimpsed through a train window on one of many train rides from Providence to New York. The two-part invention delivered the possibility of a conversational form; in lieu of a uni-directional portrait—from painter to painted—creative nonfiction offered the possibility of synchronous subjectivities, together and apart: discourses of the self in dialogue, meeting points where those selves coalesced, and linguistic fault lines where they disassembled.[5]

Yet, creative nonfiction didn't exist in my mind as a category when I wrote my discursive double portrait, my two-part invention in prose, and to call it that now seems to retrofit and tame. Over the years, my students have invented forms they've called columbaria and lagniappe, indexes, and figments, tulip forms, phalansteries (following Roland Barthes), black-outs, and studies. If you're in search of models for reinhabiting otherwise exhausted forms, try turning to Emily Dickinson for what she does with the letter, or James Schuyler and the diary, or experimental filmmaker Martin Arnold and the Hollywood melodrama, or Bill Cunningham and the fashion column: in every case, the artist reappropriates a form. But they don't call what they're doing creative nonfiction.

I once arranged for my students and me to enjoy a special viewing of a Joseph Cornell box owned by the Rhode Island School of Design in the hope that Cornell could help us to theorize and then put into practice the idea of our writing as a plastic art (language-as-material); of the box as liberating form (if an essay is a box, what kind of box would one have it be?); and of objects as auratic bearers of memory or, because of their placement and juxtaposition inside a carefully delineated fascinational field, playful odes to the most ponderous metaphysics. Similarly audacious nonfiction forms are available daily if we care to look for them. Today, Rosamond Purcell's *Special Cases* in which she writes: "This book honors the form of a slide show or an exhibition organized around associative clusters of phenomena, yielding at all times to gravitational attraction."[6] Tomorrow, Roland Barthes, who in his book, *Roland Barthes*, writes of disparate objects brought into view by contiguity. He describes his book as "not monumental" but as "a proposition which each will come to saturate as he likes, as he can."[7] He offers a curious image for how he expects the work to act upon a reader: "I bestow upon you a certain semantic substance to run through like a ferret . . ."[8]

In another book that pertains, in particular, to biography but that is not conventionally biographical, his strange and beautiful triptych (his own *Three Lives*?), *Sade/Fourier/Loyola*, he introduces what he calls a "biographeme." It appears in the opening pages: ". . . were I a writer, and dead, how I would love it if my life, through the pains of some friendly and detached biographer, were to reduce itself to a few details, a few preferences, a few inflections, let us say: to 'biographemes' whose distinction and mobility might go beyond any fate and come to touch, like Epicurean atoms, some future body, destined to the same dispersion. . . ."[9]

He closes with "Sade's white muff, Fourier's flowerpots, Ignatius's Spanish eyes."[10]

What would constitute your own life's biographemes, or those of someone you love, or would love to write about?

1. Identify the absent interlocutor ever lurking in your prose, immanent in every conversation, and write instead to someone else.

2. Gather together an uncommon archive made of home movies and Wittgenstein, your aunt's rosary beads and father's garden logs, the nubbly surface of memory's grain, the Pocketbooks that shaped your early adolescence alongside a forgotten literary theorist of your choice. Incorporate a musical soundtrack as interlocutionary base and space, then write from there.

3. Ask the question no one is asking about earthquakes in Haiti or grand theft on Wall Street. Use a shift of prepositions and a counterintuitive juxtaposition to get you there.

4. If you fear that the internet flattens difference and dulls discerning faculties, identify fine distinctions and essay from there: start with "sleep" and "slumber."

5. Rather than describe improvisatory writing as "digressive," find the word for what it more precisely does, as in, inaugurates, celebrates, and busts; synchs, surfs and dignifies; rushes, breaks, and breathes.

All these opportunities for reinvention can happen under the aegis of creative nonfiction, but there remains the question of what's at stake in gathering together these practices in its name.

There is no writing without genre, of that we can be sure; no compositional practice that is genre-free. No grouping of words on a page that doesn't emerge in some way or other from inside a preexisting envelope. It is only when institutional (and market) pressures make genre cave in rather than open that the whole enterprise makes me melancholy. Then, rivalries between otherwise entwined entities spring up from the need to compete for ever-dwindling resources. At my own institution, a new administration has introduced seemingly new discourses into the "mission" of what we're supposed to provide our students, "experiential learning" and an emphasis on the practical among them. Perhaps in an effort to show their allegiance to this plan, and in the process, distinguish themselves from "creative writing," the Writing and Rhetoric program has adopted the motto: "Writing & Rhetoric is writing that gets things done; it is writing with consequences."

I can't help but picture writing as a vacuum cleaner, Swiffer, or managerial means to an orderly end. One kind of writing cleans things up; another kind of writing (creative nonfiction) makes a mess of things. Imagine majoring in that.

One kind of writing does. Another kind of writing un-does.

Staking claims, each program agrees in the name of genre to territorialize the imagination, and so, to vanquish it.

Thematizing not just aesthetic but institutional challenges, creative nonfiction requires its practitioners to work simultaneously inside a discipline and athwart it. Because it can't be boiled down, it lends itself to lively theorizing, myriad types of practice, and invention. Creative nonfiction doesn't add up, it doesn't amount to much, it doesn't count (in more than one sense of that word). This is one reason why it is so difficult to give an account of it. And, if, at the end of the day in which breakfast is ordered in place of lunch, if, at the end of a journey through a maze, we conclude that "we've gotten nothing done" and arrived nowhere, so be it. We needn't rely on an Audenesque truism as retort to our genre's refusal to get things done—"creative nonfiction makes nothing happen"—because we know this isn't true. All writing is consequential, especially if by consequence we mean that something or someone is changed in its process; if, through it, our characteristic modes of perception and discourse are transformed.

Creative nonfiction is *without* consequence only in this sense: insofar as it relies less on sequence than on synchrony, creative nonfiction is a genre *sans-sequence*. It's the genre *sans-sequence par excellence*. It's at its best when it stops counting, even though the desire to make it count might be one of the reasons it needed, in the first place, to be named.

# Notes

1  Jacques Derrida, "The Law of Genre," trans. Avital Ronell, *Critical Inquiry* 7 (Autumn 1980): 55–81.

2  Kenneth Goldsmith, *Uncreative Writing: Managing Language in the Digital Age* (New York: Columbia University Press, 2011).

3  Mikhail Epstein, *Emory Improvisations Home Page*, Emory University, www.emory.edu/INTELNET/impro_home.html.

4  Michel Foucault, "Friendship as a Way of Life," in *Foucault Live: Collected Interviews, 1961–1984*, ed. Sylvère Lotringer (New York: Semiotext(e), 1996), 308–12.

5  Mary Cappello, "The Trees are Aflame (A Two-Part Invention in Prose)," *American Letters & Commentary* (2004): 98–107.

6  Rosamond Purcell, *Special Cases: Natural Anomalies and Historical Monsters* (New York: Chronicle Books, 1997), 7.

7  Roland Barthes, *Roland Barthes*, trans. Richard Howard (New York: Farrar, Straus and Giroux, 1977), 174–5.

8  Ibid., 175.

9  Roland Barthes, *Sade/Fourier/Loyola*, trans. Richard Miller (1976; repr., Berkeley: University of California Press, 1989), 9.

10  Ibid., 9.

# Part II

# Structures

Hermit crabs and Harvard outlines. Sestinas and spiders' webs. Computer games and encyclopedias and maps. Essays like to dress up as other things. We often tell our students that nonfiction has the fewest rules, but that kind of freedom can lead to unwieldy, amorphous masses of flung-out language. The most creative of the nonfiction writers look for ways to organize the amorphous, to upend received, traditional forms and fit them to their own purposes. Like the drag queen or the hermit crab, we borrow our shapes and shells to find a space our bodies fit.

# 10

# On Scaffolding, Hermit Crabs, and the Real False Document

## Margot Singer

In 2007, Eileen Pollack published an essay in the *Writer's Chronicle* called "The Interplay of Form and Content in Creative Nonfiction." In this essay, Pollack makes the point that while most books on creative nonfiction divide the genre according to content—"memoir," "nature writing," "travel writing," and so on—it is more useful for writers to think in terms of form. Pollack writes: "The interplay between the central question that guides a writer's research and the form that helps the writer organize his or her findings is at the living, breathing heart of creative nonfiction."[1] The way we organize our material—the *structure* we are building as the words and ideas, images and facts spool out along the page—is an integral part of what a piece of writing is "about." Form and content, *logos* and *lexis*, are interdependent, synergistic. We know this, and yet, as vital as structure is to any discussion of craft, it rarely is discussed.

I want to talk about how structure affects the way we understand genre. I want to talk about scaffolding, architecture, houses, shells. Poets understand that in writing we're not just *thinking*, but building, constructing stanzas (literally, in Italian, "rooms") that the reader moves through not just chronologically but spatially as well. Prose writers, on the other hand, tend to think of structure in terms of time, not space. From Aristotle on, we've focused on beginnings, middles, and ends—what happened first, and then, and then. Narrative requires time. And so, in fiction and creative nonfiction, we don't often stray far from organizational schemes based on the logic of sequence: chronologically ordered scenes, numbered sections, lists. Indeed, we consider it "experimental"—and are compelled to borrow terms from music and the visual arts even to describe it—when a piece of writing adopts the atemporal structure of the lyric or the collage.

The fact is that something odd and interesting happens to our expectations of genre when you play around with the conventions of narrative form. "Without time," Ben Marcus has claimed, "fiction is nonfiction."[2] To

Marcus, fiction that is "essayistic, discursive, inert, philosophical, [and] timeless"—as opposed to "storylike"—feels like nonfiction precisely because it has dispensed with the conventions of narrative time. But Marcus is thinking narrowly about nonfiction. Without time, creative nonfiction is not quite nonfiction either. Lacking the familiar structures of logical sequence and linear narrative, the essay, too, morphs into a hybrid thing. Construct an essay as a collage of lyric segments—think of John McPhee's "The Search for Marvin Gardens," or David Shields' "42 Tattoos"—and the first thing many readers will ask is, What is this thing? Where is the story? And—most tellingly—is it "true"?

One particular hybrid nonfiction form that I would like to focus on is what Brenda Miller and Suzanne Paola have dubbed the "hermit crab essay." In their textbook, *Tell It Slant*, Miller and Paola coin this term to describe

> [the] kind of essay [that] appropriates other forms as an outer covering to protect its soft underbelly. It's an essay that deals with material that seems to have been born without its own carapace—material that's soft, exposed, tender and must look elsewhere to find the form that will best contain it.[3]

It's an appealing metaphor: the reclusive hermit crab hiding in a snail or mollusk shell, a "strange, new hybrid creature"[4] wearing borrowed armor, disguised inside a borrowed home. Examples of "hermit crab essays" include pieces that appropriate the form of a how-to guide (Brenda Miller), footnotes to a critical essay (Jenny Boully), a tarot card layout (Nancy Willard), a to-do list (Joe Wenderoth), an outline (Ander Monson), and contributors' notes (Michael Martone).

Indeed, Ander Monson's essay, "Outline toward a Theory of the Mine Versus the Mind and the Harvard Outline" seems to speak directly to Miller and Paola's point about the need to find a protective shell for a certain kind of tender, personal material. Monson writes:

i.   so maybe the outline is a kind of architecture I am trying to erect
ii.  to protect myself against my family, meaninglessness, and the future
    1. an artifice to get inside the past
    2. like a cold and unlit hole—what family tragedy is there behind me glittering like a vein
iii. perhaps it is a womb
    1. and this then has to do with my mother's death

2. a protective sheath, a comfort zone

iv. or it could be a shell[5]

Monson's outline foregrounds the interplay of form and content that Pollack talks about. It provides visual and metaphoric scaffolding that contains the excavations of Monson's mind, and armors the essay against becoming sentimental or trite. But the presence of the outline also unsettles the text, for of course it is not a proper outline at all, proceeding not logically but associatively, forming more of a poem than a rationally ordered train of thought. It's a faux outline—a critique of a real outline's rigid, rationalistic way of ordering thought. Monson's outline is, in fact, a fiction. All "hermit crab shells," if you will, are fictions. But what is *fiction* doing in a nonfiction text?

The "hermit crab essay," of course, is just a new name for a very old literary device: the false document. From its earliest days, the novel has borrowed other forms of nonfiction writing—letters, diaries, memos, newspaper articles, scientific reports—as a way of creating a greater sense of realism and authenticity. Richardson's and Laclos's epistolary novels, Defoe's fictional "autobiography" of Robinson Crusoe, complete with fake publisher's note, are "hermit crab" structures too. But while the false document provides a device for making realistic fictions seem more "real," in nonfiction the false document seems to have the opposite effect. The presence of the "hermit crab's shell"—Monson's faux outline, McPhee's invented Monopoly game, Martone's made-up contributor's notes—calls attention to the constructedness of *any* organizational scheme.

Like found-object sculpture (think of Duchamp's Ready-Mades), the "hermit crab essay" is always *both* an aesthetic artifact and an ironic commentary on the material of which it's made. (Parenthetically: in certain postmodern, formalist fictions, the false document works the same way, serving as an ironic deconstruction of other, conventional forms. Examples include Rob Reiner's mockumentary, *This is Spinal Tap*, or Michael Martone's *Blue Guide to Indiana*, or many of the short humor pieces on *McSweeney's* website.) The use of "found form" in creative nonfiction reminds us that the literary text is always a construction, not a transparent window onto "reality" or the "truth." Said another way: the truth lies in the form. In the structure and the scaffolding. In the exposed ducts and pipes and beams. In space as well as time. In the reminder that all writing forms an artificial shell.

# Notes

1 Eileen Pollack, "The Interplay of Form and Content in Creative Nonfiction," *Writer's Chronicle* 39, no. 5, March/April 2007, http://elink. awpwriter.org/m/awpChron/articles/epollack02.lasso.

2 Ben Marcus, "The Genre Artist," *The Believer*, July 2003, www.believermag. com/issues/200307/?read=article_marcus.

3 Brenda Miller and Suzanne Paola, *Tell It Slant: Writing and Shaping Creative Nonfiction* (New York: McGraw-Hill, 2004), 154.

4 Ibid., 154.

5 Ander Monson, *Neck Deep and Other Predicaments* (St. Paul: Graywolf Press, 2007), 11–12.

# 11

# Text Adventure

Ander Monson

A majority of sources cite *Spacewar!* (1962), a game in which two spaceships circle a planetary body and try to destroy each other, as the first instance of a computer game, a game played on a computer. This being a project of accuracy as well as a particular brand of supergeekery, this charting of the histories of games, though, it's important to note that the first computer game is probably *OXO (Noughts and Crosses)*, a simulation of Tic-Tac-Toe (which I suspect the seminal computer-hacker film *Wargames* later references) programmed by Alexander (Sandy) Douglas, occurring a decade earlier, in 1952. It does nothing spectacular, simulating paper and pencil, a very old technology, though for the first time you the user could play a game both *on* and *against* a computer, in this case the EDSAC, the University of Cambridge's proprietary machine, perhaps for the novelty of it or just to assuage your brainy loneliness.

*Spacewar!* is multiplayer, and much sexier, in that it allows the user to perform a sort of magic, to do something they could not do before, even on paper. Two spaceships are represented on the screen, real-time. They move around a singularity at the screen's center and can thrust, maneuver, and fire. If they hit the singularity, that player loses, ship destroyed, game over. If one player hits the other, ship destroyed, game over, and you're left on the machine, wondering whether to play again, and if so, with whom.

*Spacewar!* is still surprisingly playable (Google a Java emulator for it and play in your browser). It's fun, maybe the first killer app, reminiscent of later popular games like *Asteroids* (arcade or Atari) and at least the space battle portion of *Star Control 2* (PC). Because it looks like a contemporary game, it gets more attention. All these games are simple now but must have seemed wondrous then: to think you could use these massive, expensive machines, made for calculation via vacuum tubes, for *play!*

More interesting and involving from a textual standpoint are games commonly called text adventures (or sometimes more grandly called interactive fictions). This history starts with *Adventure* (1977), followed by *Colossal Cave Adventure, Zork,* and so on, often based loosely on readings of J. R. R. Tolkien's *Lord of the Rings* series along with remembered actual campus features of MIT and an actual spelunkable Kentucky cave. Rising at about the same time as the role-playing game *Dungeons & Dragons* (and with some similar features), these text games initiated the idea of a created, fictional computer space that a character (the player, a protagonist, an I) could explore on her own in the darkness or the flickering light of the computer lab, and gave birth to the genre of the adventure game, which remains one of the most popular types of computer games, because in our adventure-poor age we love a good adventure to remind us that there are things beyond our knowledge. These games also make more apparent claims on story (hence they're called by some interactive fictions): they're first person (everything is seen from the perspective of the character, via text), they build a narrative as they go, with the reader as protagonist, deciding what to do, which verb to try to use, which direction to take out of a room, whether or not to hit another character with a rock, how to solve one textual puzzle after another. Interactive fictions are notable for being some of the first games to use a natural-language parser, in which you would type in sentences what you (the player) wanted your character to do, and the computer would render the results of that action and return the results to you (in this way these games are similar to playing real-life role-playing games like *Dungeons & Dragons,* which can be thought of as a live, collaborative story experience, also accessed via language). One game in this genre, *Mindwheel,* bears significant note as it was developed in part by former US poet laureate Robert Pinsky: as part of the gameplay, it asks the player to assemble an original poem. Pinsky worked on quite a few of these games. He is now, among other things, the poetry editor of *Slate.com.*

One of the central pleasures of any game, graphic or textual, first person or third person, is exploration. This is a familiar trope in almost every computer game (simulations of board games and card games typically excepted, since they don't offer much that the old-technology game form doesn't except maybe the temporary and false relief of our near-constant lonelinesses), whether we're moving through three-dimensional outer space via one of many sorts of spacecraft/robotic exoskeletons with many varieties of missiles, lasers, proton torpedoes, cloaking devices, and so on; or of dungeons with swords and items and cloaks and magic spells; or of other mythical landscapes, haunted houses, or simulated domestic landscapes made strange by being inside them. Though I imagine that exploration is a major element of my (and most players') experiences, adventure games are almost always framed by an explicit or implied narrative element, a story, that contextualizes the actual play of the game and gives us a stated goal. In the absence of a narrative, we'll build our own: we are after all on some sort of quest, moving through a space, even if we do not know what for. For the most part, though, game designers have concluded that, for motivation, the player should be provided with some narrative framework, however basic (see also the early Atari 2600 game *Adventure:* all we know is that we—the we in this case is a small square on a screen—need to get the chalice from the black castle and return it to our own, and that's enough to fire us up). It is only through narrating our lives to ourselves that we are able to make any sense of events we experience, after all. We can't *not* narrate our lives—that's how memories are encoded and reencoded and reconsidered and chemically recombined.

While these games are set inside stories, the pleasure we get playing is certainly not the same as the pleasure we get reading stories (or essays, or anything else). Though there are the shared pleasures of inhabiting another's world for a while, the pleasure in story is (mostly) not in agency, but in immersion inside a world, a character, a brain, to be pulled along through an arc by an author. The pleasure in play, though, is mostly in agency, the ability to control the character against or inside the narrative, to kill off every non-player-character we can find, to work against the narrative, to be punk rock, to dress our golfer in the finest virtual, digital bling we can find. The pleasure in play is in the manipulation of a system to explore and expose its elements, to achieve goals, level up, accomplish salient tasks and be duly rewarded with loot, additional story, or other perks. Some of the deepest pleasures of games are in letting the player's agency get her into complicated emotional territory. What happens when given the choice to do good or evil, we do evil, as many of us will do? Usually the game narrative doesn't turn out all that differently: we're still the hero, even if reluctantly. We can still chuck the ring in the volcano, slay the final dragonlord, etc. We're just harassed by police or guards or whoever as we go. There's pleasure in that, of course, but there's also pleasure in real narrative agency: in a game like Atlus's *Catherine*, which focuses on a romantic dilemma stemming from an indiscretion, the decisions we make change the story significantly and are designed to reflect our response to a central emotional problem: how do we handle infidelity? *Bioshock* offers multiple endings: which you get depends on how you acted in the game. In *Mass Effect* and its sequels, at points you have murky moral choices: which character will you, as commander, sacrifice?

When that character's dead, he's out of the story—and the sequels—so your decisions echo throughout the entire gameworld.

As a player I am something of a completist. Often I'll know what's expected of me narratively—it's so obvious: I just defeated A with the boomerang and I have to get inside Tower B to learn another skill so I can explore Dungeon C in order to save Princess D, which I'm told is extremely urgent—but I don't do that immediately. God, why would I? "Extremely urgent" is code for put it off as long as I can in order to explore the fishing mini-game before going to Dungeon Z, and if I can get the Ocarina to play Melody J then I can be transported to a secret, previously inaccessible place. There is pleasure in delayed gratification (the slow motion as we approach the end of a novel made apparent by the dwindling pages, the knowledge that there's only one step left before the game's narrative arc will be concluded), but also through the act of coming up against the limits of the system, its constraints, its rules. There is always the possibility that if I don't get to an area on the map now it may become unavailable, a terrible thing to know and not act on. What I want is to know, to make sure. Sometimes I'll use one of the many available online FAQ or Walkthrough documents to make sure I haven't missed some nonobvious subquest. On some level I want to touch each boundary and know I have explored the entirety of the game's imagined landscape before moving on. This is the instinct of the essay: we get to pause time and tool around in the world as player/writer, avoiding that objective, however base or obvious or narrative or argumentative, instead following tangent after tangent, the curlicues of this particular brain and its contours, lighting up new spaces on the map bit by bit, knowing where we're supposed to be going and feeling the mounting tension from playing keepaway with it, delaying our return to the subject, or maybe by the time we get there we realize that wasn't our subject at all, and we're at the bottom of a very dark well without a flashlight, looking up.

This is one reason why my book, *Vanishing Point*, has glyphs that denote words that can be typed into the website for the book, that unlock new content. In some of the new content, the careful (read: obsessive) reader can click on the period from a sentence, for instance, to open up another essay. Another essay can be read fully only if you look at the HTML source code—which contains essay text in the hidden comment fields. It's designed to destabilize the source text: to provide openings to webtext that's mutable, updatable, and potentially multilayered, and to offer the reader another avenue of exploration.

I should admit that I am not fully happy yet with the interaction between website and text: it's clunky, but the best I could do. The way it works is something of a kludge, a hack, an attempt to make something of the technology we have working at this point. This is the problem with using recent technologies for the purpose of art: one always imagines that the technology to do the thing we really want is a few years down the road. If we were smarter and wanted to spend our time this way, we might invent it. Maybe we have invented it. But we're human, thus impatient. We give it a run with what we have. Then we have to celebrate its eventual failures, the compromises we make for the sake of readability, of reader pleasure. We know that if it comes down to it we will sacrifice ourselves and our glorious plans for the reader, because we want to be read.

This pleasure of exploration is also one of the pleasures of pre-Internet Bulletin Board Systems (BBSes) or any kind of node-and-networked, mainframed culture: one system leads to another, which opens up new branches, levels of security, problems to solve in whatever way we feel fit, whether hacker or social engineer, paragraph crafter or lyric essayist, and then that leads to another space, another system, ad infinitum, cue excitement. We light up sections of the map as we go deeper in. We light up sections of our brain, too, I suspect, as we go deeper into the text and into ourselves, even as we can lose ourselves to the software of the essay and the way the engineered, artificed brain makes us submit to its will. In some ways literature is like this too as one text references another, one chapter informs and illuminates another, as we discover a new, exciting author (holy shit! Selah Saterstrom, for instance! which then strangely leads to Chris Kraus' spectacular *I Love Dick*, which is dirty, yes, but not as dirty as it sounds, a multilayered novel slash memoir stripping away a great deal of the safety net of novels, which then leads us somewhere else, doorway after doorway opening before us) and we explore their entire bibliography (world), perhaps culminating in a particularly difficult text, a literary problem, a boss to be defeated with whatever new tactic we just learned, before being eventually, blissfully satisfied by our binge, provided we haven't moved onto other drugs, Amazon recommendations, if you like X then you're really going to have your mind blown by Y, and hey, kid, try this: it's bad for you.

The reading experience is an experience of exploration of a created world. The question is how closely do you want to control your reader? What work do you want her to do? What work are you willing to let her do? Good readers like work. We like focused work, when the writer's made a thing meant to be interacted with, whether it's trying to solve a crime or understanding the subtext of an evasive bit of dialogue. We like asking questions, wondering whether what this thing is that we're reading, whether it's what it says it is: perhaps it's more of a novel than a collection of short stories? more of a fiction than a memoir? We like putting things together: oh, chapter 8 echoes chapter 1; we read pattern and motif; some assembly required is okay with us as long as the resulting toy is cool and our agency in putting it together is rewarded. Getting to these realizations is a little like leveling up. Often enough we have so little agency in what we read. We read sequentially, usually, naturally, we think, left to right, top to bottom, never mind that this is a learned behavior of the Western world. Things happen in the order they happen.

Hacker culture embraces exploration: one tracks along the perimeter of a system, to try to find ways to get around security blocks, to repurpose algorithms to do other sorts of things, opening up a new port to allow connection, retraining a system daemon to do the work of opening up the shadowed /etc./passwords file or granting us a new permission. Each dead-end is a problem asking to be solved. A copy-protected game is a problem requiring understanding and an ingenious solution (duplication of a disk, intentional bad sectors and all). The first person or group to crack the copy-protection scheme on a newly released game would be feted across BBS systems or peer-to-peer networks, their name written up in .NFO files, often with ASCII art that accompanied each game, the electronic equivalent of boast, graffiti, or book jacket blurbs. This is something like colonization or conquest if not just simple exploration. It shows up too in phone phreak culture, those of us who explored new loops and PBXs, blue box tones, cellular networks, phone trunks, unsecured wifi routers, and documented our explorations with text files as evidence that we did this and here's how. What is a poem but evidence that the poet did this, something new, she hoped, made this and left it here for you to play with, to experience, or else why bother, and maybe you can do it too, or at least run its subroutines for a while on your hardware.

The somewhat clunky term *ergodic literature*, coined by critic Espen Aarseth, refers to texts in which "nontrivial effort is required to allow the reader to traverse the text."[1] This nontrivial effort is more than turning pages and reading sequential words, scene after scene (though let's all admit, when stuck in a long book, that this effort can feel nontrivial; yet it's not of what Aarseth speaks). An example of this is B. S. Johnson's 1969 novel *The Unfortunates*, which takes the form of a series of pages, some bound, some not, presented in a box. The reader is asked to read one chunk first and one chunk last, and everything else is shuffled randomly, or as the reader wishes. As a result, the reader has a bit more agency in texts like these: we know we're involved in the making of meaning or of narrative or of whatever. The resulting interaction between reader and text in ergodic literature comes closer to approximating play, exploration, the manipulation of a system, the interaction between player and game. We have to more actively play (with) the book in order to read it at all.

Some novels have begun (smartly) to incorporate game elements, for instance Mark Z. Danielewski's oft-cited *House of Leaves*. Like other novels, it wants to move us forward page by page in the book with an overarching narrative (a mystery) that frames the action. But the book also offers us a number of side quests in the form of footnotes, which can be followed or skipped, depending on how much of a completist the reader is, how interested the reader is in touching the edge of the book's created space. Consider each of these footnotes a door that might lead to an unlit, unexplored area of a dungeon, like how in David Foster Wallace's essays we can take the long route or the short one (and if we like DFW we'll take the long route because we know it's the best). We can pass these sidetracks up or take the fork. When reading this novel we are asked to physically manipulate the book (to rotate it in our hands, to read it in a mirror, and so on: reading this book feels, more often than not, like playing). As the reader is invited to play with and explore the text, one of the more memorable portions of the narrative involves the exploration of a house that is bigger on the inside than it is on the outside. (There's an obvious analog of this particular—or maybe any suitably immersive—book as a "house of leaves," larger on the interior, taken as a whole, as linguistic system than on its outside, taken piecemeal or as physical artifact.) Characters are literally wandering around in the dark, exploring, filming, often in spaces that feel more than a little like one of the *Final Fantasy* series dungeons, barely lit, confusing, occasionally terrifying, and exhilarating. So as we read the text, we are invited to traverse the book's own physical space (on the page) and narrative space (in the story and its side-quests), even as the story frames everything, moves us inexorably forward page after page in the artifact of the book. Still, it is a novel, not a game, and unless you break the rules and skip ahead a hundred pages, it is not possible in this particular novel to experience pages completely out of the order in which they are presented (aside from these asides, some of which are still finally sequential, and some are more rewarding than others). This novel (and any novel) exerts more control over our actions than a game can or should: because reading lights us up differently, because we *only* experience worlds of books through the lens of language—of description, of described action and motivation. This is partly why *House of Leaves* is successful: it knows enough to still be a novel, no matter how much it wants to be a game.

Danielewski's second novel, *Only Revolutions*, takes this further, composed as it is of two narratives, one that goes forward in the book, and one that reads backward. The reader is invited to read them in alternating order, flipping the book over to continue with the other narrative, at whichever pace she prefers. It's more difficult to play this book, partly because the manipulations we're asked to do must be combined with the nontrivial task of parsing the book's increasingly dense language. And there's no mystery to motivate us: and this is a key consideration: how will we motivate our reader? What secret pleasures might we offer her to counterbalance the frustrations of a book that asks a lot from us? *Only Revolutions* is a more enjoyable book on the level of the sentence—which is key for this reader, but I don't know many others who have managed to make it to the end(s).

A more recent play-book is Amaranth Borsuk and Brad Bouse's *Between Page and Screen*,[2] the text of which is a series of enigmatic glyphs that are only readable when opened in front of a webcam on a computer, at which point each glyph brings up texts that are projected real-time on the video of the reader holding the book. As the reader manipulates the book, she manipulates the text onscreen: she sees herself manipulating the text onscreen. It's cool, certainly, seeing ourselves reflected onscreen holding the book, holding projected text, moving it around, though it doesn't think enough about what it means for us to be holding the text in our virtual hands just yet. Still, it's a step forward in the right direction: the text is *only* accessible if you have the book and a computer and a connection to the ether. The text is involving us in a way we hadn't expected.

At the same time some games have clearly tried to mimic a novelistic or filmic narrative experience, usually to ill effect. The commercially successful arcade game *Dragon's Lair* (1983), which had extremely impressive graphics for its time, resembles a full-motion, professionally animated cartoon. The game tells a story as you play it, but the player's interaction with it is limited to periodically having to make a choice, moving the joystick in one direction or another, like a Choose Your Own Adventure novel choosing only which page to turn to, and this action selects one of a couple possible paths. The player input is extremely restricted, and the game gives top billing to the narrative (well, really it gives top billing to the graphics, which were spectacular enough to make it one of the most successful arcade games of all time; the narrative itself was always pretty thin by any standard). As such it has almost zero replay value (nor, in this writer's opinion, did it have much actual play value; it was not really any fun at all, though it did look cool, a not unsubstantial pleasure). The notable difference between *Final Fantasy XII*, which had a large narrative and elaborately filmic cut scenes but plenty of freedom for you to wander around and do whatever between them, and *Final Fantasy XIII*, which gives the player almost no agency at all—well, the difference couldn't be more obvious. *XIII* was unplayable, no matter how slick the combat mechanics and fantastic the camerawork was. Maybe it would be better watched.

Other games with more obvious literary ambitions include those text adventures, particularly *Zork, A Mind Forever Voyaging,* and *The Hitchhiker's Guide to the Galaxy* (cowritten with Douglas Adams, author of the novel upon which it was based). These games, lacking graphics, deal exclusively in text, the province of prose, and their gameplay is strongly based on narrative, but combined with exploration, humor (sometimes), and problem-solving. And they focus on *character,* so key to our experience of literature: one of the most notable characters to come out of this or any genre of computer game is Floyd the robot, from Steve Meretsky's *Planetfall*, the first game character said to have generated an emotional response from players. As the only companion of the main character on an apparently deserted planet, when he dies, giving his life (such as it is) to perform a vital action, it is unexpectedly emotional, even on replay. This game—and its sequel, *Stationfall*, were both subsequently adapted as novels (or novelizations—which merit a weird sidetrack that we won't indulge here—we can't follow every lead into the ether).

Part of the success of these games lies in their reliance on textual rather than graphic representations, requiring players to engage their imagination to envision characters much in the way that literature does. The attentive reader relishes the opportunity to do some work in a text, whether it's the imaginative act of envisioning characters and populating worlds or simply making inferences about things told to us in passing or off-camera. In the era of the touted end of reading, which deserves but won't get (at least not from me) scare quotes, writers would do well to remember how much readers dearly want to engage with stories and essays and such, even in unofficial but intensely popular modes like fan fiction.

All of this is not to suggest that games are somehow going to replace or become literature, but that there are opportunities for useful overlap in both directions: that as games have started to take on substantially more complex literary elements, the writer might consider ways of importing game elements in their work, thinking of the reader's experience as one requiring play, a fun but nontrivial effort, and carefully considering what work our texts ask or allow our readers to do, and how we motivate them to do that work. Collage starts getting us there, with the reader's nontrivial effort required to make connections, to elide white space and fragment. When narrative happens off-screen and offstage, when we see a before and an after but not the event itself, we experience what critic and comic artist Scott McCloud terms *closure*, which is how we understand action happening between two static panels of a comic.[3] The more challenging the project for the reader, the more we would do well to consider how we can cajole, coax, beat, or tempt readers into our evil lairs: do we offer them hints of genre tease? Can we immerse them in action and character before setting them free in our labyrinth? Or do we start big with a formal conceit, as in Julio Cortazár's *Hopscotch*, and let it bounce us around?

Jenny Boully's *The Book of Beginnings and Endings* requires a lot of reader effort as we are asked to parse or assemble the collection of starts and stops into some sort of larger order, but she pays that difficulty back at least partly in the pleasures of her language. Harryette Mullen's *Sleeping With the Dictionary* requires (or at least allows and encourages) linguistic transposition in order to parse the text and experience the essential doubleness—another kind of closure. The poems therein are readable and enjoyable as is, but when the reader starts to substitute words in her own mind, she activates hidden areas, bonus rooms, in the book. Texts that use received forms (the outline, the footnote, the index, etc.) also conjure that doubleness: we're aware that we're reading an outline, but also an essay, so the reader's experience is a superimposition of the two, a double image. Maybe these ask more from readers, but shouldn't we be encouraging readers to be more ambitious? Isn't that the point of writing? And reading? What we get out of these kinds of bookplay is engagement, deeper and more complicated fun, a bigger and more immersive entertainment better suited for our age. Which is what we're all after, right?

## Notes

1  Espen J. Aarseth, *Cybertext: Perspectives on Ergodic Literature* (Baltimore: Johns Hopkins University Press, 1997), 1.
2  Amaranth Borusk and Brad Bouse, *Between Page and Screen* (Los Angeles: Siglio Press, 2012).
3  See Scott McCloud, *Understanding Comics: The Invisible Art* (Northampton, MA: Tundra Publishing, 1993).

# 12

# Adventures in the Reference Section

Kevin Haworth

*The world is one big data problem.*

Gilad Elbaz, Silicon Valley investor[1]

I was a very average child. I liked to read, sure, but who didn't in those days? Perhaps the only noteworthy thing in my reading habits was the notebook I carried with me at all times, a composition notebook, with its recognizable speckled black and white cover and its wide-spaced lines to accommodate childish handwriting. I kept this notebook with me whenever I sat down with a book. I read for story, sure, but as I did, I strained the facts. How many superheroes came equipped with wings? (Answer: more than you would think.) How many battleships did the Imperial Japanese Navy deploy in the Pacific, and, most importantly, what were their names?

I dutifully documented all this information into the composition notebook until I had filled it with lists of all kinds. At first I was just annotating, compiling the facts of my limited intellectual world. But when I looked at these lists, page after page, they took on new and imaginative readings. Didn't these winged superheroes, listed together, make their own natural and interesting team? With a headquarters, high on a mountainside, that only they could reach? In one adventure, they met up with their friends, the underwater superheroes from page 22 of the notebook, at a remote Pacific island, one team coming up from the depths, the other descending from the sky. In the distance, one feathered hero, with his eagle eyes, could see all the battleships of the Japanese navy (page 42), just bracing for a fight.

This was the beginning of my creative process. It wasn't fiction, not exactly, not to me anyway, since I built these journeys of the imagination on the facts I had compiled into my own personal reference book. I did not create new superheroes—*that would be making stuff up*. Rather, I rearranged. My understanding of them as facts gave them a solidity, a force, a legitimacy. (Yes, I know superheroes are not real. Thanks, Mom.) I enjoyed putting them next to each other in ways that broke down old associations and created new pathways, new meanings.

This, to me, is the origin story of creative nonfiction. Lists lead to narrative. Information leads to imagination. Without information, as the book of Genesis tells us, all is *tohu v'vohu*, null and void, too empty for even God to make a shape.

Reference books are inherently hybrid. They mix text and image, numbers and letters. They assert authority while hiding the authorial voice behind the editorial board, the anonymously written article. Their facts fool the eye.

In 1979 I used some of my chore money to acquire, from one of the many yard sales my family would visit each Saturday morning, *Hammond's New Supreme World Atlas* of 1954. Nothing is quite so beautiful as an outdated reference book, which shimmers in the irony of *what was true* and *is true no longer*. Even as a child I sensed the many important lessons that atlas had to teach me, lessons taught in the vocabulary of color, scale, proximity, and order. I understood that Denmark (green) had much in common with Norway (pink), Sweden (orange) and Finland (yellow), because they *all appeared on the same page*. Germany, their large and dangerous recent enemy, lay safely several pages away, divided forever into West and East. Israel and Jordan, with borders are marked only in the faintest of uncertain lines, share a half-page; above them is the squat half-page devoted to Poland (what a brutal and elegant choice). Alaska, not yet a state, receives only a half-page for all its vastness; on the half-page below sits the Panama Canal Zone, a red artery cutting across the map, while Panama itself lies north and south, off-white and barely in view. There is British Honduras and French Guiana; Ceylon and East Bengal; the Aden Protectorate and Trucial Oman; French West Africa, Anglo-Egyptian Sudan, the Belgian Congo, all names as false, and as real, as Superman's Metropolis.

Look around you. Reference forms are everywhere, and nowhere. Facebook delivers you friendship in list form. Twitter parcels your thoughts into a book of aphorisms. You know my day by my Google history. Last week it was announced that the Encyclopedia Britannica, which gave legitimacy to so many middle-class bookshelves, will no longer be printed, and its generations of known facts sent into the ethereal space that exists online.

Despite this, writers are going back to the old, dusty reference books, to remember how we used to organize our worlds. I'm here to suggest that some of the most interesting and innovative recent work in our genre is occurring in the encounter with these kinds of books, in the noisy collision between *creative* and *nonfiction*. Separated, these two words can feel like opposites: creative on one side, nonfiction on the other. But there are writers who are developing new forms by embracing and employing that duality, melding their fluid creative ideas to the hard end of nonfiction, the reference section.

See, for example, Judith Schalansky's *An Atlas of Remote Islands*. Visually evocative of the standard Rand McNally, with its two-tone cover and simple cartography, it nonetheless inverts the form, drawing our attention to these islands on the outer edges of the typical map, too distant to be connected to their political home countries, at best "granted a place at a cartographical side table . . . footnotes to the mainland, expendable."[2] Like the best creative nonfiction, Schalansky's book asks us to reevaluate what matters, what is worth our notice. It uses many of the trappings of the classic atlas: the geographic coordinates, the area in square kilometers (but what island is ever square?), and the total population of each island, here so low that it feels like a collection of individual people rather than a mere number in a book. Each map carries a story, a point of focus. Her ethnographic tone ("The Banabans' most important tool is made of wild almond wood and sharpened turtle shell"[3]) grants authority to the details, sometimes historical, sometimes mythic or outright gothic ("The Banabans do not bury their dead. They let the bodies hang from their huts until the flesh has decomposed, then wash the skeleton in the sea"[4]), and asks us to take this knowledge at face value, the way that the traditional map, with its Mercator projection, once told us that Greenland is the size of Africa.

Or take *Encyclopedia*, a collaborative enterprise in a proposed five volumes, edited by Tisa Bryant, Miranda F. Mellis, and Kate Schatz. "Encyclopedias provide historical snapshots and are not pure," they write, "They are about knowledge, but are also rife with erasures."[5] Their encyclopedia is not comprehensive; its entries are unstable, incorporating drawings, charts, interviews, memoir, definitions, song lyrics, more. It rejects that most bedrock, masculinist proposition of encyclopedias: that size matters. In a typical encyclopedia, length equals importance. Here, Eileen Myles' one sentence entry for empiricism ("Though it means practical, it sounds like 'crown'"[6]) feels as weighty as Alice Notley's eight full pages on crime fiction. The five volumes are not yet finished, which feels appropriate.

Or, finally, Rebecca Solnit's *Infinite City*, her multilingual, polyvocal atlas/essay collection/alternative history of the City of San Francisco. "A city is a particular kind of place, perhaps best described as many worlds in one place," Solnit writes. "It compounds many versions without reconciling them."[7] Does that not sound like the very definition of breaking genre? With the help of artists, cartographers, and fellow writers, Solnit investigates the many simultaneous worlds that exist in San Francisco, that most diverse of American spaces. The traditional atlas moves horizontally; it separates, one map connected only at the edges to the one before. Solnit's book is vertical, transparent, nonexclusive. It is all disputed territory.

Every breaking of genre is also an embrace of genre; we recognize the platform, even as the train rushes by.

Because information is meaningless unless we find a structure for it.

In 2002, artist and University of Maryland professor Hasan Elahi was detained by the FBI and asked to account for his activities in the days following 9/11/01. Because, you know, Muslim name. In response, he began a program of absolute self-surveillance, sending the FBI a constant stream of information—his GPS location, pictures of his whereabouts, "airports you've slept in . . . tacos you ate . . . toilets you used," in the words of NPR interviewer Brooke Gladstone.[8] *Data camouflage*, Elahi calls it: so much unmediated information that each data point becomes a black dot in a sky of black dots, a needle in a stack of needles, all meaningless, without sound or fury. *Tohu v'vohu*. Information as overflow; creative nonfiction of the most extreme sort.

"The best place to hide a sentence," the Bolivian novelist Edmundo Paz Soldán writes, "is in a book."[9]

But give us the barest elements of structure, especially in a form we recognize, and we will find meaning. Connections emerge; a story forms between and around the facts. In every humble list there is a story waiting to be encountered. Consider the Vietnam War Memorial, where the austerity of names and dates—so simple, so plain—is almost too much to bear. Or consider Ai Weiwei, whose efforts to write down the names of the children killed in the Sichuan earthquake became a stinging rebuke of the Chinese government, for whom acknowledging that such information existed meant that those people existed, and that their government had failed to protect them. Or consider, in a different timbre, this list of the songs Syrian dictator Bashar al-Assad downloaded from iTunes while his tanks and infantry attacked the city of Homs, 101 miles north of Damascus:[10]

"Bizarre Love Triangle," New Order
"Don't Talk Just Kiss," Right Said Fred

"Sexy and I Know It," LMFAO
"God Gave Me You," Blake Shelton
"We Can't Go Wrong," The Cover Girls.

Thank you for the human ability to organize, to create references for ourselves of so many kinds, and all the ways that we have found to hide or reveal our stories in these factual forms. Thank you for the *OED*, the story of our language masquerading as a dictionary. Thank you for the abstract and the annotated bibliography and the footnote and the endnote. Thank you for the author bio and the acknowledgements page, the secret history of every book. Thank you for the depth chart, the cold ranking system beautifully overlaid on the visual field of the baseball diamond, basketball court, gridiron. Thank you for the infographic and the wordcloud, the references of the digital age. Thank you for the instruction manual and the almanac, artifacts of the analog professions. Thank you for the birth notice, first scribblings in a blank notebook, and the obituary, which can never tell the whole story. Thank you for the scaffold that helps me reach the sky.

## Notes

1 Gilad Elbaz, quoted in Quentin Hardy, "Just the Facts. Yes, All of Them," *New York Times*, March 24, 2012, www.nytimes.com/2012/03/25/ business/factuals-gil-elbaz-wants-to-gather-the-data-universe. html?pagewanted=all

2 Judith Schalansky, *An Atlas of Remote Islands: Fifty Islands I Have Not Visited and Never Will* (New York: Penguin, 2010), 13–14.

3 Ibid., 94.

4 Ibid.

5 Tisa Bryant, Miranda F. Mellis, and Kate Schatz, eds, *Encyclopedia, vol. 1, A-E* (Providence, RI: Encyclomedia, 2006), 7.

6 Eileen Myles, in Bryant et al., 241.

7 Rebecca Solnit, *Infinite City: A San Francisco Atlas* (Berkeley: University of California Press, 2010), vii.

8 Brooke Gladstone, "The Art of Self-Surveillance," *On the Media*, NPR, November 11, 2011.

9 Edmundo Paz Soldán, *The Matter of Desire*, trans. Lisa Carter (New York: Mariner Books, 2003), 143.

10 Michael Hann and Matthew Taylor, "Assad's iTunes Emails Show Assad's Music Taste from Chris Brown to Right Said Fred," *The Guardian*, March 14, 2012, www.guardian.co.uk/world/2012/mar/14/ assad-itunes-emails-chris-brown

# 13

# Autogeographies

Barrie Jean Borich

One afternoon, loitering in Manhattan between the end of a conference and a plane ride home to the Midwest, I happened to walk by the Empire State Building. It was a Sunday in early February, not yet tourist season, and there wasn't much of a line, so I decided, on a whim, to take the trek up to the legendary observation deck. I navigated banks of elevators, ticket lines, security rituals, and forced detours through souvenir shops, and even stood before an Empire State Building backdrop while a man took my picture, which I thought was some new kind of post 9/11 security procedure, but no, was just an attempt to get me to buy a souvenir portrait. (Had I purchased the photo on the way out I would have departed with an ironic keepsake, documenting the inner tourist trap corridors of the Empire State Building but leaving me no proof that I had stood on the precipice of that famous view.)

Eventually, after another cramped line and another upward lurch of the elevator, I arrived on deck, a circular balcony busy with bodies, most of the visitors speaking German, everyone leaning against the fencing, peering out over the city of cities. People pointed. People peered. And below, the city spread out like an enormous jigsaw puzzle. The day was clear so I could see everything of Manhattan, sites that for me, a native Chicagoan, were equally alien and familiar. I could see the Met Life Building where my brother's wife's brother worked, and the Chrysler Building my spouse's workman grandfather had helped build. To the south I could see the clustered spires of Lower Manhattan, with the missing tooth gap where the Twin Towers used to stand. I looked over the skyscraper peaks, the valley of the park, the gray-green runner of the East River, all locations I knew better from maps and movies than my own experience, but which, from this vantage point, I could see for the first time in actual relation to each other. The view offered me everyone's story of an iconic city, and too, as a native Midwesterner, from the metropolis in the middle known as the Second City, another visual interpretation of my own story set against the purportedly premier American city.

I tell this mundane tourist's tale because it illustrates two ways geographical concepts are important in creative nonfiction. The story of any human life is a tale of quest and containment and places are both destinations and receptacles, providing interpretive context and comparison. When writers reckon with the harmonies and disharmonies of their physical, emotional, and theoretical locations they often find new ways to render their life stories.

In any narrative, report, or rumination, place has more than one function. The first and most obvious, in terms of fundamental narrative craft, is that of setting. In film this concept is called *mis-en-scene*, and refers to what the auteur chooses to contain in any single frame, the scenic characteristics and telling details that help illuminate character and do some of the visceral work of telling the story. Writers must, of course, describe rather than simply capture these details, but the role setting plays is much the same.

But the function of place in any literary work is as more than just a container of action. I frequently ask my students to try to define the feeling one gets when crossing some geographical border, whether the line is as dramatic as the difference between Indiana and India or as subtle as the shift between regions of the American Midwest. Whether or not people are actively conscious of how land, landscape, architecture and other reverberations of their public and private surroundings affect them, the human sense of, and attachment to, place is—as geographers tell us—profound and deeply embedded in our stories.

Inside a Reno casino or atop a desolate mountaintop, the air smoky and dense, or muggy and reeking of spilled beer, or traffic-bound and rainy, or so windy and dry the back of our throats itch, we all respond to the texture of the atmosphere. Standing at the apex of Times Square, at the center of a frozen Minnesota Lake, or in a difficult in-law's kitchen, we respond physically and psychologically to the ways sounds, bodies, and objects move or don't move through space. In the neighborhood where we pay rent or own a home, or passing through a strange city where we can't make out the alphabet of the local signage, we journey between alienation and citizenship. Returning to avenues we haven't traversed since graduating eighth grade or peering out over a metropolis we've only seen before in the movies, places contain meanings according to the significance we ascribe to them. Even if our nonfiction writing is not about location, the geography of actual places permeates, bringing to the sensibility of the work, and the autobiography that forms through the work, the visceral, embodied texture of involvement with living.

But often, in creative nonfiction, place—particularly our autobiographical relationship to place—is not just a story element but also our subject, carrying us partway into a slippery partnership with scholarly disciplines such as history, geography, and cultural studies. This is one of the areas where the work literary artists make of our actual attachment to places operates in much the same way as actual people exist on our pages as both character and portrait. When we work in a form where our referents actually exist, our artistic purpose is not only to compose story or impression and unearth personal meaning but also to ethically bear witness to history, the actual past. The literary nonfiction writer need not mimic the work of the scholars concerned with similar questions, but neither can we avoid the fact that we've wandered into a realm where knowledge and studied opinion does already exist and possibly even overlaps with our own concerns.

Nonfictional experience of place might also lead us to unconventional structural choices. I have taken this thinking so far as to consider some of my own essays in terms of what visual artists call map art and interdisciplinary scholars call the deep map—which in my work means longer ruminative prose passages visually and spatially interrupted by close-up and retitled narrative segments, set-off like the inset maps of cities in a road atlas, the arrangement of the page imitating the feel of a highway map—my own quirky attempt to use the visual space of textual fragmentation to help tell what I call my *autogeography*. In my book *Body Geographic*, for instance, writing which began as braided essays about the intersections of place and the body, most particularly the juncture of my body and the city and suburbs of the Chicago I knew in childhood, became, through visual structure and narrative shifts, an attempt to render something broader, more map-like, conveying at once the breadth and intimacy inherent to the human relationship to place.

I coin this term *autogeography* to define the creative nonfiction project concerned with the ways we might map our bodies and places as interdependent historical strata. Such work means to be a bird's-eye view intended to illuminate and define personal and public history, political reality, the tactile evidence of what happened at this longitude and latitude. We aim to create a particular spatial resonance, the placiness of place. An autogeography is self-portrait in the form of a panoramic map of memory, history, lyric intuition, awareness of sensory space, research, and any other object or relic we pick up along the way that offers further evidence of what does or did or will happen here.

To illustrate my meaning I will tell of two other journeys up to the observation decks of skyscrapers. One of these buildings was, compared to the Empire State, not very tall at all—the 27th floor of the World Trade Center overlooking the harbor in Baltimore, Maryland, advertised as the "Top of the World." I ventured up to this relatively unimpressive height when researching my family immigration story. My Croat grandfather, along with his parents, my great grandmother and grandfather, arrived in America at a little known entry, the B&O Railroad's Locust Point Immigration Piers. Part of my research was historical. Over 2 million Eastern and Southern European immigrants entered the United States here in the late nineteenth and early twentieth century, many immediately boarding trains that carried them to the copper and iron mines of Michigan and Minnesota.

I had come here to walk the ground of this forgotten location of history where not even a plaque commemorates the American beginnings of immigrants such as my grandfather, and I had come to better understand the threads that led into a family story in which Chicago is the nexus into which all roads lead. So first I wanted to get the history right. But I wanted to do more than understand. I wanted to connect to a story that was otherwise no more concrete than a few typed lines on copies of immigration papers. I wanted a touchable, visceral experience of my father's Croatian identity.

Of the many forays and journeys I took in order to better understand my grandfather's story, the Top of the World was one of the most successful—silly as it was with its hyperbolic name and the loop of that old Karen Carpenter song playing endlessly on the observation deck sound system. This was because I could see from the overlook both the old pilings and the railroad tracks that ran from the harbor all the way into the westward haze. I couldn't see the railroad terminus of early-twentieth-century Chicago from the floor-to-ceiling windows at the Top of the World, but I knew that's where the train tracks headed, and so I was able to imagine, and later write about, a context invisible to me from ground level, the literal tracks of my family's journey from old Europe into the steel mill plain where I was born. Speculation, the fragments of family story, and history, fused with the language I would use to bring my version of the story to my autogeographical page.

The other high rise I will describe here is more impressive. The Sears Tower in Chicago, now called the Willis Tower, as of this writing still the tallest building of the Americas, locates its skydeck on the 104th floor. I had been away from Chicago for nearly 20 years before I ventured up for a look, though every time I'd traveled home to Chicago from Minneapolis by Amtrak I'd passed the entrance, and the entry line, just a block from Union Station. I had been in the skyscraper before, just once, years back when I worked in the Loop and a good friend from high school had a job in one of the glass-walled suites halfway up the tower. Tourists, not locals, queue up for skyscraper views, but I suppose I was some kind of tourist by the time my spouse Linnea and I, killing time downtown before our trip back to Minneapolis, noticed the line was short, and so why not? I had, after all, done it in Baltimore. We lined up behind extended families visiting from India or Pakistan, no one speaking English. To this day, my first visual memory of the interior of the Sears Tower is as a country where the native garb is the sari. We all waited patiently for our big experience, riding to the top of what had recently been downgraded to the second tallest skyscraper view on earth, just a year out from being trumped by new construction in Kuala Lumpur.

What I experienced at the top surprised me; it was as if I had stepped into the deep map of my own body. This was a landscape more familiar to me than any other, by virtue of map travel, car travel, train travel, bus travel, foot travel. I'd seen this view in motion, from the tiny windows of planes as they took off or landed, but never like this, standing still like a map or a diorama, but wider and more resonant, both silent and alive. To the south I saw the gray industrial corridors I'd dreamt of escaping from as a girl, then did escape, though not in the direction I'd planned. I saw the curve of Lake Michigan, smoky from the East Side and into the mill fields of Indiana, the steel mill plain that drew the immigrant generations of my family to this city nearly 100 years before. I saw the gold and white granite glow to the north, the richy-rich side of the city where as a girl I wished to someday live, before I understood the relationship between profession, economics, and urban geography. I saw the complete tableau of my origins, but as one place, both highway and inset, not segments, not regions. The signage of the skydeck noted that the view from this height on a clear day stretched across a breadth of four states, and I could see all four from here, the urban upheaval into the peaks and cluster of the city, then the falling away at the outskirts, into first the detritus of heavy industry, then, at the horizon hem, the flat farmland that had once been the tallgrass prairie.

My autogeographical discovery was that the industrial Midwest is actually one place, and the borders between suburbs and neighborhood were only subjective markers, whether my own or that of urban politicians and planners. The land itself and my ideas about history, identity, migration, the American city, and nonfiction form remapped themselves in that moment, forming a synthesis of experiential knowledge so profound within my own body that anything I ever try to write on the subject can only hope to succeed as a readable shadow.

# 14

# "Lions and Tigers and Bears, Oh My!": Courage and Creative Nonfiction

## Brenda Miller

Recently I gave a reading of a personal essay that was, well, *really* personal; it inadvertently revealed more about myself than I'd intended. Afterward people came up to congratulate me on the piece. Some zoomed right in and shook my hand; some hung back a little, embarrassed, whispering together. And all of them used the word "brave." As in: *you were so brave to read that essay.* Or, *I could never be so brave to write something like that.*

I thanked everyone warmly, and I really did appreciate the praise, but I went back to my seat feeling suddenly self-conscious, deflated, a fraud. Brave? I'm afraid of my own shadow. And to anoint me as *brave* made me feel as if I had really done something wrong, something no one in their right mind would do: risk making an ass of myself in public. Bravery implied that I had screwed up my courage to both write and read that essay, but I had simply been in my chair writing. I had been following form and language and voice to get the essay where it wanted to go; at some point momentum had taken over. I didn't even know what I was writing until I'd written it, and I'd been chuckling the whole time, enjoying myself immensely. I'd read the piece to that audience only because I liked the form so much, loved reading that voice aloud. *Brave?* Uh oh, I thought, what have I done?

*

When I think about the evolution of creative nonfiction—and about the ways contemporary creative nonfiction has embraced radical new ways to express personal material—I tend to think about it in these terms: about how courage, a concept that seems to belong more on the battlefield than in the writing room, seems to have been superseded by form. I've come to see that at some crucial point the best autobiographical writers shift their allegiance from experience, itself, to the *artifact* they're making of that experience. To do so, they mustn't find courage; they must, instead, become keenly interested in metaphor, image, syntax, and structure: all the stuff that comprises *form*. We're hammering out parallel plot lines, not plumbing the depths of our souls, but as a collateral to that technical work the soul does indeed get tapped and gushes forth.

Case in point: that really personal essay? I wrote it in the most impersonal form: a "table of figures," where the personal narrative is told, and embedded within, the ostensibly descriptive voice of an objective table of contents. Each section of the essay is another "figure," that is:

> Figure 1.1: A girl becomes aware of herself as a girl. . . . Note the mother instructing this girl that she must now wear a T-shirt while playing in the summertime with the boys on the block. Note the girl's naked torso, her downward gaze onto an expanse of bare flesh punctuated by two flat nipples. . . .

The essay goes on to examine the narrator's sexual history—from early childhood play, to losing her virginity, to living as a single woman in her forties—all in this list of figures, speaking of this girl (myself) in the third person. I started to really have fun with the piece when I added line graphs, tables, sidebars, and photographs. All these devices enabled me to see my material not as emotional "stuff" for which I needed to muster courage, but only as the raw information that could now be shaped into an essay I hoped would be both entertaining and effective. By contrasting deeply interior material with a more outward persona, I mitigated any sense that I might be about to perform an act of indecent exposure in public.

When creative nonfiction writers choose to write in nonlinear forms such as the short-short essay, the braided essay, or the "hermit crab," (as that Table of Figures piece demonstrates, an essay that appropriates another form as its shell), they magnify the fact that they are now manipulating experience for the sake of art. They immediately signal to the reader that their intent is not necessarily to convey information or fact—or to bravely reveal a dark past—but to create the truth of literature, of metaphor, which is not always so direct.

Concrete forms allow for what I like to call "inadvertent revelations," where the writer no longer seems in complete control. Revelation, or discovery, emerges organically from the writing; the *essay* now reveals information about the writer, rather than the writer revealing these things directly to the reader. So the writer doesn't need courage; the *essay* does.

My students understand this instinctively. In my lyric essay class, we begin our experimentations with short-short essays, where the restricted space of a single page forces my students to look for the small things, to magnify small details until they yield meaning. There's no runway on which to build up your courage, and so experience is now shaped to give precedence to image, scene, detail, subtle metaphor—not necessarily "feelings" or bare emotion. We use the online journal *Brevity*, edited by Dinty Moore, to seek out models for this form. Essays such as "The Sloth," by Jill Christman, may have their impetus in deep emotion, but the writing goes far beyond that, finds the mettle to explore this emotion through keen observation, precise language, and organic metaphor. It begins:

> There is a nothingness of temperature, a point on the body's mercury where our blood feels neither hot nor cold. I remember a morning swim on the black sand eastern coast of Costa Rica four months after my twenty-two-year-old fiancé was killed in a car accident. Walking into the water, disembodied by grief, I felt no barriers between my skin, the air, and the water.
>
> Later, standing under a trickle of water in the wooden outdoor shower, I heard a rustle, almost soundless, and looking up, expecting something small, I saw my first three-toed sloth.[1]

Notice how Christman's description of grief is not so much an emotional feeling as a physical one: "no barriers between my skin, the air, and the water." The information about the situation is given quickly—a fiancé killed—a context that lets us know our foundation, but her most effective move is that *she does not start with that line*. No, we start with a fact external to her own experience, a physical fact that will become the focal point for Christman's overarching metaphor. From the very first line, Christman is translating experience into artifact, and by doing so, the writing takes on its own courage.

Noticing the sloth, the narrator is taken outside of her introspection and so, in the end, this story becomes not a polemic about her own personal grief, but about new insights into the *nature* of grief, an articulation that does not necessarily arise from one's own experience, but from a literary perspective on the world.

After watching the sloth move in his slow yet deliberate progress through the branches, Christman ends the essay with:

> What else is this slow? Those famous creatures of slow—the snail, the tortoise—they move faster. Much. This slow seemed impossible, not real, like a trick of my sad head. Dripping and naked in the jungle, I thought, *That sloth is as slow as grief*. We were numb to the speed of the world. We were one temperature.[2]

From a statement of fact about equilibrium of temperature, we've come full circle, but this fact is now imbued with much more meaning. Because the essay is so short, every image must be precise, every word must further the narrator's discovery in a focused and measured way. The essay must move like the sloth—slowly, deliberately—opening up space for this grief to manifest. Christman didn't need courage; she needed that sloth. She needed that sloth to carry the weight of her grief for her, and eventually for us.

*

Writing a braided essay offers a slightly different kind of armor when venturing into dangerous or risky material. In these essays strands form, disappear, and reappear at strategic moments, creating a lively, interactive structure in which one's personal material now can interweave with material the world offers. The personal and the more "impersonal" can play off one another to create new meaning.

In Sherry Simpson's essay, "Fidelity," for example, she begins an emotionally wrenching piece about the complexities of marriage not with a scene of that marriage—the fights, the doubts, the ambivalence—but with a bear:

> I saw the bear first. I turned from the ocean's calm edge toward the dusky blue of Reid Glacier, and there it was, striding over the spit in the honeyed evening light, stiff green stalks of beach rye parting against its flanks. The bear was coming toward us. It was looking at us.
>
> "There's a bear," I said. My voice was low. My husband was standing by the kayak and turned around to look. I did not know what else to say.[3]

In this vivid first scene, we readers do not yet know what territory we'll be heading into (though the title gives us a good clue, plants the theme in our consciousness); we're simply hooked to know what will happen with that bear. As the essay progresses, Simpson interrupts this scene repeatedly to play it against the narrative strand of her marriage, so that it quickly becomes clear that this one vivid, extended scene with the bear—and the way husband and wife must face this danger together, the different ways they face this danger together—becomes emblematic of marriage itself. In that first section all the themes are planted for the essay to come: the lurking presence of danger, the impossibility of words to ward off that danger, the different directions these partners face, and how eventually they reconcile those differences to work together in order to survive.

The scene with the bear becomes what I like to call a "container" scene; not only does it provide narrative momentum (we want to know what physically happens), it "contains" the strong emotions involved in dealing with sensitive, emotional material. We come back to the bear four times in the narrative, and in between Simpson gives us scenes from the marriage, difficult scenes rendered quickly, with just the right detail. For example: "One night in bed, thinking of all I'd been learning without him, I said, *You're a speed bump in my life.* It may have been the cruelest thing I've ever said. He looked at me and replied, *I love you with all my heart. Why isn't that enough?* I couldn't say, but I knew the failure was in me, in wanting to make him something he was not and never would be."[4]

These reflections on her own culpability, the portrayal of the husband with his vulnerabilities and flaws, and her gradual insight into the essential nature of this relationship are all subsumed in the context of this one bear who seems to keep stalking the couple on this trip through the wilderness. The bear provides the narrator with an outer, concrete image that both bolsters and buffers the emotional material to come. The narrator and her husband, once they shake the bear, end up in the last sections of the easy in camaraderie, having survived both the ordeal of bear and long marriage:

> Such a relief to be still and quiet, to lie there open to the world and returned to ourselves. I slept with one hand tucked into his sleeping bag, one palm pressed against that steady warmth. In the morning, we sat and watched the clear light fill the stormy basin, grateful that for once there was nothing more to say.[5]

I know it can seem a paradox: that writings imbued with qualities of what we recognize as "honest" or "brave" may actually be so strong because they focus *away* from that material directly. This refocus can be on form, yes, but these forms also urge us to hone in on details that exist at an oblique slant to the center of the piece. These essays employ what I call "peripheral vision": turning the gaze to focus on something that seems peripheral to the emotional center or ostensible topic. Instead of facing your "stuff" head on, you turn away from it, zero in on something that has fluttered up on the side, and see what angle it gives you.

Case in point: For years I tried to write about two miscarriages I'd had as a very young woman: ectopic pregnancies that left me unable to bear children. Most of that writing was tortured, anguished, and very, very brave. I wept when I wrote. I felt the pain of it all over again. But one day, after traveling to Vermont in autumn, I remembered a small detail: the needlepoint kit my mother had bought for me as I recovered from emergency surgery.

So, instead of writing directly about pregnancy and miscarriages and lost love, I wrote about that needlepoint. I found myself looking not at my scarred belly, but at all those numbered squares, on the needle dipping in and out, feeling that thread moving through my fingers. While my mind was so occupied, the essay found all sorts of things to blab to the reader. And it turned out to be an essay not *about* pregnancy or miscarriage or infertility, but about how we keep bearing our lopsided fruits in spite of great loss and pain. I didn't need courage. I didn't need to be brave. I only needed that grimy piece of muslin in my hands.

✳

In Bernard Cooper's memoir *Truth Serum,* he describes his experiences growing up as a gay boy in Los Angeles, coming to terms with his sexuality, and then living as a gay man in the era of AIDS. In the eponymous essay "Truth Serum," a visit to his therapist's office (where he is seeking a "cure" for his homosexuality), becomes the through-line for an essay that goes back in time to his first sexual experiences with women, up to the present moment when he is living with a woman, and into the future, when he will settle into his identity as a gay man. Throughout it all, we periodically return to the doctor's office, where the narrator is compelled to tell the truth through the injection of truth serum. The onset of this drug leads to some pleasant physical sensations, and, "with the sudden candor of a drunk," he writes:

> I wanted to tell the doctors how happy I felt, but before the words could form, I heard what I thought was a receptionist typing in another room. Her typing would quicken—faster, manic, superhuman—and invariably I would think to myself: A million words a minute! What nimble fingers! The keys must be shooting sparks from the friction! And then I'd realize it wasn't the sound of typing after all, but something more miraculous—chattering watts of light showered down from a bulb on the ceiling. Stirred to the verge of tears, I wanted to shout, "Hold everything doctors. I can hear light!"[6]

The serum amplifies everything, sets his senses on high, and in the aftermath of the initial rush he is supposed to be able to express his essential truths. Throughout the essay, Cooper honestly explores his sexual feelings, coming to a conclusion that will disappoint his doctors but will be the launch pad for the rest of his life. The doctor's office becomes the anchoring point of this complex narrative, a supposedly safe place where he is encouraged to plumb the inner depths; late in the essay we return to the doctor's office, where Cooper muses: "I suppose I understood that no behavioral modification, no psychological revelation, was going to take away my desire for men, but in the end I went back to Dr. Sward's office because—this is the hardest confession of all—I wanted to hear the light."[7]

In a book full of hard confessions, this may seem like a trivial one. But I'd like to posit that the real "truth serum" in this essay is the writing itself: a prose that goes beyond the facts and gets at a truth accessed only through this artistic interpretation of experience. Truth serum activates when we find the right voice, the right form; when we've practiced enough so that we can tell when we're onto something. We "hear the light." We become candid as drunks. This truth serum loosens our lips, discretion be damned.

In his essay "Marketing Memory," Cooper expresses his befuddlement at the reaction to his memoir. Of course, he responds with pleasure at praise, but he tells us:

> After a reading, people would sometimes commend me for my "honesty" and "courage" in writing about sexuality. . . . I thanked these people, but tried to explain that I felt neither honest nor brave when I worked with personal subjects because the rigors of shaping sentences and paragraphs overwhelmed any sense that I was dealing with risky or revealing subject matter. In the end, my history became so much raw material to temper in the forge of craft. . . . Since "honesty" in writing is so often artless and indulgent, and since mere audacity so often masquerades as "courage," I was actually a little bothered by the suggestion that these were the work's most notable qualities. I'd hoped that the formal aspects of my autobiographical writing—its structure, language, and juxtaposition of images—were what made it worthwhile.[8]

I would like to propose that we—as readers, as writers, as appreciative members of an audience at a literary event—continue to appreciate more fully that "courage" often can be conveyed only when a writer is not feeling courageous at all. Honesty, authenticity, bravery: all these traits emerge under cover of form, voice, metaphor, syntax. The brave writer is the one who cares more about words, about sentences, about discovering significant detail, than about the feelings or experiences that engendered these words in the first place. The evolution of nonfiction, for me, means that we have become adept at recognizing that artifact owes a debt to experience, but that experience itself no longer has the upper hand.

## Notes

1   Jill Christman, "The Sloth," *Brevity*, no. 26, Winter 2008, www. creativenonfiction.org/brevity/past%20issues/brev26hotcold/christman_ sloth.html.

2  Ibid.
3  Sherry Simpson, "Fidelity," in *The Accidental Explorer: Wayfinding in Alaska* (Seattle: Sasquatch Books, 2008), 165.
4  Ibid., 166.
5  Ibid., 173–4.
6  Bernard Cooper, *Truth Serum* (New York: Mariner Books, 2007), 98.
7  Ibid., 106.
8  Bernard Cooper, "Marketing Memory," in *The Business of Memory: The Art of Remembering in the Age of Forgetting*, ed. Charles Baxter (St. Paul: Graywolf Press, 1999), 112.

## 15

# Traumatized Time

## David McGlynn

Near the end of my first year of graduate school at the University of Utah, I saw a flyer advertising a luncheon hosted by a sales representative from a textbook company. "Free food," the flyer promised. "Free books." My income that year, including my teaching stipend and the other various odd jobs I did around town, came out to a little more than $8,000. When an event offered free food, I went, regardless of who was throwing the party. The fact that this event promised not only free food but also *free books*—my favorite thing in the world—made it irresistible. I canceled my morning class and showed up 15 minutes early. When I walked in the door, the sales representative greeted me cordially. She pointed to the banquet of sandwiches and her far more elaborate display of glossy textbooks and anthologies. She told me that if I saw a book I liked, I could take it home with me.

By the end of the luncheon, I'd eaten at least fifty dollars worth of Subway sandwiches, and carried away a hundred dollars worth of books— all of which, I promised myself, I was going to read. The sales representative hadn't wasted her time and effort on me. When the weekend came, I lay on my bed with my window open and began to read. The first section of the first anthology I picked up was devoted to "memoir"—a genre I rarely ever read. Memoirs were the books politicians wrote after they'd left office. I was a fiction writer, and fiction writers considered memoir too self-indulgent, too interested in the banal and the mundane, too bereft of imagination. I believed, like a lot of naïve fiction writers, that the memoirist did little more than shine a flashlight into one ear and then write down whatever images and memories were projected from the other side. I'd even read a scathing essay about the genre by the writer William Gass, in which he says, "Why is it so exciting to say, now that everyone knows it anyway, 'I was born ... I was born ... I was born'? 'I pooped in my pants, I was betrayed, I made straight A's.'"[1] Up until that day, I'd felt duty-bound to not only avoid but to scorn memoir. But I was impoverished and earnest and intent on fulfilling my promise, so I shrugged and figured, *what the hell.*

One of the first stories in that section was "Family Album" by Mikal Gilmore, a music critic for *Rolling Stone* magazine. Gilmore's story, however, wasn't about music; it was about his brother, Gary Gilmore, the infamous murderer of two young men in Provo, Utah in the late 1970s and the first person sentenced to death in the United States after a ten-year moratorium on the death penalty. The event had made national headlines, and had inspired several films and books, including Norman Mailer's *Executioner's Song*. The iconic Nike slogan, "Just Do It," is an allusion to Gary Gilmore's alleged last words before meeting the firing squad.

Even after nine months of living in Utah, I still knew the state mainly through its clichés. The mountains were filled with ski resorts, the Great Salt Lake was . . . salty, and Salt Lake City was the headquarters of the Mormon Church. Like a lot of people, including a number of my graduate school classmates, I saw Utah as overwhelmingly homogenous, excessively wholesome, and, well, boring. But as I read Mikal Gilmore's account of his brother Gary's life, crime, and execution, I felt as though I was seeing Utah for the first time, and in a light far starker and more violent than I'd ever dared to imagine. I'd never read a story that struck so close to the bone, or that felt so urgent. I gasped at the final scene, then immediately turned back to the beginning and read the story straight through again. I stood up from my bed and paced about my bedroom reading whole paragraphs aloud. I lived in the attic of an old house high on a hill above downtown Salt Lake; when I at last closed the book and set it down, I crawled out my bedroom window onto the roof, where I sat for a long time staring at the valley: the copper-colored Wasatch mountains rising right out of the desert floor, the Great Salt Lake as flat and metallic as a sheet of foil, the bleached alkaline flats of the Great Basin—the sink drain of the North American continent— disappearing over the horizon. The orderly grid of Salt Lake City's streets ran in a straight line all the way to the southern tip of the valley. Right at the point where the mountains turned out of view, I could make out the lights of the Utah State Prison, where, 20 years earlier, Gary Gilmore had faced the firing squad.

Close to the end of "Family Album," after recounting the myriad ways his brother's crimes and infamous execution wreaked havoc in his life, all of which gets told in the past tense, Gilmore steps out from the plot in order to meditate, this time in the present tense and the plural first person, about the larger stakes of his tale. Gilmore writes:

> Murder has worked its way in our consciousness and our culture in the same way murder exists in our literature and film: we consume each

killing until there is another, more immediate or gripping one to take its place. When this murder story is finished, there will be another to intrigue and terrify that part of the world that has survived it. And then there will be another. Each will be a story; each will be treated and reported and remembered as a unique incident. Each murder will be solved, but murder itself will never be solved. You cannot solve murder without solving the human heart or the history that has rendered that heart so dark and desolate.[2]

One of the magical qualities of creative nonfiction—a magic first revealed to me in this story—is its ability to travel through time, to leap without preamble or warning from the narration of particular past events to the immediate and universal present. Because the writer who pens a memoir is contiguous with both the narrator who tells it and (in most cases) the character who lives through the events, she earns the right—by her survival and her reflection—to teach the reader a thing or two about the world. And by inhabiting the lives of other real people, memoir readers are able to discover new ways of understanding their own worlds, their own lives.

So it was with me. That Saturday in my Salt Lake City apartment, Gilmore's "Family Album," gave me a vocabulary for understanding my own world and life. Not only was I able to see Utah in a new and different light, I began to realize that I had my own complicated relationship to murder. When I was 15 years old, my closest friend was shot and killed in a home invasion, along with his father and older brother, a bizarre and incomprehensible crime that has never been solved. I'd talked to my friend on the phone just 20 minutes before he died; his mother and younger sister were sitting in their car, in my driveway, when the gunmen arrived. I'd spent the decade following the murders not exactly trying to forget them, but definitely trying to convince myself that they no longer affected me, that I was, in the jargon of pop-psychology, "over it." Sitting on my roof, I realized I wasn't over it at all: the murders had never stopped intriguing and terrifying me. I'd long ago abandoned the hope that the killers would ever be identified or brought to justice; instead, it was the absence of motives or suspects, the utter dearth of answers, that had informed my life, fastening to my eyes the lenses through which I viewed everything from friendship and love to religion and rationality. Sudden, unforeseen disasters had informed my storytelling for years, but before that day I'd never considered the possibility that I might have something to say about murder. But now I felt a story taking shape: what was once a knotted jumble of inarticulable emotions and surreal memories was metamorphosing into language, and into a communicable order. I climbed down from the roof, back inside my window, and that night I began my first attempt at what would become, eleven years later, my own memoir, *A Door in the Ocean*.

In the dozen or so years that have elapsed since I first encountered Gilmore's "Family Album," I've learned to keep an eye out for dangerous stories lurking in unexpected places. These days I teach at a small, liberal-arts college in northeast Wisconsin, a school of about 1,500 students, smack in the center of a town of about 75,000 people. Twenty-five miles south of Green Bay, the Packers are a local religion; so are deer hunting and the Friday fish fry. When I tell my neighbors where I work, they frequently assume my students are spoiled kids from the big city suburbs who have never suffered hardship or had to work a day in their young lives. It's true that a number of my students hail from the suburbs of Chicago or Minneapolis or Milwaukee, but nearly all of them have substantial scholarships and student loan bills. And a surprising number have been through some amazingly harrowing and traumatic ordeals. I've had veterans of the war in Afghanistan, cancer survivors, and political refugees. In one nonfiction workshop, I had a student whose family was persecuted in the early 1970s during the Bangladesh Revolution, a student whose sister was missing for several years, a student who was diagnosed with bipolar disorder when she was just 14, and a student with an eating disorder so severe she twice dropped out of college. Each of these young writers was drawn to nonfiction because they understood, in a way more instinctive than conscious, that they had stories to tell.

Yet even the students who recognize their stories' dramatic potential struggle with the telling. In the early going, most tend toward exposition— the old, clichéd problem of telling instead of showing—a phenomenon that can be partially chalked up to inexperience and impatience, but also stems, I believe, from a deeper fear about devolving into melodrama or pimping their hard experiences for gratuitous attention. It's an apprehension common among memoirists: Michael Ryan, author of the highly acclaimed *Secret Life*, says, "Any autobiographer who does not constantly torment himself with the question, 'Is this interesting to anyone else?' is probably going to write a book that isn't."[3] Rarely, though sometimes, my students fret about injuring the people they're writing about; more often, they worry that the elements from which a story is made—language, plot, character—cannot adequately capture or express the events as they were experienced. Simply telling of the story threatens to turn suffering into schmaltz.

Some students circumvent these concerns by writing in the present tense. It's a logical solution, for the present tense allows the author to inhabit the point of view of her younger self, even if the narrator's diction and tone remain unambiguously adult, and allows the reader to ride shotgun as the action unfolds. And yet the present tense also exudes a timelessness that allows the narrator to move backward and forwards in time. The narrator can be a child in one paragraph, the storytelling urgent and immediate, then in the next, a reflective and clinical adult who attempts to make sense of what the reader experienced only a moment before. The present tense's timelessness, moreover, mirrors the traumatic experience, which often disrupts the orderly progression of chronological time and intrudes, without warning, on the victim. Psychiatrist Dori Laub notes, "Trauma survivors live not with memories of the past, but with an event that could not and did not proceed through to its completion, has no ending, attained no closure, and therefore, as far as its survivors are concerned, continues into the present and is current in every respect."[4]

Perhaps the most famous, and unquestionably the most controversial, example of a trauma memoir told in the present tense is *The Kiss*, Kathryn Harrison's 1997 memoir about her incestuous affair with her father. After a short preamble, the story unfolds in more or less linear time, from the author's early childhood, to her teenage years, to her fateful reunion with her father her freshman year of college—all told in spare, staccato-like declarative sentences. Harrison writes on the opening page:

> One of us flies, the other brings a car, and in it we set out for some destination. Increasingly, the places we go are unreal places: the Petrified Forest, Monument Valley, the Grand Canyon—places as stark and beautiful as those revealed in satellite photographs of distant planets. Airless, burning, inhuman.
>
> Against such backdrops, my father takes my face in his hands. He tips it up and kisses my closed eyes, my throat. I feel his fingers in the hair at the nape of my neck. I feel his hot breath on my eyelids.[5]

By comparing the locations of her rendezvous with images of distant planets, the narrator announces that her own story will take place at a great remove, through a wide-angled lens. In Harrison's case, present tense is an effective device. *The Kiss* is a swift and haunting read. But the present tense isn't without pitfalls. Though it seems more "immediate" than the past tense, the present tense calls even greater attention to itself as an artificial construction. No memoir—indeed, no story—is ever written in real time, as the action actually happens. Indeed, human consciousness itself unfolds in the past tense: we're only aware of an action or a sensation after it has occurred (even if the time between the event and our comprehension of it is miniscule). The fact that the narrator of *The Kiss* and her father go, in the same sentence and in the present tense, to the Petrified Forest in California, Monument Valley in Utah, and the Grand Canyon in Arizona, signals the author's deliberate efforts to manipulate time and distance, which in turn raises questions about the veracity of the narrative—whether the author is really telling the truth. Critic Leigh Gilmore points out, "The history of American autobiography strongly suggests (at least in the American tradition) that autobiographical subjects are judged in part by whether they are appropriately representative."[6] A memoir's resonance and its truthfulness are inextricably entwined. James Frey's *A Million Little Pieces* is a testament to how deliberately duping a reader—especially if the reader is a billionaire talk-show host—can lead to negative consequences.

At this point, someone in my class usually raises her hand and asks, "What intelligent reader really forgets that she's reading a story—a made and invented thing, a different kind of narrative than a newspaper article? Isn't the story more important?" Perhaps the better question is: is there anything better than forgetting? Michael Ryan again: "Without invention, he [the autobiographer] must fascinate us as much as a novelist with the endlessly interesting interactions between character (people) and plot (what happens to them), just as we are fascinated in and by our own lives."[7] Good stories, be they works of fiction or nonfiction, generate for the reader the pleasurable illusion of inhabiting a different time and place, along with all its concomitant foreign sights and sounds and smells. Good stories turn on the imagination, which is why those of us who love stories love them more than movies or television, which do our imagining for us.

But *The Kiss* and *A Million Little Pieces* aren't famous for their powers of illusion. They're famous for their scandalous confessions, or the scandals produced by their false confessions. They're famous for what they reveal rather than how they reveal it. It's interesting that Kathryn Harrison describes *The Kiss'* unreal locations as "airless, burning," and "inhuman." Over time the memoir itself starts to feel similarly airless and inhuman, the senses ignored. For example, the moment of consummation with her father—the moment the book has been building toward for 136 pages— practically sounds like a Freudian case study:

> The sight of him naked: at that point I fall completely asleep. I arrive at the state promised by the narcotic kiss in the airport. In years to come, I won't be able to remember one instance of our lying together. I'll have a composite, generic memory. I'll know that he was always on top and that I always lay still, as if I had, in truth, fallen from a great height. . . . No matter how hard I try, pushing myself to inhabit my past, I'll recoil from what will always seem impossible.[8]

James Alan McPherson has argued that Harrison's critics "tend to ignore the mystical threads that parallel the sexual theme of the book."[9] Specifically, McPherson argues, Harrison delves into her painful memories "in order to connect with what Augustine called the place 'beyond memory.'"[10] Harrison's movement "beyond memory" is clearly evident here; memories of having sex with her father elude her. It's possible, following McPherson's argument, to read Kathryn Harrison as channeling Saint Catherine of Siena, and to view Kathryn's falling asleep at the sight of her father's body as an ecstatic vision, similar to Saint Catherine experiencing a vision of God. McPherson's analysis is convincing and seems to bolster Laub's argument that for the victim, the traumatic experience remains "current in every respect." The trancelike sleep that allowed Harrison to lie down in darkness now obscures her ability, years later, to remember.

But, as a reader, as a lover of stories, I must confess I'm disappointed. It's not that I want a graphic sex scene between a middle-aged father and his teenage daughter, but I'm nevertheless bored by the author's "composite, generic memories." I can't think of a single great literary work, from Augustine's *Confessions* to Styron's *The Confessions of Nat Turner,* made of anything composite or generic. The composite and the generic, by definition, aren't very memorable, nor do they help capture or mitigate the trauma at the heart of the story. Psychiatrist Judith Herman argues, "A narrative that does not include the traumatic imagery and bodily sensations is barren and incomplete."[11]

Harrison's "composite, generic memories" aren't simply incomplete. They're also self-conscious. The author analyzes her story as she tells it, and so prevents herself, and her reader, from disappearing into the details. If a reader is to feel as fascinated by the characters and events in the story as she is with her own life, as Michael Ryan insists, she must be allowed to suspend her disbelief that the characters are the puppets of an author standing above the theater with her fingers on the strings.

If the goal is to generate the illusion of immediacy and intimacy while expressing the traumatic experience as accurately as possible, manipulating time isn't the only option. Narrative form itself might be bent. When it comes to bending form, especially where trauma is concerned, there aren't many examples better than Tim O'Brien's *The Things They Carried.* Despite the fact that O'Brien calls the book "a work of fiction," it frequently calls attention to the problems of distinguishing "true" from "false" as well as "real" from "not-real." The first story in *The Things They Carried,* which shares the book's title, is the most famous, the most widely anthologized, the most often read, but it's in the rest of the book that O'Brien most deliberately confounds the border between fiction and nonfiction.[12]

O'Brien's confabulations of fact with fiction are both informed and expressed by narrative structure of *The Things They Carried*—a structure that denies a linear trajectory between a beginning and an end and instead constructs a text laid out like shrapnel from a bomb, with fragments scattered across time and geography. In the same way that a kaleidoscope twists and disperses sunlight, the individual stories in *The Things They Carried* bend a fragmented shard of the larger narrative, braided it into a fractured whole. O'Brien provides insight into his own narrative strategy:

> In any war story, but especially a true one, it's difficult to separate what happened from what seemed to happen. What seems to happen becomes its own happening and has to be told that way. The angles of vision are skewed. When a booby trap explodes, you close your eyes and duck and float outside yourself. When a guy dies, like Curt Lemon, you look away and then look back for a moment and then look away again. The pictures get jumbled; you tend to miss a lot. And then afterward, when you go to tell about it, there is always that surreal seemingness, which makes the story seem untrue, but which in fact represents the hard and exact truth as it *seemed*.[13]

By presenting his story through "skewed" and "exploded" angles, O'Brien allows for a conjoining of emotions that under other circumstances might be prevented from intermingling. When O'Brien tells the story of Curt Lemon stepping on a booby-trap and blowing up into a tree, he writes: "I remember pieces of skin and something wet and yellow that must've been the intestines. The gore was horrible, and stays with me. But what wakes me up twenty years later is Dave Jensen singing 'Lemon Tree' as we threw down the parts."[14] Curt Lemon's death is both horrible and humorous. The horror draws its force from the humor and vice-versa; as a result, the reader experiences, by way of the book's form, the contradictions of war, the same confusions and mysteries and explosions the characters experience. The kaleidoscope disallows the disjunction between form and content, for it is the content that produces the form, while the form enriches and deepens the experience of the content—the vertigo and horror and hilarity of war. Moreover, O'Brien's "surreal seemingness" and the kaleidoscopic narrative form that contains and expresses it mirrors Judith Herman's observations that reconstructing traumatic experiences "resembles putting together a difficult picture puzzle" and "is often based heavily . . . upon paradigmatic incidents, with the understanding that one episode stands for many."[15]

Experimenting with the puzzle pieces of storytelling—time, structure, form—has helped many of my students find their way through the reservations and hang-ups that roadblock the telling of their stories. The young woman with bipolar disorder struggled to write about her time in an in-patient psychiatric facility until she devised a structure she termed "scattershot": dramatic scenes interspersed with highly compressed moments of reverie, journal entries, and letters from her family. Though chaotic at first, she was stubborn with the form and over time worked her story into a finely tuned and lyrical narrative that both captured the experience of her condition and the eerie sensation of living outside her body, which, too, is part of the disease. Granted permission to bend the form of her story, she, like a number of her classmates, was able to set aside her worry about what her story left out instead to concentrate on the scenes she cared most about. By exploding the story's structure and traumatizing its use of time, she found a way to not only tell but, more importantly, truthfully represent the story of her young life.

I, too, felt like a puzzle worker during the many years I worked on *A Door in the Ocean*. Though each event in the story occurred in a specific time and place, I initially found myself unable to write the story chronologically or in a singular, uniform tone. Some sections of the memoir, such as the account of the events immediately surrounding the murders of my friend and his brother and father, felt most natural and most dramatic in the present tense, which allowed me to reimmerse into that strange, surreal, and painful time. Certain images—the police sirens flashing in my friend's window when his house appeared on the ten o'clock news or the white September sky as I wandered listlessly around my high school courtyard the next morning—returned to my memory as vividly as if they'd just occurred, as open and unresolved as Dori Laub suggests. Yet the chapters detailing the longer-term effects of the murders, including the way the shock and confusion pushed me toward my father and stepmother's fervent evangelical Christianity, begged for refraction through a distanced, academic, kaleidoscopic lens.

As a result, the memoir's early chapters rushed forward, heedless and headlong, while the later chapters were more essay-like, fueled more by a desire to mediate and reflect than to narrate or dramatize. It was only with the help of several readers and two editors that I managed to align the disparate sections into a cohesive whole. And it was only during the process of wrangling the different sections together that I began to truly understand just how not "over" the murders I really was. They'd haunted and informed every big event in my life since they'd happened, from my college graduation to my wedding to the day I leaned over the isolette that held my newborn son, born with weak lungs and pneumonia, and begged God to save his life. Now arranged chronologically and narrated in the past tense, *A Door in the Ocean* might be described as possessing a traditional structure and tone. But the memoir's final form is only the floating peak of the berg. Beneath the waterline lurks the trauma that the story itself helped me to first face, then tell, then understand.

## Notes

1 William H. Gass, "The Art of Self: Autobiography in an Age of Narcissism," *Harper's*, May 1994, 43–52.

2 Mikal Gilmore, "Family Album," in *The Granta Book of the Family*, ed. Bill Buford (New York: Granta Books, 1997), 334.

3 Michael Ryan, "Tell Me a Story," in *The Business of Memory: The Art of Remembering in an Age of Forgetting*, ed. Charles Baxter (St. Paul: Graywolf Press, 1999), 139.

4 Shoshana Felman and Dori Laub, M. D., *Testimony: Crises of Witnessing in Literature, Psychoanalysis, and History* (New York: Routledge, 1992), 69.

5 Kathryn Harrison, *The Kiss* (New York: Random House, 1997), 3.

6 Leigh Gilmore, *The Limits of Autobiography: Trauma and Testimony* (Ithaca: Cornell University Press, 2001), 49.

7 Ibid., 139.

8 Ibid., 137.

9 James Alan McPherson, "El Camino Real," in *The Business of Memory*, ed. Baxter, 69.

10 Ibid.

11 Judith Herman, M. D., *Trauma and Recovery* (New York: Basic Books, 1997), 177.

12 Tobey Herzog's "Tim O'Brien's 'True Lies' (?)," *MFS: Modern Fiction Studies* 46, no. 4 (2000): 893–916 discusses O'Brien's propensity for creating "literary lies"—by which Herzog means, ironically, works of fiction so convincing they seem like nonfiction. Herzog recounts a reading O'Brien gave at Wabash College in Indiana:

O'Brien began his evening presentation to an audience of students, faculty, and townspeople, including some Vietnam veterans, with what he labeled a "personal war story." As he told (not read) this story, O'Brien recalled his difficult decision to enter the United States Army despite his strongly held belief that the war in Vietnam was wrong. "Certain blood was being shed for uncertain reasons," he explained, using his oft-repeated refrain. He went on to describe his summer of 1968, the time immediately after his graduation from Macalester College and subsequent receipt of a draft notice. The internal conflict surrounding his moral dilemma—avoid induction by fleeing to Canada or serve his country by entering the army—culminated in his trip to the Rainy River, which forms part of the border between Minnesota and Canada, where O'Brien was compelled to choose his future. . . .

At the end of his storytelling, O'Brien paused as the Wabash audience nodded knowingly at the story's conclusion: Tim O'Brien had chosen to enter the army, to fight, and not to flee across the river into Canada. Then, after a dramatic pause, O'Brien confessed: the story was made up; he had lied to the Wabash audience—well, sort of. Real life soldier-author Tim O'Brien had indeed considered fleeing to Canada in the summer of 1968, and the thoughts, questions, and fears of the real man did mirror those of the fictional narrator in the story. Yet the incidents on the Rainy River, so realistically described, simply did not occur in O'Brien's own life. The result: after the reading, some audience members expressed their frustration to me about O'Brien's seemingly unnecessary lie. For example, a few veterans, who perhaps came with unrealistic expectations, felt manipulated by O'Brien's presentation of this "personal war story." Wanting to bond with him, they expected their fellow veteran to share some of his actual war-related experiences. Other audience members, present to hear O'Brien read from his fiction, felt tricked without understanding the purpose for this deception. Their trust of him as a person and as an author was undermined.

13  Tim O'Brien, *The Things They Carried* (New York: Broadway, 1990), 71.
14  Ibid., 83.
15  Herman, 184, 187.

# 16

# Split Tone

## Lee Martin

One of the things I've always valued about creative nonfiction is the fact that it refuses to be owned by any one special interest group. The poets don't own it, the fiction writers don't own it, the journalists don't own it. The genre, so supple, resists any attempt to claim and tame it, to bend it to fit anyone's more rigid notion of what it should be and how one should go about making it so. Sassy lad or miss that it is, it reinvents itself in response to the material that calls out for its container.

Let's begin with the word "sepia," and how I thought I knew something about it and then found out there was more to know. Isn't that always the way? More facts to gather. More knowledge to acquire. I've long known about sepia photographs—of course, known them, at least, when I've seen them—but I had no idea about the origin of the term or what happened in the dark room to achieve that sepia effect. Brown. That's what I knew. Brown pictures. Not black and white, but shades of brown. I had no idea that the word sepia had anything to do with the cuttlefish and the squid, that sepia is actually a secretion extracted from their ink sacs, that the chemically inert pigment is used as a drawing ink and a watercolor. I had to go looking for those facts.

Which then made me curious about exactly how a sepia photograph comes to be. More research told me more than my non-scientific brain could process, but I think I understand correctly that sepia toning is the result of three stages of chemical baths: one to bleach the metallic silver of a print to silver halide, a second to wash away excess potassium ferricyanide, and a third to convert the silver halides to silver sulfide. Incomplete bleaching creates a multi-toned image with sepia highlights and grey mid-tones and shadows. This is called *split toning*.

It's this term, "split toning," that helps me think about texture and dramatic effect in creative nonfiction. I imagine that we all expect certain things of the genre depending on how we've defined and are willing to adjust our aesthetics, but I'm guessing we can all agree that the genre, no matter our individual aesthetic, demands some degree of allegiance to fact. We have, then, at the start an impulse centered in the importance of something factual that brings us to the page—a replication of event, a recreation of character, a meditation on the nature of this or that; a report, in other words, from some part of the known world, even if what's known is known only in memory.

But once we get to the page, something factual in tow, we're faced with all sorts of choices for how to present the facts, how to use them, how to create an experience for readers that will depend not only on the reporting of fact but also on the stylistic presentation—the coloring and shading and texture, we might say—of what the writer has come to document. This is what excites me about the genre—this expectation that fact, so styled, will create an emotional experience for the reader. To look upon a color digital photograph, I'd suggest is one thing, particularly such a photograph taken by a photographer whose only intention is to document, not interpret or style via choices in lighting, perspective, etc., what he or she sees in what we used to call the viewfinder and now in our digital era, the LCD screen. To look upon a black and white photograph, printed from the same shot, even if the black and white is still merely representational, is quite another thing. The use of sepia tones creates yet another experience for the viewer, and for me the difference often lies in how my emotional response is "arranged" for me by the way the print uses depth and texture and shading to create something that the representational shot isn't able to manage.

So "split-toning." That's what I admire in creative nonfiction, no matter whether we're talking about the memoir, the personal essay, literary journalism, or any of the other major sub-forms of the genre. I admire the way the textures and shades of a piece can make me feel something. I like the way a piece of nonfiction can feel like a poem, a story, a novel. And this is the point where I begin to wonder whether we can take a fact in a piece of nonfiction and overlay it with any one of a number of techniques to achieve an artistic and emotional effect that the fact alone might not be able to convey. I could argue, for example, that lying, imagining, or subverting might pay off in any given piece.

I was thinking about all of this lately when I was going through one of my own essays, "All Those Fathers That Night," in preparation for a reading I was about to do.[1] It's an essay about parenthood, about fathers and sons, about the fact that I have no children and the fact that when my father first found out my mother was pregnant with me he asked the doctor, "Can you get rid of it?" But before all that, it's an essay that comes from my obsession with a story from my hometown when I was a boy, a story that didn't involve me in its facts. An alcoholic man, the father of six children, including a set of triplets, came by the barber shop one summer evening, and, when the barber told him that a state trooper had been in earlier asking about him, the man went into the alley between the post office and barber shop, broke the Pepsi bottle from which he'd been drinking, and used the jagged end to cut his throat.

This suicide became a story, so rich in mystery, I couldn't let it go. Eventually, I wrote this essay to try to explore the questions of why the man did what he did and also what it all had to do with me. My factual source for the essay was a childhood friend whose father was in the barber shop at the time of the suicide, was one of the men, as a matter of fact, who found the man in the alley. My friend, via his mother—his father is no longer living—was able to report many of the details to me, details I used to imagine the event. I make clear that I'm speculating by early on making reference to the fact that the story was one of those stories that gets told and told again in a small town until you start to feel like you were there—right there—at the time it happened. The one thing I couldn't do, though, was claim any knowledge whatsoever about the man's motivation. That was the one thing I didn't know. "I don't know why the law was looking for the drunk man," I say toward the end of the essay. "I don't know whether that was the reason he cut his throat." Then I admit that, if I chose, I could get in touch with the barber and ask him questions. I could get in touch with the triplets and ask them questions. I could, you see, do more research, gather more facts. I confess that I have that option, and, then, despite what the creative nonfiction police might think, I turn my back on the time-honored base of the genre. I refuse to find the fact that's waiting for me. I discard the representational in favor of something that is, to my way of thinking, more textured and expressive. "As long as I don't know why the drunk man did what he did," I write, "I can fit the story to my own—the story of an only child, born to a father, who may have come to love me, but at first was willing to let me go." By overlaying the factual with the imagined and then refusing to do the research that could have privileged the former, I allowed the form to be expressive, not only of the event itself, but how that event cast a light into my own interior as connected to this issue of parenthood in general and fathers in particular. The story of the man, then, became necessary to what I had to explore about my own father and the fact that I've never been a father. If I knew the facts of why the man did what he did, you see, it might very well not have fit into my own story, might not have been expressive of that story, would have only been the reportage of facts, expressive of something else in their own right, but probably not the story that mattered to what I needed to say about the self. I needed to know less, not more, to be able to honor the purpose for writing.

The refusal to find all the facts flies in the face of what many expect of creative nonfiction, but I'll argue that this refusal made possible a more layered form, one where, through the techniques of fiction and poetry, three genres converse and come to bear on one another in a way that transcends hybridity—a term, by the way, that has its origins in biology: an offspring of two animals or plants of different races, breeds, varieties, species, or genera. An offspring. Exactly. Both part of (a hybrid) and separate from (a highly evolved form) that which gave it birth.

## Note

1   Lee Martin, "All Those Fathers That Night," *Gulf Coast* 22.2 (2010): 33–42.

# 17

# My Mistake

## Nicole Walker

A fair number of people know that I have a serious problem with typos. It seems that my once strong typing skills are disintegrating and my never strong proofreading skills are getting worse. Even more troublesome, I feel schizophrenic: that I'm writing one thing while transcribing something entirely different through my fingers. With homophones, I write the one I don't mean almost every time. It is an uncomfortable position to be in a writing department, teaching writing to students, and asking them to write better when every third time I spell write R-I-G-H-T.

And when I'm proofreading, I end up revising, which is a very different sort of activity that relies on the invention part, not the careful detailed retooling part of my brain. And when I go to revise, I tend to mess things up more than they already were. Or I get distracted. I fall into a line of thought I did not intend. I'll go in to change one word, possibly fixing the R-I-G-H-T to the more accurate W-R-I-T-E and begin to think—what if I, instead, talked about right as in correct rather than talking so self-obsessively about my own mistaken writing practices. I'm sure I have things to say about right: the correct and proper way to set a table, fill a dishwasher, drive a car. Propriety, rather than navel-gazing, can become my subject now. I could be known as the Proper Writer—she who details the right way to sauté spinach, eat an oyster—with horseradish and mignonette sauce, not the flavor-obliterating cocktail sauce, the right way to French an onion, the right way to sear fish—high heat, grape seed oil.

Apparently, most of my opinions about right are food-based.

I think food might be my moral compass.

And yet, how did I get here?

Queen of etiquette. Which fork is my salad fork? Which fork in the road did I take to get here? When homophones are also homographic, it's hard to keep a forward focus.

I arrived at right R through write with a W. I arrived at hear meaning the birds followed me in my ears until I was at the place I am at now. I came to there by pointing to *their* special piece of writing. They are writing me back. They're telling me, in their contraction ways, what's wrong with the piece.

I don't mean to suggest, quite, that I write without volition or with some kind of Yeatsian automatic writing. But I do think creative nonfiction's playfulness takes some of its cue from surprise and mistake. Letting the language drive the piece, letting the course of the essay turn like so many rivers, letting your flow of thought be interrupted by a question for instance: do you know why rivers curve? It is not just a matter of making it around big rocks (which is what I mistakenly thought). Factors, a number of them, including gradient, soil density, soil composition, and the characteristics of rainfall cause a course to change. A river might turn because three pieces of sand shifted when a frog hopped out of the riverbed and onto the bank. A website called Happy News claims that "A river bends as it adjusts to disturbances, such as increases in water volume or obstacles that deflects its current. The diverted current follows a new path, bumps into a bank, encounters bank resistance, and erodes the bank—eventually carving a bend."[1] (Shouldn't it be "obstacles that deflect its current"? Is this the way sentences run these days?) Still, the river is still the river, the course is still the course. You have to adjust for the interruption of sand, the mistake of rain, the coincidence of a bank.

A course in a river. A course in semantics. If I happen to be standing in the river listening to you, I can only take my circumstance as the subject matter.

Making mistakes may be a Freudian thing, or maybe just a too tiny keyboard or a too easily moved cursor, or maybe a brain whose hemispheres of between see of vision and sea of waves is starting to crash. But maybe there's a pattern to this accident.

Paul Auster in his memoir-type thing *The Invention of Solitude*, finds a pattern in images of his son.

On page 107 (unless I typed that wrong) Auster, who has just finished describing his son's asthma attack, notes that the very moment the end of his marriage occurred was when, after trying to keep their son occupied while the boy spent three days in an oxygen-tent-covered crib, the wife made the mistake of saying "I give up. I can't handle him anymore. I have to get out of here."[2] Auster says that he turned against his wife then. He says he wanted to punish his wife for such selfishness. The marriage fails right at that turn. Auster doesn't dwell on that failure just then. Instead, thanks to the catapult that is white space, he leaps to a story about Mallarmé. He talks about poems Mallarmé wrote at the side of his dying son's bed. Auster translates these poems, publishes them in the *Paris Review*.

About one year later, no white space leap necessary, he's at a bar with his good friend R., a poet from Amsterdam, who remarks that he'd been reading Mallarmé in the latest issue of the *Paris Review*. Next to the poems was a picture of Mallarmé's son. R. was musing about how much alike he thought the picture of Mallarmé's son was to Auster's son, whom R. had met many times. Auster interrupted—those poems you were reading. Those were my translations. Didn't you notice? R. said he hadn't noticed. He hadn't read that far. The coincidence propelled him out of himself almost as much as his wife's mistake had. So much, it punched him into another leap of white space. No comment necessary.

Coincidence in nonfiction is the foreshadowing. It's the narrative arc. It's the belief in literary Gods that suggests if you study the patterns between two things, the thing they have in common will reveal itself to you. The patterns begin to resonate into some kind of meaning. In fiction, coincidence reads as contrived. And anyway, you have the tools of foreshadowing and recurring images, character development and coming full circle to give the reader satisfaction.

But in nonfiction, the images returning in surprise are all the pattern you have to trace.

At the end of his memoir *Speak, Memory*, Nabokov reveals how much he believes or wants to believe in coincidence. He believes there is a pattern behind the places he visited, the people he knew. The coincidences form their pattern in images of broken shards of pottery:

> I do not doubt that among those slightly convex chips of majolica-ware found by our child there was one whose border of scrollwork fitted exactly, and continued, the pattern of a fragment I had found in 1903 on the same shore, and that the two tallied with a third my mother had found on that Mentone beach in 1882, and with a fourth piece of that same sort of pottery that had been found by *her* mother a hundred years ago—and so on, until this assortment of parts, if all had been preserved, might have been put together to make the complete, the absolutely complete, bowl, broken by some Italian child, God knows where and when, and now mended by *these* rivets of bronze.[3]

That assertion that these pieces of clay are pieces of one big puzzle is on page 308. The number 308? A coincidence?

Mistake is the stuff of memoir. It's the stuff of narrative and plot. It's the way current nonfiction justifies itself, makes a claim to fame. But mistakes are also the stuff of sentences—the way Nabokov's observational skills led him to see other facts, the way Auster uses his wife's mistakes and R.'s unknowing to shift the angle of light. Mistakes are where perspective takes place. I tell my students it's serendipity but really, being wrong can lead you to see what's right over here, and then what's right over there, multiplying perspective right by write by right.

## Notes

1  April Holladay, "Why Do Rivers Follow Lazy Loops and Bends?" *Happy News*, August 25, 2007, www.happynews.com/news/8252007/why-rivers-follow-lazy-loops-bends.htm.
2  Paul Auster, *The Invention of Solitude*, revised ed. (New York: Penguin, 2007), 107.
3  Vladimir Nabokov, *Speak, Memory* (1947; repr., New York: Vintage, 1989), 308–9.

# 18

# Play-Doh Fun Factory Poetics

Wayne Koestenbaum

*That is the way memory serves us, details return ill assorted, pell mell, in confusion.*

Ezra Pound, *Gaudier-Brzeska*[1]

My poetics—anal, alimentary, abstract—resembles a Play-Doh Fun Factory.

I practice what Foucault called, in reference to the history of sexuality, "the care of the self."[2] I trim, slash, shape; I perform askesis. But my material is not "self." It's words: Play-Doh.

Last night I dreamt my mother showed me her vagina: an offering.

Each new paragraph interrupts the previous. Paragraphs have the privilege of parataxis.

In 1913, Pound demanded: "Direct treatment of the 'thing,' whether subjective or objective."[3]

Without my sexual compulsions, my penis would sit inert in my pants and endure a dull, nonmonumental existence. Without my sexual compulsions, I would have no poetics.

In a brand-new poem, I wrote: "Play-Doh Factory, / I loved your poop / ambience, extruded quadri- / laterals vast yet squat."

As a youngster, I liked the smell of Play-Doh, an odor of chalk and vanilla, enriched by cardamom and pavement. Play-Doh smelled like the Pentateuch, or the golem, or a Robert Ryman painting—abstract, blank, complex, eerie, bumpy.

Difficult to remember whether it was more fun to push the Play-Doh out the Factory's chute or to lop off the Play-Doh after it had been extruded and formed. Maybe the greatest pleasure lay in choosing the shape—the filter—through which the Play-Doh would be forced.

Today, on the piano, I warmed up with a Brahms exercise ("broken arpeggio figuration in contrary motion with repeated notes") and an etude from Czerny's *The Art of Finger Dexterity:* "Changing the Fingers in Rapid Playing." Then I worked on Albinez's naive, forgotten "Sonata No. 3." I love the fact that it is forgotten.

Each book, poem, or paragraph I produce is a physical machine, generated by hand movements. I like to put my fingers to work. I value diligence, facture, momentum.

I write to experience inner folds. Call them psychological and spiritual contortions; or call them abject, self-debasing, self-enlarging contractions. José Saramago (in *The Gospel According to Jesus Christ*) describes such a contraction: "In self-abasement his soul shrinks into itself like a tunic folded three times, surrendering his defenseless body to the mercy of the mothers of Bethlehem . . ."[4] When I write, my soul shrinks into itself like a tunic folded three times.

I write longhand in a diary, for no reader, nearly every day. I have done so, daily, for 33 years. My diary, the longest book I've ever written, is a lifelong experiment in accretion—a scroll, remote from audience, coherence, or plan.

In my diary, on Sunday, November 8, 2009, I wrote: "Dream: I tried (energetically) to explain to my mother the gay scene in Berlin. I mentioned *Taxi zum Klo.* All this conversation was occasioned by a foreign film (French: Agnès Varda or her ilk?). My mother stood in the Augusta Way garage, by the front step. She momentarily concealed herself behind a curtain. Neighbors had three scrawny trees. The neighbors either praised or disapproved of our property's shrubbery. They were working their land, we were working ours." If this dream finds its way into a poem, I'll probably use the words "Agnès Varda" and "*Taxi zum Klo,*" and maybe the neighbors' disapproval of my property's shrubbery. I like the musical affinity between the words "property" and "shrubbery." And I could use the phrase "scrawny trees," and the pathetic scene of trying (with futile zeal) to describe to my mother the gay scene in Berlin, my father's birthplace.

These days, for first drafts of poems, I use a manual typewriter, and colored construction paper—red, orange, yellow, beige, purple. I type quickly, without forethought, usually in quatrains. Each quatrain is a box, an arbitrary module, a friendly lump, of an accommodating size. Later, I scavenge clumps of language from these construction-paper improvisations, and turn these clumps into poems—reassembled, like Frankenstein's monster, from pilfered parts.

Recently I found my first diary—from 1968. I was 9 years old. Here are a few entries. "Thursday January 29. I get in a play which Brad made. I have the 4th biggest part! I am going to record it with a movie camera." "Monday March 18. I find my long lost library card. And it was right in front of me.

We have the play today." "Wednesday March 20. Today I film it! It is very fun to film a movie. I have to memorize a poem." "Saturday June 29. A fat girl babysits today. Mommy and Daddy go to *The Odd Couple*. It's their anniversary." Why did I say "fat girl," but not give her a name? Already I was interested in shameful singularity, in abject exemplarity. Here's another entry: "Wednesday June 5: Robert Kennedy was shot. Not dead yet. He won the primaries. No [Cub Scout] den meeting."

A paragraph is a container for sentences—like a shadow box, a bureau drawer, a coffin, a laundry hamper, a diaper hamper, a time capsule. I put as many sentences in the box as will fit. Sometimes I keep the box relatively empty. I shake the box and let the sentences fall into different positions.

I write for solitude's sake, not for companionship or communication. My writing may seem chatty but its aims are inexpressive and abstract.

I write to wallow—to feel a soaring upward and then a crash downward. Adjective or noun or verb or adverb can be *anagnorisis* and *peripeteia* happening simultaneously. Diction should hurt. I like to twist a word into its dirty groove.

I like em-dashes, parentheses, semi-colons, line-breaks—any form of stoppage or interruption. A short utterance, or an interrupted one, is a gasp rather than a statement. Short sentences—words conspicuously crammed together or omitted—remind me of a finger pointing, either to indicate or condemn.

I write inside a bleak, turgid morass; I peer out from the muck, sometimes with clarity, forgiveness, or curiosity, but sometimes with recursive distaste for the self-made muck I'm peering through.

I wrote my undergraduate thesis on the relation between "word" and "thing" in the early poetry and prose of Ezra Pound. The core of the thesis was a chapter on his *Cathay* poems: "What is the use of talking and there is no end of talking . . ."[5] My epigraph came from Emerson's *Journal*: "In good writing, words must become one with things."[6] I palpate a word's thingness with my eyes, mouth, and fingers.

Between words, I seek sonic similarities. I like chunky words, chunky adjacencies—monads crammed together, without a gap. My favorite Ezra Pound line: "Quick eyes gone under earth's lid."[7] A death line. Chunky words, or strongly stressed words ("Quick eyes gone"), each vowel a different pitch and mouth-shape, are mausoleums: the emphatic, chunky concentration of stresses is at once an elegiac sigh and a violent mimesis of war's murderousness.

A William Wordsworth line that kills me begins with a trochee: "Breathless with adoration." "The holy time is quiet as a Nun/Breathless with adoration."[8] I love the chasm between "Nun" and "Breathless." The stoppage. And then the reemergence, with "Breathless," into activity. But a sliver of silence has intruded between "Nun" and "breathless." A simple effect. But it kills me. He breaks the line because he wants to slay me, and I want to be slain: we participate together in this funeral rite.

I teeter between graphomania and a laconic thwartedness—the drive toward excess is not estranged from the drive toward death.

For prose, my rule is: revise nine times. Stations of the cross: the ritual practice of nine drafts is itself a temporal event—the construction of a tomb but also a paring-away, a self-shedding.

I stare hard at each sentence, nine times, to find the fat. Always nine times.

When I write, I feel spasms of self-disgust. I try to do something productive with the self-disgust: make it bloom. Extract a nugget from it, a calcified chunk.

Swimming is part of my poetics. As a child, I feared water; through practice, I overcame terror. I know only two strokes: crawl and breast-stroke. I alternate strokes: one lap breast, one lap crawl, one lap breast, one lap crawl. Back and forth, breast, crawl, breast, crawl. Without variation. These repetitive movements pare away at consciousness, empty it of specificities.

Schmutz and its removal are part of my poetics. Too much schmutz in my language. A trench coat has a stained collar. A pink shirt has ruined sleeves. A fuchsia shirt is too blowsy. A favorite black shirt is now grey. A pair of boots has chipped toes. My boyfriend rips up underwear and socks when it's time for them to die.

I cook dinner every night. I spend as much time preparing food as I spend writing. (At the greenmarket today, I bought parsley, arugula, romaine, Russian potatoes, broccoli rabe, cauliflower, carrots, celery, radishes, yellow cherry tomatoes.) Cooking, swimming, piano-playing, and writing are dumb bodily necessities, exercises of Play-Doh Fun-Factory-esque mechanicity.

Play-Doh, apparently nontoxic, is made from flour, salt, water, boric acid, silicone oil, and other substances.

Last night I dreamt that I was a graduate student again, taking a seminar in modern poetry: this week we were reading George Oppen, but I needed to skip class because there were fatal errors in my health insurance eligibility form. I love Oppen. I once stole his *Selected Poems* from a bookstore in San Francisco. I also stole Anaïs Nin's *House of Incest* and Yukio Mishima's *Confessions of a Mask*. But the best theft was Oppen. I read him while standing on a San Francisco bus. The bus swayed: I concentrated on his line-breaks, their abruptness and probity. On a different bus, I read Robert Creeley's poems—purchased, not stolen. I loved Creeley's omissions, his bluntness. I appreciated how much he discarded, and the interrupted lumpiness of what remained.

My mother's father grew up on the Lower East Side and from that fertile nothingness he spurred himself to get a PhD in English Literature from NYU but no college would hire a Jew so instead he taught English and disciplined the boys at Brooklyn's Abraham Lincoln High School. Hypercritical, he sent me vocabulary lists, so I could study for the SAT. From him I got my taste for words like "rodomontade."

In grammar school, I hated wearing hard shoes—stiff leather. I only wanted to wear soft shoes—Keds sneakers. Poems are soft shoes. Prose is a hard shoe.

Once my mother caught me wearing sneakers to school. Out the kitchen window she saw me cross the street in forbidden footwear. She called me back to the house and wrote a note to the teacher. I'll reconstruct it: "Wayne is late to school today because he refused to wear the shoes that give his feet the proper support." My parents worried that my feet would grow deformed. Because our family doctor said that going barefoot would lead to disease, my mother's repeated exclamation—a household mantra—was "I step on bare feet." Five strong-stressed monosyllables. Not unlike Pound's "Quick eyes gone under earth's lid." The girls across our street were pigeon-toed. My mother said "Gail and Sharon are pigeon-toed because they go barefoot outside."

Pound wanted "words that hover above and cling close to the things they mean."[9]

I grew up among orchards. Gradually, during my childhood, developers cut down the trees and built tract houses and shopping malls. I remember driving by the remaining orchards and enjoying the instant when the trees line up—when the eye can make of the arbor a parallel, uninterrupted arcade. In our backyard we had a peach tree, but I remember not the fruit but the galvanized steel bucket in which we put the fruit after it was picked. When my fingers touched the schmutzy bucket, I felt neurasthenic shivers of horror.

Play-Doh smells like oranges mixed with ashes. When the Play-Doh canister's lid closes, it locks the substance in a dark cavern. Rilke, in *The Notebooks of Malte Laurids Brigge,* described the relationship of lids to jars. The jar longs for its lid, desires the tight fit of closure and containment. Rilke: "Let us agree on one point: the lid of a can—or let us say, of a can that is in good condition, whose edge curves in the same way as its own—a lid like this should have no other wish than to find itself on top of its can . . ."[10] Emily Dickinson knew about lids. "If ever the lid gets off my head/ And lets the brain away . . ."[11] I should summarize. My subject is lids— earth's lid, mind's lid, Play-Doh's lid, the I's lid, what holds the "I" in place. Autobiography is not a defunct practice. Please don't prematurely put the lid on its fragrant complexities.

I didn't own a Play-Doh Factory. I encountered the toy at the house of a friend—a freckled, redheaded Mormon, whose penis was the first uncircumcised specimen I'd ever seen. I wondered why he had a deformed flap hanging from the end of his wienie. His tract-house street was infinitesimally fancier than mine. No one could accuse my street of being opulent.

Sentences are Play-Doh constructions, shaped, chosen, extruded, timed, enjoyed, rejected. Sentences—or lines, or word-groups—are pushed out, through a filter, or attachment, which controls the shape into which the sentence's dough will be formed. I am a sentence factory.

I look coldly upon my sentences. I expect them to please. If they don't, I'm disgusted. I wish I could describe more luxuriantly the varieties of disgust I feel when I appraise my sentences and try to figure out which words should live and which should die.

Because I'm rereading Giorgio Agamben's *Remnants of Auschwitz* (which acknowledges the impossibility of testimony), I'm moved to tell you the following story. My father's cousin Wolfgang survived Auschwitz, though Wolfgang's parents were gassed upon arrival. I wasn't nice to Wolfgang. That's part of my poetics—not being nice (not being a mensch) to Wolfgang and not being nice to his wife Luisa who also survived Auschwitz, I wasn't nice to her, either, I wasn't a mensch, and that is part of my poetics, not being nice to survivors of death camps, my permanent culpability and rottenness is part of my poetics, an integral part. I could go into detail about my not being nice to survivors; going into detail would be part of my poetics. (I wrote this final paragraph while eating chocolate cake at a hotel restaurant.)

## Notes

1  Ezra Pound, *A Memoir of Gaudier-Brzeska* (London and New York: John Lane, 1916), 39.

2  Michel Foucault, *The History of Sexuality*, vol. 3, *The Care of the Self*, trans. Robert Hurley (New York: Vintage, 1986).

3  Ezra Pound, "A Few Don'ts by an Imagiste," *Poetry* I, no. 6, March 1913.

4  José Saramago, *The Gospel According to Jesus Christ*, trans. Giovanni Pontiero (New York: Harcourt, 1991), 185.

5  Ezra Pound, "Exile's Letter," in *Personae: Collected Shorter Poems* (New York: New Directions, 1971), 134.

6  Ralph Waldo Emerson, in *The Topical Notebooks of Ralph Waldo Emerson*, vol. 2, ed. Ronald A. Bosco (Columbia, MO: University of Missouri Press, 1993), 376.

7  Ezra Pound, "Hugh Selwyn Mauberly," in *Selected Poems* (New York: New Directions, 1956), 64.

8   William Wordsworth, "It is a Beauteous Evening, Calm and Free," in *William Wordsworth: The Major Works*, ed. Stephen Gill (Oxford: Oxford University Press, 1984), 281.

9   Exra Pound, "I Gather the Limbs of Osiris," in *Selected Prose, 1909–1965*, ed. William Cookson (New York: New Directions, 1973), 28–9.

10   Reiner Maria Rilke, *The Notebooks of Malte Laurids Brigge,* trans. Stephen Mitchell (New York: Vintage, 1990), 182–3.

11   Emily Dickinson, "If Ever the Lid Gets Off My Head," in *The Poems of Emily Dickinson*, ed. Ralph William Franklin (Cambridge, MA: Harvard University Press, 1999), 264.

# Part III

# Unconventions

Fiction has scene, plot, character, narrative arc. Poetry has meter, lineation, volta, assonance, consonance, and (sometimes) rhyme. What tropes and conventions does nonfiction rely on? The most common answer is that nonfiction operates with the devices of fiction: narrative and character-driven, but with an "I" for the protagonist and fact for plot. But nonfiction has its own techniques and "unconventions": montage, juxtaposition, toggling, fragmentation, white space, etymological exegesis, the weave, the tangent, and the digression. None of these devices is exclusive to nonfiction, of course, but nonfiction propels them to the fore—continually reinventing the generic space where the writer plays.

# 19

# On Convention

## Margot Singer

For many years now, the conversation about creative nonfiction has focused almost exclusively on questions of definition and legitimacy. What is this thing we're writing? We can't even settle on a name. Tacking the word "creative" or "literary" or "narrative" in front of "nonfiction" feels defensive or pretentious or redundant or all three. "Essay" conjures the specter of the term paper, "article" connotes journalism, "belles-lettres" is lovely but no one can pronounce it, "memoir" is too limiting, and plain "nonfiction" is too big. And the trouble of nomenclature is only a symptom of a larger problem: where to draw the borders of this Thing-That-Cannot-Be-Named? Every phony-memoir scandal provokes a fresh boundary skirmish. Some of us duck behind parked cars.

We love creative nonfiction, of course, *because* of its blurry borders, the way it toggles back and forth between fact and the imagination, between expository and lyric modes. We love its ability to blend scene, description, meditation, raw fact, speculation, and reportage. Creative nonfiction casts aside journalism's formulaic "five W's" and inverted pyramid structure and neutral third person invisibility for a vast array of forms. This plasticity, of course, makes some people nervous. If a piece of nonfiction reads like fiction or poetry, how can you tell it's true? You have to take the truth on faith—not form.

Creative nonfiction, some say, is defined by a lack of established conventions.[1] But I would suggest that what's going on is more complicated than that. Creative nonfiction may be polymorphous, and may resist easy categorization, but it's rooted in convention all the same. It may be obvious, but perhaps worth repeating, that *all* writing is conventional. Not "conventional" in the pejorative sense of "unoriginal" or "trite," of course, but meaning a customary way of doing things, or norms. Convention is what we talk about when we talk about craft. As every creative writing student knows, it's *conventional* to fill one's prose with sensory imagery and concrete, significant detail. It's conventional to shape dialogue in zippy bursts, to portray scenes from a specific point of view, to "show, not tell." We tend to talk about these elements of craft as givens—laws of nature, almost—but they're not. They're simply the familiar attributes of one particular type of narrative, one that is used, to varying degrees, by historians and scientists and journalists as well as by fiction and nonfiction writers to tell stories that feel "true" and "real."

Often misconceived as techniques "borrowed" from fiction, the conventions of *narrative realism* underpin *any* kind of writing that seeks to portray the world as it "really" is. These conventions, quite simply, help us *feel*, deep in our guts and in our bones, that we are "there" in a way that exposition can't, and we feel this because of the artfulness (the artifice) of narrative, which for better or for worse operates independently of the inherent truthfulness, or lack thereof, of any given text. Creative nonfiction both builds on the conventions of narrative realism and at times bends and reinvents them, and it is the *tension* between these dynamics, I propose, that distinguishes creative nonfiction from other literary genres.[2]

As the scholar Doug Hesse has rightly pointed out, narrative feels realistic or lifelike not because it *is* lifelike but because it's "storylike."[3] But realistic narrative has a way of naturalizing the operation of its conventions so that we forget they're there. To Tsvetan Todorov, realism (what he calls the *vraisemblable*) "is the mask which conceals the text's own laws and which we are supposed to take for a relation with reality."[4] In other words, we forget that we're reading a linguistic representation and imagine instead that the narrative is literally holding up a mirror to the world.

This naturalizing effect is, I think, especially strong in creative nonfiction. Never mind that the dialogue presented in a memoir is obviously not a transcription of actual speech. Never mind that the order of presentation in a narrative is rarely linear, that time is dilated or compressed. Never mind that the myriad details of experience must be selected, filtered, ordered, and re-presented in a way that imposes meaning onto what would otherwise be chaos. We accept the conventions of narrative realism as indicative of the truthfulness of a piece of writing, when in fact they're what makes it art.

In shifting its emphasis from exposition to story, from summary to scenes rich in dialogue and descriptive detail, creative nonfiction creates an artful illusion of the real. Susan Orlean's *The Orchid Thief*, for example, plunges us into the murky depths of Florida's Fakahatchee swamp, slogging away beside Orlean as she searches for elusive bromeliads. No one would mistake the following passage for a newspaper article, but nevertheless we trust that journalist Orlean's account is true. Even more importantly, we *feel* that it is true—because of its vivid, sensory detail:

> The fact is that the swamp is so grabby that even though I was covered from neck to foot I felt stark naked. The water was freezing cold and mosquitoes sneaked in and out of my shirt by way of my collar and sleeves, and every plant with prickers snatched at my leggings, and the gritty sinkhole muck passed right through my socks and sneakers and stained my ankles and toes. I had mosquito bites on my stomach and face, and toward the end of that first hike I got so nervous and exhausted that I broke out in hives for the first time in my life.[5]

Orlean's prose puts the reader "there." The long string of coordinating conjunctions replicates the endlessness of the hike, and the repeated consonance of hard "k" sounds ("neck," "stark naked," "cold," "mosquitoes," "sneaked," "prickers," "sinkhole muck," "socks and sneakers," "ankles," "stomach," "hike," "broke") mimics the insects' and thorns' relentless pricks. Do we believe that's what it feels like to slog through the Fakahatchee swamp? You bet.

Similarly, one of the most moving scenes in Rebecca Skloot's *The Immortal Life of Henrietta Lacks* occurs when Skoot and Lacks' adult children visit the Johns Hopkins laboratory where the HeLa cancer cells, taken decades earlier from their deceased mother's body, are cultured and kept:

> Christoph leaned over the microscope again and began moving the cells quickly around the screen until he shrieked, "Look there! See that cell?" He pointed to the center of the monitor. "See how it has a big nucleus that looks like it's almost pinched in half in the middle? That cell is dividing into two cells right before our eyes! And both of those cells will have your mother's DNA in them."
>
> "Lord have mercy," Deborah whispered, covering her mouth with her hand. . . . Deborah and Zakariyya stared at the screen like they'd gone into a trance, mouths open, cheeks sagging. It was the closest they'd come to seeing their mother alive since they were babies.[6]

This five-page scene, narrated in a dramatic third person (except for the first and last sentences, which subtly remind us of Skloot's presence in the lab), puts the reader, like Skloot, in the position of bearing witness to an emotional event.

Orlean's and Skloot's narratives may read as vividly as fiction, but we never forget that they are *not* fictional, and one of the reasons for that is voice. Voice, I propose, is one of the few formal conventions that distinguishes creative nonfiction from other kinds of prose. Since the heyday of the New Journalism in the 1960s and '70s, writers of creative nonfiction have adopted an intimate, reflective, self-reflexive narrative voice, in marked contrast to the "omniscient" third person of the news story or history book. I call this point of view the "Naked I": "Naked" because the "I" is a pronoun with a concrete referent, the living body of the author, and not just a narrative construct. (Again, I don't mean to imply that *all* creative nonfiction is narrated in the first person. Even in second or third person narratives, as we'll see in a moment, the identity between narrator and the author crucially influences how we read the text.)

The "Naked I" places writers like Orlean and Skloot squarely on the page. They not only narrate, but participate in the stories they tell. As in science, the act of observing inevitably changes the nature of the thing observed. *The Orchid Thief* is as much about Orlean's obsession with obsession as it is a profile of obsessive orchid dealer John Laroche. *The Immortal Life of Henrietta Lacks* draws Skloot into the lives of Lacks' family just as it draws them into her journalistic quest. As Skloot puts it: "Slowly, without realizing it, I'd become a character in [Deborah's] story, and she in mine."[7] There is no pretense of objectivity here, no invisible "fourth wall." Instead the detail-rich, descriptive scenes of narrative realism blend with the limited, one-sided, fallible, fundamentally human perspective of the "Naked I." There are both hubris and honesty in this technique, which is both contemporarily postmodern and the direct legacy of Montaigne.

What happens, then, in creative nonfiction when the convention of the "Naked I" is cast aside in favor of an "omniscient" third person point of view? Truman Capote famously championed this approach as a way of heightening the vividness of the "nonfiction novel." "My feeling," he told George Plimpton in their famous 1966 interview, "is that . . . the author should not appear in the work. Ideally. Once the narrator does appear, he has to appear throughout, all the way down the line, and the I-I-I intrudes when it really shouldn't."[8]

The intrusive "I-I-I," of course, is precisely what reporters and biographers and historians have long banished from the page. It's when the hidden third person narrator slips beyond reported fact into the realm of the imagination—for example, dramatizing scenes that the author could not possibly have witnessed, recreating dialogue that the author could not possibly have overhead, clairvoyantly representing real-life characters' most private feelings and thoughts—that the genres really blur. Again, what interests me is not so much the ethics of invention, but its effect on how we read and make meaning of the nonfiction text.

Take, for example, Sebastian Junger's reconstruction in *A Perfect Storm* of the unknowable last days and hours of the *Andrea Gail*. The book may be "completely factual,"[9] as Junger insists, but it is also an act of the imagination, in Junger's own words, "as complete an account as possible of something that can never be fully known."[10] Junger performs a deft balancing act of speculation, extrapolation, and invention in describing the ship's last moments after it is struck by a rogue wave:

> Whether the *Andrea Gail* rolls, pitch-poles, or gets driven down, she winds up, one way or another, in a position from which she cannot recover. There's no time to put on survival suits or grab a life vest; the boat's moving through the most extreme motion of her life and there isn't even time to shout. The refrigerator comes out of the wall and crashes across the galley. Dirty dishes cascade out of the sink. The T.V., the washing machine, the VCR tapes, the men, all go flying. And, seconds later, water moves in.[11]

Notice how quickly Junger slides away from the equivocal "or" and "one way or another," foregoing the conditional for a vivid, present tense description of an utterly imaginary scene.

Dave Eggers, that wunderkind of postmodernist self-reflexivity, also uses an "omniscient" third person narration in *Zeitoun,* his nonfiction account of an Arab-American family's experience of Hurricane Katrina. In *What is the What*, Eggers goes even further, using what you might call a ventriloquist's first person as he channels the voice of the real-life Sudanese Lost Boy, Valentino Achak Deng. Sounding an awful lot like Capote, Eggers told an interviewer from *Salon*: "I don't want my voice in this book. I don't want to be a character."[12] The *New York Times* critic Timothy Egan called the result "an odd hybrid."[13] Eggers published *What is the What* as a novel and left it at that.

Like Junger, Eggers devotes a substantial amount of energy to explaining his methodology and defending the thoroughness and credibility of his reporting and research. And we buy it. Just as we're sold on Junger's version of what it must have been like aboard the lost ship *Andrea Gail*, we're sold on Egger's rendition of Valentino's experiences, feelings, and thoughts. But this use of third person omniscience raises questions. Ethical questions, maybe, but also questions of genre. We *don't* read *A Perfect Storm* as fiction, even though it "reads like a novel," even though we know Junger had to speculate. We don't read *What is the What* as a novel either, even though it claims to be one, despite the oddness of Eggers writing in Valentino's voice. The unconventionality of the narrative voice doesn't destroy our trust in these stories' truth.

In his 1987 essay "Toward a Theory of Literary Nonfiction," Eric Heyne usefully distinguishes between the terms "factual status" and "factual adequacy."[14] "Factual status," Heyne argues, is a matter of authorial intention: is the work intended to be read as fact-based or not? "Factual adequacy," on the other hand, is a function of the reader's judgment as to whether a "work is good or bad fact" according to the text's own terms.[15] In his analysis of *In Cold Blood*, Heyne rightly rejects John Hersey's narrow dictum that "the journalist must not invent," and applauds Capote's use of innovative form.[16] He also rejects the notion that the inaccuracies in Capote's account mean that we should read the book as fiction.[17] Heyne's reasoning rests on the book's "factual status"—on the understanding that Capote intended his account of the Kansas killings to be read as true. In evaluating the literary merit of works of nonfiction, Heyne concludes, we must consider the nature of the specific "truth-claims" being made.[18] Heyne, therefore, finds Capote guilty not of invention, or even of lying, but of "factual inadequacy"— of violating "his *own* rules."[19]

By breaking with convention, innovative works of creative nonfiction get at "reality" in powerful, new ways. The intrusive "I-I-I" of the first person narrator reaches for a deeper kind of truth by shattering the illusion of journalistic objectivity and putting the author's subjective experience squarely on the page. Likewise, concealing the author's presence behind a dramatic, third person narration works to create a camera-like illusion of unmediated reality. Neither approach is a guarantee of factual accuracy (you still have to take that on trust). Most importantly, both approaches serve to remind us that even the most scrupulously fact-based, truthful writing is always also an imaginative act, a work of art.

Much has been written about experimental fictions that break narrative convention in a way that shatters the illusion of reality. The metafictions of Robert Coover and John Barth, for example, call attention to their own fictionality and the artifice of form.[20] Other anti-mimetic fictions center on a dislocated narrator (Robbe-Grillet's *Jalousie*), depict a physically or logically impossible space (Danielewski's *House of Leaves*), present contradictory storylines (Calvino's *If On a Winter's Night a Traveler*, Atwood's "Happy

Endings") or illogical sequencing (Cortázar's *Hopscotch*, Coover's "The Babysitter"). But what about works of *nonfiction* that similarly transgress mimetic bounds? Creative nonfiction that's not "realistic"? Isn't that a contradiction in terms?

When creative nonfiction messes with conventions of narrative level, presents an unreliable narrator, or breaks the narrative frame, something very different happens than when fiction plays such "games." When in Martin Amis's novel *Money*, for example, a character named Martin Amis walks into a bar, it jolts us out of the seemingly realistic story world. (If you're of a theoretical bent, you might call it a "metaleptic joke."[21]) But when Michael Martone publishes a series of "Contributors' Notes" written in the third person that present contradictory information about Martone, you get a joke that works in a completely different way. The character "Martin Amis" reveals the presence of the author, Martin Amis, pulling the puppet's strings behind the text. In *Michael Martone* by Michael Martone, there are no puppet strings. Instead of reminding us that fiction writers invent imaginary characters, Martone reminds us that we are always creating and re-creating ourselves. The nonfiction text's fictionality is a comment not on the nature of fiction-making, but on the nature of the truth.

When a fictional narrator is "unreliable," we understand that the text is asking us to negotiate the gap between the world as we know it and the world as it's presented through the narrator's (skewed) eyes. So when a supposedly omniscient third person narrator turns out to be unreliable, as in Ian McEwan's novel *Atonement*, we experience a kind of shock. The shock calls attention to the subjective and provisional nature of narrative, to authorial manipulations of all kinds. But when Lauren Slater opens *Lying: A Metaphorical Memoir*, with the statement "I exaggerate";[22] when she tells us that this is "a book in which in some cases I cannot and in other cases I will not say the facts,"[23] we experience an altogether different kind of shock. With "unreliable" nonfiction narrator there's not only a gap between perceived realities, there's no firm ground at all. And yet Slater's project, infuriating as it may be, compels us to confront our desire to know the "truth," and to consider whether "[using] invention to get at the heart of things" can be more powerful than even documented fact.[24]

Creative nonfiction, to sum up, is far more than prose that feels like fiction with a special claim to truth. It's a genre that, at least in its more innovative forms, exposes many of the unexamined expectations we bring to the so-called realistic text. It foregrounds the slipperiness of representation. It makes us ask fundamental questions about the nature of storytelling, memory, "reality" and "truth." Building on the conventions of other prose forms, it bends those conventions to offer fresh literary perspectives on our experience of the world.

# Notes

1 See Chris Anderson, Introduction, *Literary Nonfiction: Theory, Criticism, and Pedagogy*, ed. Chris Anderson (Carbondale: Southern Illinois University Press, 1998), ix–xx.

2 This is not to claim that all creative nonfiction is narrative, or even realistic, of course, but only to acknowledge that mimetic prose narrative remains creative nonfiction's dominant mode.

3 Douglas Hesse, "Stories in Essays, Essays as Stories," in Anderson, 191.

4 Tsvetan Todorov, Introduction, *Communications* 11 (1968): 3, quoted in Jonathan Culler, *Structuralist Poetics* (Ithaca: Cornell University Press, 1975), 139.

5 Susan Orlean, *The Orchid Thief* (New York: Ballantine, 1998), 130.

6 Rebecca Skloot, *The Immortal Life of Henrietta Lacks* (New York: Crown-Random House, 2006), 265.

7 Ibid., 7.

8 Truman Capote, interview with George Plimpton, "The Story Behind a Nonfiction Novel," the *New York Times*, January 16, 1966, www.nytimes.com/books/97/12/28/home/capote-interview.html.

9 Sebastian Junger, *The Perfect Storm* (New York: Norton, 1997), xi.

10 Ibid., xii.

11 Ibid., 140.

12 Dave Eggers, interview with Sara Corbett, "Lost and Found," *Salon*, November 13, 2006, www.salon.com/2006/11/13/eggers_38/singleton/.

13 Timothy Egan, "After the Deluge," *New York Times*, August 13, 2009, www.nytimes.com/2009/08/16/books/review/Egan-t.html?pagewanted=all

14 Eric Heyne, "Toward a Theory of Literary Nonfiction," *Modern Fiction Studies* 33, no. 3 (1987): 480.

15 Ibid.

16 John Hersey, "The Legend on the License," *Yale Review* 70 (Autumn 1980): 1–25.

17 Heyne, 482.

18 Ibid., 488.

19 Ibid., 485.

20 See, for example, Coover's "The Babysitter" and "The Magic Poker," in *Pricksongs and Descants,* 1969 (New York: Grove, 2000) and Barth's *Lost in the Funhouse* (New York: Anchor, 1988).

21  Suzanne Keen, *Narrative Form* (New York: Palgrave MacMillan, 2003), 110–11.

22  Lauren Slater, *Lying: A Metaphorical Memoir* (New York: Penguin, 2001), 3.

23  Ibid., 219.

24  Ibid.

# 20

# 42 Tattoos

## David Shields

A tattoo is ink stored in scar tissue.

*

Archeologists believe, based on marks they've seen on mummies, that human beings had tattoos between 4000–2000 BC in Egypt. Around 2000 BC, tattooing spread to Japan and from there to Burma.

*

In 1998, 35% of NBA players had tattoos. Now, well over 70% have tattoos. Twenty percent of American adults have tattoos.

*

Asked by *Playboy* what he'd like people to know, NBA star Allen Iverson, now retired, said, "Tell them not to believe what they read or hear. Tell them to read my body. I wear my story every day, man." At the very end of the interview, Iverson said, "The minister at [his close friend] Rah's funeral said to look at your life as a book and stop wasting pages complaining, worrying, and gossiping. That's some deep shit right there."

*

In body-contact sports, such as basketball or football, there's a much higher percentage of tattooed players than in "cerebral" sports such as baseball, golf, or tennis.

*

While watching a basketball game on TV, Dakkan Abbe, founder of Fifty Rubies Productions, came up with the idea of NBA players selling space on their bodies to plug products with temporary tattoos. Abbe wanted someone with "bad-boy" appeal, so he approached Rasheed Wallace, who once set an NBA record for the most technical fouls in a season, about a candy-bar tattoo. Wallace's agent, Bill Strickland, said there's "nothing in any basic agreement [between the players' association and the league] that forbids advertising on the human body." An NBA spokesman said, "We don't allow commercial advertising on our uniforms, our coaches, or our playing floors, so there's no reason to think we'll allow it on our players." Abbe said, "The NBA is defining tattoos as part of the players' uniforms, but a player's skin is not part of his uniform. I find it offensive that the league would not allow something on someone's skin. Whenever the topic of tattoos comes up, the league says things like, 'We prefer if players didn't have tattoos.' The NBA scared people off. The very nature of tattoos is disturbing to the NBA. The league is a little bit out of touch with the players and fans. Tattoos are a very explicit example of that. They just don't understand what tattoos are about." Strickland said, "Being a lawyer, I thought it presented some interesting free-speech issues," but he finally decided not to press the case. Stephon Marbury, who used to play in the NBA and now plays for the Beijing Ducks, asked if he'd wear a tattoo advertisement, said, "Depends on how much money they'd pay. If they're paying the right money: yeah." Selling, say, his left shoulder to a shoe company, would Marbury be losing control over his body or exerting control over capitalism?

*

In the *Tattoo* magazine supplement to the New Orleans tattoo convention, an inordinately buxom but somehow slightly demure-looking blonde babe is on the cover, wearing a sailor hat, fishnet stockings, a short red skirt, white gloves, a bra top, and a couple of tattoos. Behind her in black shadow is a dark-haired woman dressed in a leopard costume. The function of the blonde babe's tattoo is to portray her in the process of being transfigured from sailor-girl to jungle-cat and back again (and to portray as well the Eros of this tension between civilization and savagery).

*

"As for the primitive, I hark back to it because we are still very primitive. How many thousands of years of culture, think you, have rubbed and polished at our raw edges? Probably one; at the best, no more than two. And that takes us back to screaming savagery, when, gross of body and deed, we drank blood from the skulls of our enemies and hailed as highest paradise the orgies and carnage of Valhalla."—Jack London

*

According to a third-century account of the Scythians' defeat of the Thracians, the Scythians tattooed symbols of defeat upon the Thracians, but as a way of turning "the stamp of violence and shame into beautiful ornaments," the Thracian women covered the rest of their bodies with tattoos.

*

On my thirtieth birthday, under my then-girlfriend's influence, I got my left ear pierced and bought a diamond earring. I wore various earrings over the next ten years, but wearing an earring never really worked for me, and on my fortieth birthday, under the influence of Natalie, who thought it made me look like a pirate, I took out the earring I was then wearing—a gold hoop—and haven't worn an earring since. Earrings forced me to confront the nature of my style, or lack of style. I'm certainly not macho enough to wear an earring as if I were a tough guy, but neither am I effeminate enough to wear an earring in my right ear as if I were maybe gay-in-training. Instead, I'm just me, muddling through in the middle, and the earring forced me, over time, to see this, acknowledge it, and respond to it.

*

Marcus Camby's first name is tattooed on his arm; Kirby Puckett also had his first name tattooed on his arm. Scottie Pippen has small tattoos on his biceps and legs. Michael Jordan has a horseshoe-shaped fraternity tattoo. Dennis Rodman's tattoos include a Harley, a shark, a cross (the loop of which encircles his pierced navel), and a photo of his daughter. Mike Tyson has a tattoo of Che Guevara on his abdomen, a tattoo of Mao on his right hand, and one of Arthur Ashe on his left shoulder. Shaquille O'Neal has a Superman tattoo on his left shoulder. Ben Wallace has a tattoo of the Big Ben clock tower on his right bicep, with basketballs for clock faces; he also has two tattoos of Taz, the Tasmanian devil from *Bugs Bunny.*

*

"Human barcodes are hip," declared that arbiter of hip, the *Wall Street Journal.* "Heavy-metal band Slipknot has a barcode logo, with the stripes emblazoned across their prison-jumpsuit outfits. Barcode tattoos are also big, says New York tattoo tycoon Carlo Fodera."

*

Who owns these words?

*

In Galatians 6.17, St Paul says, "From this time onward let no one trouble me; for, as for me, I bear, branded on my body, the scars of Jesus as my Master."

*

"Since a tattoo to certain levels of society is the mark of a thug, it becomes also the sign of inarticulate revolt, often producing its only possible result: violence."—Amy Krakow

*

In order to demonstrate their corporate loyalty, many Nike employees wear on their leg a tattoo of a swoosh.

*

The Greek philosopher Bion of Borysthenes (ca. 300 BC) described the brutally tattooed face of his father, a former slave, as "a narrative of his master's harshness."

*

Orlando Magic guard Jason Richardson says, "If you're a good basketball player, you've got to have some tattoos to go with the package. Basketball players have tattoos; that's the way it is. It's a way of showing who I am."

*

Asked what his tattoos mean, Iverson replied, "I got CRU THIK in four places—that's my crew, that's what we call ourselves, me and the guys I grew up with, the guys I'm loyal to. I got my kids' names, Tiaura and Deuce [Allen II], 'cause they're everything to me. I got my wife's name, Tawanna, on my stomach. A set of praying hands between my grandma's initials—she died when I was real young—and my mom's initials, Ethel Ann Iverson. I put shit on my body that means something to me. Here, on my left shoulder, I got a cross of daggers knitted together that says ONLY THE STRONG SURVIVE, because that's the one true thing I've learned in this life. On the other arm, I got a soldier's head. I feel like my life has been a war and I'm a soldier in it. Here, on my left forearm, it says NBN—for 'Newport Bad News.' That's what we call our hometown of Newport News, Virginia, because a lot of bad shit happens there. On the other arm, I got the Chinese symbol for respect, because I feel that where I come from deserves respect—being from there, surviving from there, and staying true to everybody back there. I got one that says FEAR NO ONE, a screaming skull with a red line through it—'cause you'll never catch me looking scared."

*

Aaron McKie, a former NBA player who is now an assistant coach with the Philadelphia 76ers, said, "A lot of guys get tattoos because they think they look nice and sexy wearing them, but I don't need them. One reason is because of my old college coach, John Chaney. He didn't allow players to wear tattoos or earrings or stuff like that. The other reason is because I guess I'm old-fashioned. I don't see any good reason to pierce or paint my body. I'm comfortable with my natural look."

*

"The publication of *International Archives of Body Techniques* would be of truly international benefit, providing an inventory of all the possibilities of the human body and of the methods of apprenticeship and training employed to build up each technique, for there is not one human group in the world that would not make an original contribution to such an enterprise. It would also be a project eminently well fitted to counteracting racial prejudices, since it would contradict the racialist conceptions which try to make out that man is a product of his body, by demonstrating that it is the other way around: man has, at all times and in all places, been able to turn his body into a product of his techniques and his representations."— Claude Lévi-Strauss

\*

What Lévi-Strauss means, I think, is this: before we started, she said she needed to tell me something. She had herpes. Madly in love with her witchy bitchiness, I found occasional enforced celibacy insanely erotic, the way a chastity belt glamorizes what it locks out. We wound up living together, and as we fell out of love with each other, her herpes became a debate point between us. She suggested that we just get married and then if I got it, I got it, and who would care? I suggested she at least explore some of the possibilities of which modern medicine avails us. For a multitude of reasons, the two of us didn't belong together, but what interests me now is what, for a lack of a better term, a free-floating signifier the virus was. When I was in love with her, it eroticized her. When I wasn't, it repelled me. The body has no meanings. We bring meanings to it.

\*

Ex-NFL fullback Brock Olivo, who has only one tattoo—an Italian flag, on his back, to honor his ancestry—said, "That's my last tattoo. No more. I don't want to scare my kids or affect things in the business world by having all kinds of crazy stuff on me."

\*

According to *Rolling Stone*, Paul Booth is "the tattoo artist of choice for rock stars who love death, perversion, and torture." His "black-and-gray tattoos of blasphemous violence echo the same nihilist madness of the metalheads he inks," musicians from Slipknot, Mudvayne, Slayer, Pantera, and Soulfly. His East Village shop features cobwebs, rusty meat hooks, a moose head, a mummified cat, medieval torture devices, a gynecologist's black leather chair with silver stirrups, a human skull given to him by a Swedish gravedigger, a note from a customer written in blood. His arms are covered in tattoos, his face is studded with silver loops, and he's enormously fat.

Some of his most popular tattoos are "weeping demons, decapitated Christ figures, transvestite nuns severing their own genitals, cascading waves of melting skulls, muscled werewolves raping bare-chested women." He has a two-year waiting list. His clients—including the "hardcore-metal elite"—come to him "because they share his frustration and rage, his feelings of anger and alienation. He understands those emotions and brings them to the surface with his needle. His gift lies in transforming the dark side of his clients—their hurt, their torments—into flesh." Evan Seinfeld, the bassist for Biohazard, says, "We're all trying to release our negative energy, our frustration with the world. Through our art and our music, we're getting it all out." Shawn Crahan of Slipknot says, "I have a lot of dark ideas in my head. Paul develops these same emotions in very powerful pieces." Booth says, "If I woke up one day and became happy, I probably wouldn't tattoo anymore, because I wouldn't see a need to do it. I would lose my art if I became happy."

*

"In Samoa there is a legend that tattooing was introduced there by the goddesses of tattooing. They swam to Samoa from Fiji, singing on the way their divine message, 'Tattoo the women but not the men.' With constant repetition the message became confused and twisted. When the goddesses finally arrived on the Samoan shore, they found themselves singing just the reverse, and so, says the legend, the tattoo became the undeserved prerogative of the men and not the women."—Albert Parry

*

Who owns these paragraphs?

*

"Revelation 17.5 says of the Scarlet Woman: 'And upon her forehead was a name written, MYSTERY, BABYLON THE GREAT, THE MOTHER OF HARLOTS AND ABOMINATIONS OF THE EARTH.'"

*

NBA veteran Jud Buechler, now retired, said Michael Jordan wanted "me and Steve Kerr [Jordan's then-teammates, both of whom are white] to get tattoos" after the Bulls won their fourth championship. "I thought about it but didn't do it because I knew my mom, wife, and mother-in-law would kill me."

*

"The human body is always treated as an image of society."—Mary Douglas

\*

"By the early seventeenth century [in Japan], a generally recognized codification of tattoo marks was widely used to identify criminals and outcasts. Outcasts were tattooed on the arms: a cross might be tattooed on the inner forearm, or a straight line on the outside of the forearm or on the upper arm. Criminals were marked with a variety of symbols that designated the places where the crimes were committed. In one region, the pictograph for 'dog' was tattooed on the criminal's forehead. Other marks included such patterns as bars, crosses, double lines, and circles on the face and arms. Tattooing was reserved for those who had committed serious crimes, and individuals bearing tattoo marks were ostracized by their families and denied all participation in the life of the community. For the Japanese, who valued family membership and social position above all things, tattooing was a particularly severe and terrible form of punishment. By the end of the seventeenth century, penal tattooing had been largely replaced by other forms of punishment. One reason for this is said to be that at about that time decorative tattooing became popular, and criminals covered their penal tattoos with larger decorative patterns. This is also thought to be the historical origin of the association of tattooing with organized crime in Japan. In spite of efforts by the government to suppress it, tattooing continued to flourish among firemen, laborers, and others at the lower end of the social scale. It was particularly favored by gangs of itinerant gamblers called Yakuza. Members of these gangs were recruited from the underworld of outlaws, penniless peasants, laborers, and misfits who migrated to Edo in the hope of improving their lot. Although the Yakuza engaged in a variety of semi-legal and illegal activities, they saw themselves as champions of the common people and adhered to a strict code of honor that specifically prohibited crimes against people, such as rape and theft. Like Samurai, they prided themselves on being able to endure pain and privation without flinching. And when loyalty required it, they were willing to sacrifice themselves by facing imprisonment or death to protect the gang. The Yakuza expressed these ideals in tattooing: because it was painful, it was proof of courage; because it was permanent, it was evidence of lifelong loyalty to the group; and because it was illegal, it made them forever outlaws."—Steve Gilbert

\*

"You put a tattoo on yourself with the knowledge that this body is yours to have and enjoy while you're here. You have fun with it, and nobody else can control (supposedly) what you do with it. That's why tattooing is such a big thing in prison: it's an expression of freedom—one of the only expressions of freedom there. They can lock you down, control everything, but 'I've got my mind, and I can tattoo my body, alter it my way as an act of personal will.'"—Don Ed Hardy

*

Didn't American slave-owners brand slaves so they could be identified like cattle? I've always thought there was a connection between the gold jewelry worn by rap artists and the chains of slavery—transformation of bondage into gold, escape from slavery, but not quite . . .

*

During the early Roman Empire, slaves exported to Asia were tattooed with the words *tax paid*. Words, acronyms, sentences, and doggerel were inscribed on the bodies of slaves and convicts, both as identification and punishment. A common phrased etched on the forehead of Roman slaves was *Stop me—I'm a runaway*.

*

Peter Trachtenberg, the author of *Seven Tattoos: A Memoir in the Flesh*, told me, "The most obvious reason African Americans didn't get tattooed until recently was that the old inks didn't show up on black skin. Newer, clearer pigments didn't come into use until the mid- to late eighties, which coincides with the introduction of tattoos into the African American community. I also wouldn't be surprised if tattooing's association with working-class culture—redneck culture in particular—made it unpopular with African Americans. You don't come across many black country-music fans, either. (Charlie Pride's fan base is entirely white.) My guess is that there were two principal routes of diffusion: the first from rap, the second from black college fraternities (some of which also used branding as an initiation rite). Starting in the late '80s, a number of gangsta rappers adopted tattoos, most notably Tupac Shakur, who had THUG LIFE tattooed in block letters down his torso. It would be interesting to go back through magazines of that period and see if photos of tattooed rappers predate those of tattooed ballplayers." They do, by a lot. "Also, to find out what percentage of NBA players belonged to black college fraternities." Some, but not a lot. "There's some irony at work here. The tattoos mark their wearers as gangstas or gangsta-wannabes, but one of the hallmarks of black gangsta rap is its appropriation of white organized-crime terminology, e.g., the group BLACK M.A.F.I.A. and admiring references to John Gotti in several songs."

*

A decade ago, Charles Barkley said, "White folks are not going to come see a bunch of guys with tattoos, with cornrows. I'm sorry, but anyone who thinks different, they're stupid."

*

In 1999, the shoe company And1 created a controversial advertisement in which Latrell Sprewell, who was suspended from the NBA for a year for choking his coach, said, "People say I'm America's worst nightmare; I say I'm the American dream." In the background, a blues guitar played "The Star-Spangled Banner" in imitation of Jimi Hendrix's version of the anthem (And1 couldn't afford the rights to the original). Seth Berger, the cofounder of the company, said that MTV created a youth market in which blacks and whites are indifferent to color: "It's a race-neutral culture that is open to endorsers and heroes that look different. These people are comfortable with tattoos and cornrows."

*

Who owns these statements—the people who said them or the people who wrote them down or the person who has gathered them together here or the person who reads them?

*

Concerning the people who are featured in the book *Modern Primitives*, and who are devoted to body modification, mutilation, scarification, and tattoos, *Whole Earth Review* said, "Through 'primitive' modifications, they are taking possession of the only thing that any of us will ever really own: our bodies."

*

In the 1890s, socialite Ward McAllister said about tattoos, "It is certainly the most vulgar and barbarous habit the eccentric mind of fashion ever invented. It may do for an illiterate seaman, but hardly for an aristocrat."

*

Upon being told that the NBA's *Hoop* magazine had airbrushed his tattoos off the photograph of him on the cover of the magazine, Iverson responded, "Hey, you can't do that. That's not right. I am who I am. You can't change that. Who gives them the authority to remake me? Everybody knows who Allen Iverson is. That's wild. That's kind of crazy. I personally am offended that somebody would do something like that. They don't have the right to try to present me in another way to the public than the way I truly am without my permission. It's an act of freedom and a form of self-expression. That's why I got mine."

*

When John Allen, who now plays professional basketball in Finland, was a high school star in Philadelphia, he said, "I think that on the court, if I didn't have as many tattoos as I do, people would look at me as—not being soft—but people would look at me as average. When they see me come in with my tattoos and the big name that I've got, before you even play a game, it's like, 'Whoa, this guy, he must be for real.'"

*

In the nineteenth century, Earl Roberts, Field Marshall of the British Army, said that "every officer in the British Army should be tattooed with his regimental crest. Not only does this encourage *esprit de corps* but also assists in the identification of casualties."

*

I recently had the pin removed from my left leg, for no particularly compelling reason other than it spooked me to think of one day being buried with a "foreign object" in my body (for one thing, it's a violation of Jewish law). Not that I'll be buried; I'll be cremated. Not that I'm religious; I'm an atheist. Still, leaving the pin in seemed to me some obscure violation of the order of things. As one tattoo artist has said, "The permanence really hits other people, and that is linked to mortality. And that is why skull tattoos really ice it."

*

Who owns this body, this body of work?

# 21

# Creative Exposition—Another Way that Nonfiction Writing Can Be Good

## Dave Madden

"I know this is going to make some people in this class angry," the student said. "But I feel like nonfiction can get away with bad writing a lot more than fiction can." We were sitting in a very tiny room talking about the book we'd all read—a debut work of nonfiction that had become in the two years since its hardcover release a force in the culture—and many of us had problems with the book's writing. The *writing* wasn't very good. The story that was being told was *interesting*, many of us were ready to allow, but the writing *itself* wasn't very good. Examples of writing that wasn't very good weren't so much forthcoming as vaguely alluded to. The writer had done too little work to vary the sentence structures. The writer had been repetitive and overly cautious in informing us what time period we were in.

I was more unhappy than angry. Not because I disagreed, but because I could feel that amid everything we were talking about there was something fundamental that was not being talked about.

"Wait, so: do we all agree?" I asked.

I looked out at the rest of the class. We all seemed to agree.

I want in this essay to parse out what led both my student to share this idea, and the rest of us to know what it seemed to want to mean. I want to figure out how nonfiction gets away with anything that fiction cannot, what "getting away with" means in this context, and who has been doing all the policing. Just one week before the class came to this agreement, I'd posed a hypothetical question: without any informing apparatus—on the cover, say, or as a disclosure in the text itself—how could we tell a work of nonfiction from a work of fiction? One student ventured that she didn't much care. "I don't care," she said. "I just want to know whether it's good." It was another sentiment with which we all seemed to agree. Why should it matter? Our job as people in a writing classroom is not to corral genre so much as to learn generic husbandry. To help our writing grow, whatever the genre, we need to come to a set of values—"good writing"—we can use to produce it.

That identifying genre doesn't matter and that we should aim more to discover whether a text is good seem to imply that whether writers go to fiction or whether they go to nonfiction they are using the same set of tools to get the job done. And in my experience of writing fiction and nonfiction this feels inaccurate. Of the many trays in my toolbox maybe there are one or two shared by these genres, but there are many—interiority, argument, the conflated *I*—that I save for one or the other. If this is the case, if the attempt at making fiction writing good incorporates a different methodology from the attempt at making nonfiction writing good, then it follows that we shouldn't use the same set of tools to evaluate that writing. Or even just to read it. Just as much as we don't reward a piece of fiction because of its nonfictional qualities, such as they might be, we ought not reward a piece of nonfiction when it starts to read like fiction.

This, though, is what so much of the writing on the writing of nonfiction wants to do. (It's what so often accounts for the frequent appearance of the word *creative* in front of the word *nonfiction*.) Forefather of the genre's new breed, Tom Wolfe wrote essays in magazines pointing out the ways reporters were borrowing from novelists to write their New Journalism, and Lee Gutkind, now the genre's godfather, writes in *Keep it Real* that creative nonfiction "presents or treats information using the tools of the fiction writer."[1]

The trouble is that only sometimes does nonfiction want to be read like fiction, absorbing its readers into a narrative by recreating scenes through sensory detail. But many times it does not. Many times nonfiction has been the gone-to genre not so much because what is being told is true but because what needs to be said can benefit from the immediacy and intimacy between author and reader that nonfiction allows. If we're to come to some understanding, then, of how to talk productively about nonfiction writing, we're going to need to sort out these different motives.

I propose we stop looking at the divide between fiction and nonfiction and start looking at the divides within nonfiction. It's been the habit among recent writings on this genre to do this subgenerically—to carve out little niches for travel writing, memoir, the personal essay, science writing, and so on—describing how each subgenre differs on a content level. In order to get at different differences—differences of form—I'd prefer to look at how nonfiction writing divides among modal lines. Namely, I want to look at the differences between narrative nonfiction (writing that tells a true story), lyric nonfiction (writing that aims foremost for vocal and sonic effects), and expository nonfiction (writing that delivers fact-based information). It's no less arbitrary a division, and indeed many if not all nonfiction writers work among these three modes sometimes in the same piece, but in making this division I've found a way to understand what happened in my classroom that day. Nonfiction "gets away with bad writing" when it goes through its expository modes. As long as we're getting facty content, we don't seem to mind the slovenliness, such as it may be, of the form. It's almost like we writers of expository nonfiction never have to worry about a single word. Expository nonfiction gets a pass. Spend your creative energies elsewhere.

At the risk of dating this essay, here's a lede from a story on the front page of today's *New York Times*:

> LOS ANGELES — Michael Jackson, among the most famous performers in pop music history, spent his final days in a sleep-deprived haze of medication and misery until finally succumbing to a fatal dose of potent drugs provided by the private physician he had hired to act as his personal pharmaceutical dispensary, a jury decided on Monday.[2]

Such sentences historically have been the very thing keeping *straight journalism*, as it's often called, out of the big "creative nonfiction" tent. Stephen Minot opens his book, *Literary Nonfiction: The Fourth Genre*, with such an ousting, writing that "[j]ournalism stresses accuracy above all else," whereas literary nonfiction "tend[s] to be more personal."[3] He comes up with an example of "how a reporter might begin a local story":

> Mildred Gray of 238 Canal St. stared in disbelief as flames leapt from her apartment window three stores above her. The fire, of suspicious origin, broke out at 1:35 A.M., rousing some 23 residents, forcing them to the street. The fire department was not notified until 2:02.[4]

And then Minot rewrites the passage as "described by a writer of literary nonfiction":

> I was stunned into silence when I first saw two dozen people on the street, some in bathrobes or wrapped in blankets, staring at flames leaping from their apartment house. My first reaction was rage: this was the very building the notorious landlord Harry Cutter had tried

to burn the previous week. Why wasn't he being held in jail? Then, like someone waking from a dream, I realized that there were no fire trucks there. Where were they? "Hey," I cried over the crackling of flames, "[h]asn't anyone called 911?"[5]

The second passage differs from the first modally. Minot's journalist writes in an expository mode, whereas his writer of literary nonfiction writes in a narrative mode. The idea here is that "literary" or "creative" nonfiction (hereby abbreviated as CNF to indicate this hyper-corralled nonfiction subgenre of recent vintage) should at every moment tell a story with actions and sensory detail. But to limit CNF to just this narrative mode seems strange given that nonfiction is, technically, everything ever written that's neither fiction nor poetry. Which is, probably, a lot.

Minot's not the only one pointing to the personal as putting the *creative* in "creative nonfiction." Sondra Perl and Mimi Schwartz write in their nonfiction textbook, *Writing True*, that "until recently [i.e. until CNF started showing up in MFA programs], 'creative' in writing has meant poetry, drama, and fiction."[6] This implies that the simple choice of working within one of these genres affords a piece of writing the label *creative*. It does not. There are wildly uncreative poems, stories, and plays written maybe every day. *Creative* is not a genre but a qualifier. It carries a sense of imagination, of original ideas. I like to tie it to its root word and understand creative writing—no matter the genre—as writing that forms something new in the mind of its reader. Why I like this definition is that it allows for creativity in nonfiction genres usually denied access to the big tent: journalism, scholarship, instruction manuals. How this is so is what I hope in this essay to uncover. For now I'll point to an old complaint (referenced in Gutkind's *The Art of Creative Nonfiction*)[7] about the genre: "*Creative nonfiction?* Isn't that an oxymoron?"

*No,* should be our collective answer. *It's just redundant.*

Minot argues that "journalism [. . .] does not generally use literary devices such as fresh and original metaphors or prose rhythms. It rarely if ever creates symbolic suggestions. It almost never indulges in wry understatement."[8] And he's right. Bad, flat journalism does do this. But look again at that *Times* lede. Here's creativity if you allow for it. The detail and use of assonance and alliteration. The "personal pharmaceutical dispensary" metaphor. The clause tacked on at the end that saves the paper from libel while not getting in the way of the image of an ailing MJ. In a CNF workshop, this sentence would be called out as being too *impersonal* or not *expressive* enough. And perhaps by needs the prose is flatter—with a distant, more objective point of view—than when held up against poetry, say. But even if this is true, to say it's not creative is to show a total incomprehension regarding the work reporters do once they're back at the desk.

But creativity as I'm trying to understand it involves more than stylized prose. To return to the problem, I want to try to figure out how, other than through info-delivery or a certain artful style, expository nonfiction can create something new in the reader's head. How can *this* nonfiction—often impersonal, rarely expressive—be creative in form?

One way is through what I'll clunkily call *productive juxtapositioning*, which happens when placing two different bits of information next to each other results not just in contrast, but in creation. It's exposition as montage. And *montage* in the classic Soviet sense. In the 1920s, filmmaker Lev Kuleshov became obsessed with US filmmaker D. W. Griffith's work, screening the latter's *Intolerance* so much at his cinema workshop that reportedly the print disintegrated before he was done studying it. In trying to understand how Griffith's film (and film in general) achieved its greatness, Kuleshov ran some experiments in front of live audiences. In one, he intercut the still image of a famous actor's face with other still images. Audiences would see the face. And then they'd see a bowl of soup, say. And then the face again. Both times: same expressionless expression. Kuleshov would ask the audience: what are you seeing? The audience would say: *He is pining for some lost bowl of soup!* Kuleshov intercut the face with a shot of a woman in a coffin. The audience would then say: *He is distraught over the death of his beloved!* This from *the same face*. The experiments unlocked for Kuleshov some new notion of cinematic grammar, and the birth of what some film critics call "the Kuleshov effect." Here's how David Cook characterizes it in his *History of Narrative Film*: "[T]he shot, or cinematic sign, has two distinct values: 1) that which it possesses in itself . . . and 2) that which it acquires when placed in relationship to other shots."[9]

Kuleshov's audiences made of two separate images some theretofore-unformed set of emotions, memories, and experiences. This is how cinema is creative. This is what it creates. Compare this effect to what happens in the following block of text, from the December 2011 *Harper's* "Findings" column:

> Dutch doctors have better odds of securing organ donation if they first wait briefly, in accordance with the *Hersendoodprotocol*, before they discuss donation with the next of kin of catastrophic-brain-injury victims. Research into the spread of selfishness through human history found that egalitarian societies have more difficulty expanding in times of crisis than societies in which the poor suffer disproportionately. In Britain, where one sixth of cell phones were infected with fecal

bacteria and gonorrhea was becoming drug-resistant, scientists noted an uncoupling of the brain's "hate circuit" in 92 percent of depressed Chinese. Canadian psychologists concluded that "moral disengagement" leads to workplace rumor-mongering and collegial sabotage. Psychopathic Canadian murderers, when describing their crimes, more frequently use conjunctions and employ the past tense than do their non-psychopathic counterparts. Racially ambiguous janitors are more likely to be seen as black. The nose smells what it expects.[10]

What I love about the "Findings" column—printed always on the mag's last page, covering conclusions made by recent scientific studies—is how almost brattily non-narrative it is. The front-of-the-book expository field day that is *Harper's* famed "Index" is always very careful to cite each figure it quotes. One can go and find the whole story, so to speak. "Findings" doesn't bother with this. "Findings" doesn't want the story, it wants the facts. The things done. The things observed. Each of the facts in the above text has its own distinct value (criterion no. 1 of the Kuleshov Effect), which refers to a new understanding of the world some scientists somewhere have come to. I want to look at the value *acquired* by each sentence in its position relative to those around it. I want to look at Kuleshov's criterion no. 2.

How much of this text is about the challenges of living in the world! And I'm not talking about shitty cell phones or sneaky gonorrhea (although I intend to come back to those). I'm talking about the sense, as we move from disparate fact to disparate fact, of interconnectivity this text creates. We move from nation to nation, sure, but as we do so we're led through notions of courtesy, selfishness, egalitarianism, suffering, hate, rumor-mongering, and racism. "The nose smells what it expects" caps off the passage as a kind of warning. No language in the passage itself exhorts that we should take care when encountering other people. That we should withhold judgment. That regardless of nationality we should identify some shared existence. But as they continue to rub together, these sentences create a larger message than they do in sum.

This notion of productive juxtapositioning involves more than the creative sequencing of factual sentences. The sentences themselves can have a kind of internal beauty and logic and creativity. Look again at this sentence in the middle: "In Britain, where one sixth of cell phones were infected with fecal bacteria and gonorrhea was becoming drug-resistant, scientists noted an uncoupling of the brain's 'hate circuit' in 92 percent of depressed Chinese." Here we have a classic case of the periodic sentence, in which the sentence's chief element is saved for the end. To aid in the suspense and delay intrinsic in the periodic sentence, the writer throws in that long appositive, which has the extra value-added job of presenting us with a Britain we may not have been ready to consider from just the words "In Britain." It's a contrast, another productive juxtaposition, formed by the writer's sense of how his or her sentences can move.

I've been perhaps cheekily taking my examples thus far from traditionally un-creative nonfiction genres, but this sort of creative exposition can be found in writers that we in CNF Nation would (perhaps begrudgingly) call our own. To finish up I want to look at John D'Agata's *About a Mountain*. As another arbitrary example, it's not without its problems. In 2012, around the release of his *The Lifespan of a Fact*, CNF Nation went through a mild online uproar over D'Agata's insistence that certain bits of data—for example, the number of strip clubs in Las Vegas—were amendable given the lyric, rhythmic, or otherwise associative needs of the author. To readers of this essay, his stance may render as groundless what points I hope to make. But why I'm using *About a Mountain* is that, invented or not, D'Agata's "facts" operate in an expository mode. What's more, he's got a way of composing his expository prose such that it ends up being both lyric and narrative as well.

*About a Mountain* looks at Las Vegas through two lines of inquiry: the Yucca Mountain project, a one-time plan to deposit the nation's nuclear waste in a mountain outside the city; and the suicide of Levi Presley, who jumped off the top of the Stratosphere, Vegas' tallest building. Around the middle of the book, in the midst of a discussion about the city's unfavorable crime and quality-of-life statistics, D'Agata points to how little of the truth of Las Vegas is ever written by Las Vegas journalists, mostly because so many of those journalists have ties to casinos.

In 1983, for example, when Las Vegas casino owner Steve Wynn decided to apply for a gaming license in Britain, *The Independent* of London reported that an investigation by Scotland Yard drew links between Wynn and the Genovese crime family, an investigation that subsequently was referred to in advertisements by the publisher of a new book about Steve Wynn, *Running Scared: The Life and Treacherous Times of Las Vegas Casino King Steve Wynn*. However, even though *The Independent*'s report was never challenged, Wynn still sued the publisher of *Running Scared* for what he considered "libelous statements," winning $3 million in a Nevada state court, bankrupting the publisher of the biography in question, and somehow winning support from Las Vegas journalists, such that the allegations that initiated his suit were covered by the daily *Las Vegas Review-Journal*— arguably the most influential paper in the state—for only one day, in only one article, on page 5, section B, under the quarter-inch-high headline "Wynn Sues Local Writer."[11]

If we look at the form and style of the paragraph we find, foremost, long sentences. They're not longly poetic or longly meditative, they are long and they are filled with facts. But there's something else going on. This is not a paragraph that deploys its sentences to tell each stage of a narrative or to outline, incrementally, some argument. This is a paragraph that enlists its sentences as repositories for its fact-packed clauses. As such, the relationships between these events seem more apparent, and kind of cemented. The sentences' grammar forms stronger links of causality.

Fine, so the paragraph is composed toward certain rhythmic and interrelational strategies. What, though, does it create on its own? It's just facts. And not only is it just facts, but it's facts that have *already been covered by the press*. D'Agata attributes the facts behind this paragraph to a 2,700-word article in the November 2000 issue of *Columbia Journalism Review*. Here, in order of their appearance, are the passages from the original article D'Agata used in his paragraph:

> *The Independent* of London revealed that Wynn had nearly lost his license in Atlantic City "after a Mafioso called Tony Castelbuono was caught recycling the profits of heroin trafficking at the gambling tables." The March 9, 2000, article referred specifically to a lengthy, 1983 Scotland Yard file alleging Wynn's "links to the Genovese Cosa Nostra family." Scotland Yard had investigated Wynn when he sought a gaming license in Great Britain, and Wynn had subsequently withdrawn the license application.
>
> . . .
>
> Notably missing from local coverage of the Kerkorian-Wynn deal was the Wynn biographer John L. Smith. Smith's 1995 biography, *Running Scared: The Life and Treacherous Times of Las Vegas Casino Kind Steve Wynn*, had detailed accounts of Wynn's continuing proximity to organized crime, and promptly drew down a sweeping libel suit in which a Las Vegas jury found for Wynn in August 1997, bankrupting the publisher, Barricade Books.
>
> . . .

the litigation was over the wording in the publisher's catalogue

. . .

The *Review-Journal* reported the case on page 5B, under the headline WYNN SUES LOCAL WRITER.

. . .

A Las Vegas jury initially awarded Wynn $3.1 million for punitive and compensatory damages.[12]

These facts are unearthed and sequenced in the service of a story about how MGM Grand owner Kirk Kerkorian's $6.4 billion takeover, in 2000, of Wynn's Mirage Resorts went mostly unreported in the Las Vegas press. D'Agata's also interested in this reporting failure, but notice how his passage creates lines of causality that aren't in the original. You can find these lines in such sneaky-vital clauses as "However, even though *The Independent*'s report was never challenged" and "somehow winning support from Las Vegas journalists." In other words, D'Agata is using expository language to piece together a sequence of events—a narrative—that had not before been so sequenced. This is creativity, in the sense I'm getting at in this essay, not fabrication. D'Agata's not drawing connections where none exist, he's creating something new from the factual record. There's a kind of accretive effect to the paragraph as he's composed it. As we move between these sentences, relationships and notions of character, scandal, and corruption build and build to the final understatement—"Wynn Sues Local Writer"—a kind of inevitability that, as another writerly attempt at getting at the story, suddenly appears as woefully inadequate.

There's a chance I've just rendered this essay on nonfiction as redundant as the term "creative nonfiction" itself. For what else is a narrative made up of if not facts? And what other option for us expository nonfiction writers than as careful an attention paid to language as that of the lyricist? As separatable as these modes may be in a craft essay, any effective piece of nonfiction is going to have to employ all three at some point. But here's one last plea for giving each mode its rightful place. We have canon-approved literature (novels, poems) to look to as models in assessing the narrative or lyric successes of nonfiction writing. But as long as CNF continues to cling to these two modes as a way to distinguish itself from its older, dirtier expository-nonfiction siblings, any appearance of expository modes in nonfiction is going to be treated like some vestigial limb—the -ectomy of which we haven't yet found a way to pay for.

# Notes

1 Lee Gutkind, ed., *Keep It Real: Everything You Need to Know About Researching and Writing Creative Nonfiction* (New York: Norton, 2008), 12.
2 Jennifer Medina, "Doctor is Guilty in Michael Jackson's Death," *New York Times*, November 8, 2011, A1.
3 Stephen Minot, *Literary Journalism: The Fourth Genre* (Upper Saddle River, NY: Pearson Education, 2003), 2.
4 Ibid., 2–3.
5 Ibid., 3.
6 Sondra Perl and Mimi Schwartz, *Writing True: The Art and Craft of Creative Nonfiction* (Boston: Houghton Mifflin, 2006), 2.
7 Lee Gutkind, *The Art of Creative Nonfiction: Writing and Selling the Literature of Reality* (New York: John Wiley & Sons, 1997), 9.
8 Minot, 2.
9 David Cook, *A History of Narrative Film*, 2nd ed. (New York: Norton, 1990), 145–6.
10 Rafil Kroll-Zaidi, "Findings," *Harper's*, December 2011, 100.
11 John D'Agata, *About a Mountain* (New York: Norton, 2010), 139.
12 Sally Denton and Roger Morris, "Big Deal in Vegas and How the Local Press Missed It," *Columbia Journalism Review,* November/December 2000, 46–9.

# 22

# Ostrakons at Amphipolis, Postcards from Chicago: Thucydides and the Invention and Deployment of Lyric History

Michael Martone

## K-4 Pacific vs J-1 Hudson

Each night at Englewood Junction on Chicago's south side the Pennsylvania Railroad's Broadway Limited leaving from Union Station and the New York Central's 20th Century Limited leaving from LaSalle Street Station, both bound for New York City overnight, meet to race on their paralleling rights-of-way to the Indiana line.

*He begins his History of the Peloponnesian War this way—"Thucydides, an Athenian wrote the history of the war . . ." but eases into the first person halfway through the paragraph.*[1] *It is as if the tradition of invoking the muse has now transmuted to invoking the self. Is Thucydides the source or its receiver, the inspiration or the action, subject or object, the new or the news?*

## Time begins in Chicago

On the Chicago block bordered by Quincy, LaSalle, Clark, and Jackson stood the Grand Pacific Hotel. On October 11, 1883, 60 delegates representing the principal railways of North America met to standardize time. Up until this time each major city set its own time, often by means of a time ball—the last remaining example of such is the one used in Times Square to indicate midnight. Because of the Chicago convention, the midnight we see indicated in New York is not New York's real midnight but Philadelphia's midnight as Eastern Standard Time is set at noon on the 75th meridian, the meridian that runs through Philadelphia, the headquarters of the Pennsylvania Railroad. The 90th meridian in Memphis, the 105th in Denver, the 120th in Fresno are the other noons we now live by. November 18, 1883 is the day known as the day of two noons when telegraphic signals were sent to reset all the local times and time became the time we think is time.

*In the eleventh year of the war he writes: "The history of this period has also been written by the same Thucydides, an Athenian." Only a few sentences later Thucydides writes: "I lived through the whole of it being of an age to comprehend events and giving attention to them in order to know the exact truth about them. It is also my fate to be an exile from my country for twenty years after my command at Amphipolis."²*

## Platonic harvests

In the back corner of the now old new wing of the Art Institute of Chicago is the reconstructed Chicago Stock Exchange Trading Room designed by Louis H. Sullivan in 1893. The elaborate stenciled applications, art glass treatments, and molded plaster capitals were preserved when the Stock Exchange was demolished in 1972. The Art Institute was able to recreate the room in 1976 using the original salvaged elements. In the corner of the trading room, hard against the coffered quarter-sawn oak wood paneled walls, is an empty table. When the exchange was active, displayed on this table were several piles of grain—wheat, oats, corn, barley—as an illustration to the traders on the floor. The puts and calls being exchanged, the bids being bid, were connected to an actual thing, real cereal, a commodity that had not, as yet, evolved to pure algebraic abstraction. These products were, already, part of the communal imagination of the traders who traded future futures, where real futures were already bargained for in a now already existing, unreal present. The vast, severely modern bay of pits that replaced Mr Sullivan's Beaux-Arts guildhall was built without such a display table. There, even that slim reed of graphic connection snapped, the real real cornered now only in the tangled snapping ganglia of the shouting brokers, the synapses of their electronic devices mimicking memory.

*In Book Four, Thucydides narrates the action of Thucydides at Amphipolis, describing there his own defeat that precipitated his own exile. He records objectively, dispassionately, the story of General Thucydides as he rushes to defend the city against the Spartan army led by King Brasidas but arrives too late, the fall of the city sparking a regional revolt against Athens. He is ostracized. Had he won the battle, the history of the battle would have been different, of course. Had he won the battle, the history of the battle would never have been written.*[3]

## North by Northwest is not a real direction

Mistaken identity. Masquerade. Camouflage. You remember. George Kaplan played by Roger Thornhill played by Cary Grant arrives on the 20th Century Limited at LaSalle Street Station disguised as a red cap assisted in his escape by Eve Kendall played by Eve Kendall played by Eva Marie Saint. He shaves in the station restroom using a miniature travel razor—the scene prefiguring the finale's scramble on the cliff faces of Mount Rushmore. *North by Northwest*'s original title was *The Man in Lincoln's Nose.* But now we are in Chicago and Roger Thornhill is sent by Eve Kendall to a cornfield in Indiana there to meet up with his nonexistent double George Kaplan, or so he thinks. You remember the rest. He do-si-does instead with the deadly crop duster, a pas de deux in the dusty flat fields outside Prairie, Indiana. Of course the scene was shot near Bakersfield, California, which appears on film as more Indiana than Indiana or an exaggerated Indiana, an amplified Indiana. In the film, the pretend Indiana pretending to be Indiana becomes Indiana. But more striking here for our purposes is to realize this famous scene makes no sense. What machinations to lure the victim out to a remote cornfield to be killed by an admittedly ungainly and inaccurate weapon system. If you think about it, how did Martin Landau playing the evil Leonard throw such an elaborate operation together on such short notice and with what cost-benefit analysis to guarantee the desired result? The assassins themselves seem confused on the deadliest delivery device. Propeller decapitation? Automatic weapon strafing? Actual crop-dust dusting? No, the famous scene is a lark, a tour de force, is in the movie as a complete out-of-whack whack, a lyric moment in spite of, to spite, the picture's narrative oomph. The scene is the movie's made-up movie. *North by Northwest*'s theme dwells on the slippery nature of reality—I am but mad north-north-west. This crazed scene is the real movie's madness. It makes make-believe make believe.

*The nineteenth year of the war. Thucydides, writing of the exhausted Athenian army's slaughter in the Assinarus river near Syracuse, is first to use the image of a river running red with blood. "The Peloponnesians came down and butchered them . . . in the water which was thus immediately fouled but which they went on drinking just the same, mud and all, bloody as it was,*

*most even fighting each other to have it." Perhaps, he was not the first to write*
*such a set piece, but his is the first to survive. The river of history inked from*
*now on with blood.*[4]

## It's okay in practice, but what about theory

He's an undergrad upperclassman showing prospective students and their
families the University of Chicago's Hyde Park campus. His group is near
the field where once the Manhattan Project ignited the first chain-reacting
atomic pile when one of the kids asks what the students here do for fun.
This kid has been to Northwestern to tour as well, has there heard about
the dance marathon and the rock that gets painted over and over again by
students who protect the rock's topmost coat. The rock has its own website
and rock cam. "A scavenger hunt," the tour guide tells his glassy-eyed crew.
"We have a scavenger hunt each spring. Last spring," he says, "a dozen
teams of students searched the campus for parts to construct an atomic
reactor." He turns and takes a step or two leading them toward the Econ
building and the abstract sculpture designed to cast, on May Day, a shadow
of the hammer and sickle. Perfectly timed, he stops and turns back to his
following. He says, "Two of them worked."

*Ostrakons were potsherds, broken pottery Athenians used to vote for exile.*
*One's name was scratched into the shard. The ballot cast. Thucydides. I*
*imagine an ostrakon with his name on it on Thucydides' table, a paperweight,*
*a souvenir, as he writes his history and his History.*

## Notes

1  Thucydides, *History of the Peloponnesian War*, trans. Rex Warner (London:
   Penguin Books, 1954), 35.
2  Ibid., 363.
3  Ibid., 328–9.
4  Ibid., 352.

# 23

# On Fragmentation

Steve Fellner

Once I developed a severe case of urticaria. I can still remember the ER nurse surveying the red splotches all over my skin. I asked her if I should be worried. "You're still breathing. That's always a good thing," she said. That's when I knew I was in trouble.

What was weird about these hives was that they would move. You'd see a rash on my upper neck; if you closed your eyes for a second, they'd disappear and show up somewhere else: my lower neck, arm, or even forehead. They wouldn't stop moving.

You couldn't trace a definite trajectory—the appearance of the hives seemed almost arbitrary. After I accepted the fact that this urticaria was going to continue indefinitely, my relation to Time became different. I couldn't pinpoint the moment when something revealed itself and then when it vanished. Everything was blurry and fragmented.

*

I never trust people who love Sappho. It seems cowardly. It's always easy to say that you like something based on a few fragments. Or maybe I'm the coward. I always want to fill in the blanks with unambiguous solutions. I always believe that if you look hard enough, you can find something else that you see as definite, essential.

*

Four years ago, I had a nervous breakdown, culminating in a diagnosis of bipolar disorder. What bothered me the most was sleeplessness. Before I received the proper diagnosis, it turned out I was wrongly diagnosed and given an anti-depressant, jettisoning me into mania.

I didn't fall asleep for three days. I lost track of time. Wakefulness never seemed to end. I needed to experience time in smaller stretches. Little fragments of eternity.

\*

When I grade freshman composition essays, I sense that I always become more annoyed when I spot a sentence fragment as opposed to a run-on sentence. How American is it to assume that more is more?

\*

When I was manic, I couldn't sit down. I didn't know what got into me. I didn't know how I was going to continue at the rate I was going. I thought I was going to die.

I decided that if I was going to die I had to write my mother a love letter.

The best way I knew how to write someone a love letter was to write a book.

How to begin?

I sat down at the computer and typed a single quotation my mother had once said to me.

I had been excessively apologizing to people for things I didn't have any control over.

She slapped me and said: "Don't live your life like a woman. Don't live your life as an apology."

I read my mother the quotation. "I said that?" she said, "That's pretty damn good."

"That's part of a new book I'm writing," I said, "It's the first sentence."

"Whatever happened to Once Upon a Time?"

\*

It seems that more and more people are structuring their essays into piecemeal sections. Little bits. Sometimes enumerated, sometimes not. Sometimes titled, sometimes not. When you ask them why they structured the essay the way they did, they'll say something like, "I want the reader to draw their own conclusions." Which always sounds like a cop-out. Isn't that why you became a writer in the first place? To draw someone else's conclusions for them in an artful, honest way?

\*

During the course of writing my memoir, I showed my mother my fragmented notes, all from childhood.

We made a pact. She would write one of three things next to my scribblings. I told her to tear up the sheets of paper and place each fragment in one of three piles: one marked "O.K.," one marked "You're making things up," one marked, "Too personal." Without asking for explanation, I gave her back the ones she labeled "Too personal." "You can burn those if you want," I said. For the ones marked "You're making things up," we talked about them, trying to reach a compromise. We always did.

I took the fragments marked "O.K.," and "You're making things up" and turned them into full-length scenes. It oddly didn't take much time to add transition, descriptions of place, elaborating on characters and conversations. Before I knew it, all those fragments that were in the end finally agreed by both of us as the "acceptable raw material" for my book were transformed. My fragments had become whole.

I sent them to my mother for approval.

She brought them all back to me in a big disorganized pile. Now they all had the same comment: "You're making things up."

Then she handed me back the stack of sheets she'd marked "Too Personal." She hadn't thrown them away. "Use these," she said.

*

One of my creative writing teachers once said to me the digressions in a piece of writing are almost always the most interesting parts. If you create an essay-in-fragments, you never really have time to digress. You're always looking for the end. You have no time to go anywhere other than forward. Detours aren't acceptable.

*

What is complexity but a lot of simple things strung together?

*

Does illness always preclude form? Does illness always preclude the fact that memories needed to be forgotten? Is trying to create a coherent narrative a sickness in and of itself?

*

A memoir-in-fragments invites non-sequiturs. Accepting a life as a series of non-sequiturs may be the most honest way of not only writing but also living.

*

A fragment is in itself incomplete. The conundrum: no matter how many fragments you assemble you can never create the actual thing.

*

A memoir-in-fragments always encourages me *not* to read it from beginning to end. Once I told a friend that.

"That's not cool," she said.

"What isn't?"

"You read it from beginning to end. That's the way the author intended it. If he meant for you to read the thirty-fifth fragment, then he would have put that first. The first is always the first. I hope you feel bad about what you've been doing."

"Now I do," I say.

"Good."

*

A creative writing teacher about essays-in-fragments: "If you write the perfect fragment, you won't need the rest of the essay. All you'll need is the fragment."

*

I hate jigsaw puzzles. So many little tiny pieces. So many fragments hopeful to find themselves in a completed puzzle. Once a potential boyfriend told me, "I hate jigsaw puzzles. Why would you want to create an image someone else has already created?"

That's when I knew I was in love.

*

Ever since my nervous breakdown, I've lost some of my short-term memory. My husband and I will be watching a TV show, and 5 minutes after a pivotal scene occurs, I'll have to ask for clarification as to what happened. Our nights usually consist of him stopping the DVR, rewinding, offering a synopsis, and then replaying. I'm not just talking about shows everyone sees as intricate and complicated, like *The Wire* or *Game of Thrones*. I'm even talking about *Gossip Girl*. He's a patient man so he doesn't get too angry. He even sort of enjoys it.

Our viewing is so fragmented that it can take 3 hours to finish one show. Which isn't a bad thing. Now finding our way from the beginning through the end feels like more than an experience. It feels like a feat. Like we accomplished something big.

This has made us grow even closer.

*

A memoir-in-fragments confesses the disposability of literature. Let's face it: there's always something you can cut out that no one will notice. And if they do notice: they'll just assume it's in the white space, begging for their attention.

*

When I first started sending my mother fragments she said, "What are you going to do with all these things?"

"I don't know," I said. "Maybe I'll keep them the way they are."

She said, "That's crazy. Everyone will think you've written a book of poetry."

"Maybe I have," I said.

"Oh no!" she said, "No one reads poetry. How am I supposed to become famous? Respect your mother. Turn me into prose. You owe me that."

*

When you're writing an essay-in-fragments, should each fragment be a complete thing in and of itself? Or does it need to transcend itself, existing for something larger? Should we even think of transcendence as a goal in literature? Should the goal simply be to *allow*?

*

I wrote an essay-in-fragments for a creative writing teacher. During the workshop, he said: kill all your darlings.

I raised my hand and asked, "Can you be a little more specific? They're all my darlings."

# 24

# Positively Negative

Dinty W. Moore

Of what use, really, is white space on the page?

One answer might be found by asking you, the reader, what you made of the space that separates this paragraph from the one-line paragraph above. Possibly you were annoyed or suspicious of my gimmick. That's understandable.

The answer I am hoping for, however, is that you found yourself momentarily filling in the blank, inserting your own tentative response to the opening question. Or at least giving your possible response some brief consideration before jumping down to the paragraphs you are reading now.

I'm trying to better understand the ways in which a reader absorbs nonfiction prose, and especially how that reader participates in the making of meaning. The writer has an enormous responsibility to shape the words, the sentences, the paragraphs, the chapters, the metaphors, the language, the texture of every written artifact, but the reader is no passive dummy. The reader, especially the reader who seeks out literary work, comes to the page with an active brain, chock-full of ideas, referents, and connections.

I'm not—absolutely not—trying to re-open the deconstruction debate. Theory does not much interest me. But as a writer, it is important to think about what you are presenting to a reader, to acknowledge the simple fact that what you experience reading your own words is going to be substantively different from what someone else, someone who does not live inside of your brain, will experience.

And thinking about this brings me to my main questions: how do our choices about something as simple as white space influence how readers engage with our essays? Are we making conscious decisions about our use of spacing, taking full advantage of this essential element of craft?

Poets may be scratching their heads at this point, because they've been thinking of white space, negative space, the distance between thoughts and words, since the time they first took up the pen in a serious manner. Poets love the line
> Break, and they love their
> Enjambment
> And they love it for good reason.

There is a palpable, tactile difference to what happens in my brain when I settle in with these lines from Mary Oliver:

> You do not have to be good
> You do not have to walk on your knees
> For a hundred miles through a desert, repenting
> You only have to let the soft animal of your body
> Love what it loves[1]

Versus this:

> You do not have to be good. You do not have to walk on your knees for a hundred miles through a desert, repenting. You only have to let the soft animal of your body love what it loves.

The difference is hard to categorize, of course, which is why poetry is art and not engineering. But in the poet's version, with the line breaks intact, reactions rise up in my mind—like cartoon thought bubbles—after the word "good," after "knees," after "repenting," and certainly after her vivid phrase "the soft animal of your body."

Because Oliver is the writer that she is, she retains full control of that back and forth—whatever I come up with is trumped by what she offers in return—but the back and forth is a significant part of the pleasure.

I am already in beyond my depth where poetics is concerned, so let me turn instead to prose writers, who in my experience seldom if ever articulate how white space works in our literary realm. We use it, certainly, but I very seldom find it discussed in craft books or writing classrooms.

Traditionally, each chunk of prose—anywhere from one paragraph to one thousand paragraphs—is (though the term is rapidly becoming extinct) a "crot." Consider the crot to be our version of a stanza. Back in the typewriter days, when a writer would decide to hit the carriage return twice instead of once, she would end one crot and begin another, creating what is variously called a space break, section break, segment break, crot break, line break, line space, double drop, or line drop.[2] The mere fact that an informal survey of my writer friends turned up all of those terms makes my point: this is something we seldom discuss, and thus, we don't even have a common language.

In my fiction workshops in grad school, I learned that space breaks— that's what *we* called them—most often indicate a passage of time or scene change, or both, such as a jump from the protagonist's front lawn to a moment later that same day in the protagonist's kitchen. Fiction writers might use the simple break for other purposes as well: change in point-of-view, change from scene to summary, movement into the character's thoughts, and of course, for flashback.

In every case however, the "double drop" is not just a symbol for "scene change," it is a moment where the reader is given a breath, and in that breath, the reader is invited to think "What did I just read, and where do I think this might all be going?"

Nothing earth-shattering there, but it does bring the reader into the story and offers some room for participation, like the line break in a poem. Oral storytellers accomplish this same effect with a pause. Actors do it with a pause and perhaps a change of expression: what they call a beat.

There is also opportunity (actually, obligation) for the writer to carefully choose what occurs on either end of the space break. The ending of one section—the word or the moment chosen—inevitably interacts with where and how you choose to begin the next section. As John McPhee points out, ". . . two parts of a piece of writing, merely by lying side-by-side, can comment on each other without a word spoken,"[3] so whatever is happening in the protagonist's kitchen after that brief jump should also illuminate or advance whatever was being tossed about earlier out on the lawn.

Novelist and New Journalist Tom Wolfe takes it one step further, choosing "crazy leaps of logic" over comment and illumination:

> As each crot breaks off, it tends to make one's mind search for some point that must have just been made—*presque vu!*—almost seen! In the hands of a writer who really understands the device, it will have you making crazy leaps of logic, leaps you never dreamed of before.[4]

In memoir or literary journalism, this rudimentary space break or section break is used much as it is in fiction: a scene change, a flashback, a switch from scene to reflection or exposition. The personal essayist might use the break to signal a fresh angle, a logical jump, or another piece of the intellectual mosaic. Montaigne did it constantly.

But there are more radical examples.

Consider Lawrence Sutin's *A Postcard Memoir*, which uses duotone reproductions of postcards as occasions to pen 400-word memoir snippets. We readers are given a challenge: pull together the pieces of this engaging jigsaw puzzle to assemble one man's life.

Or Jenny Boully's *The Body: An Essay*, which is nothing *but* white space. Boully leaves the entire text of the book blank, except for 157 footnotes which readers must use as clues to imagine what the text might have contained.

In her book-length essay *Bluets*, Maggie Nelson demonstrates how grave personal losses can shatter us into pieces by splintering her nonfiction musings into 240 lyrical prose entries focused on grief and the color blue.

And of course David Shields makes an extreme statement with his manifesto, *Reality Hunger*, a series of 618 very brief aphorisms, quotes, and observations on narrative and reality, reminiscent perhaps of the index cards one might collect preparatory to beginning one's dissertation. Shields further complicates his work, and demands further reader participation, by refusing to acknowledge his sources of the quotes (though in the end, his publisher compelled him to put an appendix at the back of the book; an appendix he begs us to ignore). *Here is the source material*, Shields seems to be saying. *You write the book.*[5]

Anyone toiling in the creative nonfiction fields lately knows of the ongoing popularity of the collage essay, variously criticized as a lazy writer's way of avoiding the need to write transitions or lauded as an experimental innovation that allows for, as Wolfe suggested, "leaps of logic, leaps you never dreamed of before."

I think both are true. I'm a fan of the collage form, though I certainly see it used lackadaisically on occasion. But weak collages do not condemn the form entirely. We have, after all, plenty of weak villanelles, weak sestinas, weak novels, and weak pieces of narrative journalism.

Composition theorist Peter Elbow lays out pretty well why collage is inappropriate for the academic or informative essay:

I try to teach thinking, and thinking *does* mean figuring out hierarchy and subordination: what are your main points and what are the sub points and how do they relate? Make it all explicit. After all, the whole point of an essay is . . . no, wait, that's not quite right. The whole point of the *school* essay or *academic* essay is to *say* what you are saying, not to leave it implicit. And complex, hierarchical prose is good to learn and can be lovely.[6]

But Elbow *does* value the collage approach for the literary essay, citing reader participation as a main advantage:

> It is *not* always syntactically immature to lay out unconnected sentences or units and let them rub up against each other without connective tissue. There is more energy in unconnected sentences, more drama. They tend to be an enactment of something going on rather than a record of a past event—something conceptually finished. Let the reader feel the energy of the jump.[7]

The energy of the jump.

The moment for the reader to absorb.

And possibly add a thought of their own.

Annie Dillard, in *Living by Fiction*, notes that "the use of narrative collage is particularly adapted to various twentieth-century treatments of time and space. Time no longer courses in a great and widening stream . . . passing fixed landmarks in orderly progression . . . Instead time is a flattened landscape, a land of unlinked lakes seen from the air."[8]

It is now the twenty-first century, and, oddly, Dillard's words sound like an advertisement for Facebook or Twitter. One might argue her assertion that time no longer courses "in a great and widening stream," but information certainly does not, and the contemporary reader seems increasingly comfortable absorbing information from various blogs, news sources, and social media posts in order to form their own view. Does this mean that today's reader is more comfortable with cutting and pasting moments from a nonlinear literary narrative and reassembling the pieces inside the brain? Probably yes.

And what of the future reader? That is difficult to answer. White space has an altered connotation when reading on a Nook or Kindle. Technologies yet to be discovered will change the "act of reading" in ways we can only guess at, and the moment where the reader pauses, the energy of the jump, will no doubt be changed as well.

But returning a moment to the present:

A beginning writer, I've observed, often falls short of the goal by telling the reader too little, until said reader becomes lost and annoyed and wanders off to another story. Or the beginner tells too much, hitting the reader over the head with every connection, every irony, every telling moment, until the reader feels that her intelligence has been insulted, or underestimated at least.

Readers are smart. They want to participate and want the pleasure of putting two and two together themselves, of making discoveries along the way—sometimes along with the writer and sometimes a step ahead of the writer.

The break, the space, the interruption, allows for that to happen.

The energy of the jump.

Why don't writers talk more about the crafting of white space, space breaks, double drops? I don't know. Like poetry, literary prose is art, not engineering, but there are things to be said, things to be learned, about how this negative space—small to large—operates on the page, and in the reader's experience of the page.

"Each word is a rock I've placed personally into a wall—five go in and I pick through a pile and find another, shift them all around until it's right," Dagoberto Gilb offers in the introduction to his essay collection *Gritos*. "I've chipped and nicked at most so they look to me like good sentences, good paragraphs. . . ."[9]

Indeed. But nothing says that wall will have no gaps.

As Leonard Cohen once reminded us, "There is a crack in everything."[10] Better to let the light come in.

## Notes

1  Mary Oliver, "Wild Geese," in *Dream Work* (Boston: Atlantic Monthly Press, 1986), 14.

2  In Microsoft Word, the writer hits the "enter" key twice, instead of an old-fashioned carriage return, although the default formatting options in Word complicate the matter. In many student essays I see these days, Word inserts an annoying space break between *each and every* paragraph, meaning no distinction is made between paragraph change and a deliberate section break. But that's a software issue. I can only hope that anyone serious about their prose has a handle on how to make the choice deliberately, not by default.

3 John McPhee, quoted in Norman Sims, Introduction to *Literary Journalism*, ed. Norman Sims (New York: Ballantine, 1984), 13.

4 Tom Wolfe, introduction to *The Secret Life of Our Times*, ed. Gordon Lish (New York: Doubleday, 1973), xxv.

5 Here of course, the artifice of nonfiction comes into play. Shields already "wrote" the book, of course, by deciding in which order the reader encounters the 618 disparate snippets.

6 Peter Elbow, *Everyone Can Write: Essays Toward a Hopeful Theory of Writing and Teaching Writing* (New York: Oxford University Press, 2000), 309.

7 Ibid., 309.

8 Annie Dillard, *Living by Fiction* (New York: Harper & Row, 1982), 20–4.

9 Dagoberto Gilb, introduction to *Gritos: Essays* (New York: Grove Press, 2004), xiv.

10 Leonard Cohen, "Anthem." *The Future*. Columbia studio album, 1992.

# 25

# Study Questions for the Essay at Hand: A Speculative Essay

Robin Hemley

1. Is it the aim of this essay to allow wonder and speculation and not one fact?

2. Is it the aim of this essay to speculate about topics of which the essay is not expert?

3. Might the essay be overly self-conscious and coy? Does it concern this essay that it cares too much for form and has nothing to state (formerly known as "meaning"), that it actively avoids meanings, messages, interpretations, that it has no author, that it might be a trick that someone is playing on you, that you have always suspected that God was out to "get you," and now here is your proof, that perhaps you should not follow that line of inquiry?

4. Are words measurable? Do they have a pulse? Is this essay *really* writing itself or is it even now being written by someone on a plane going to Turkmenistan while the essayist tries to shield what he is writing from an inquisitive seatmate? Does that mean you, buddy?

5. Will the essay work the Friday shift if the Manager calls unexpectedly?

6. Is the essay a bit of a narcissist? A solipsist? A mensch? (Circle all that apply.)

7. How did the essay do on the Essay section of the Foreign Service Exam?

8. If the essay were stranded on a desert island, would anybody notice?

9. Is the essay concerned that it might be getting too self-serious as it matures, that even the terms "essay" and "essayist" are a little overused? Does it long to have lines that don't blend fact and fiction?

10. Do essays have feelings? Are there little starving essays on other continents? Would you sponsor an essay for as little as five cents a day?

11. What will the quiz cover?

Fact: the Treaty of Tordesillas
Fact: type B Blood
Fact: from 1953 to 1975.
Fact: the Tang Dynasty

A Slight Digression: the essay has apparently failed in its original intention not to admit a fact. But it does not care. Because essays are full of contradictions. This is what makes the essay more essayistic. It essays onward because it feels empowered. This essay has agency.

12. What if everything is a digression? Certainly, if there is no afterlife, then our lives are a digression. But this essay believes in an afterlife, so for the time being we're all safe.

A Second Digression: this essay has been considering a topic lately though it isn't sure it can afford one. The topic has something to do with good health, but the essay is having difficulty settling between Bernarr McFadden, a health guru of the 1920s as well as a media tycoon, and the *We-Di-Co Peptomist*, an in-house newsletter published in the 1920s by The Western Distributing Company of Chicago, Illinois. The Western Distributing Company published health encyclopedias and its employees sold them door-to-door throughout the country. One of the features of the *We-Di-Co Peptomist* was a monthly column titled, "My Hardest Sale" in which various members of the sales team recounted their hardest sale.

13. Why does the essay care at all about Bernarr McFadden, a forgotten health guru from the 1920s and the *We-di-Co Peptomist*, an in-house publishing organ of which there are probably no extant copies remaining other than the ones to which the essay's putative author bought in a Chicago bookstore over 25 years ago?

This essay has no idea why it cares or why anyone else should care (what is commonly known as the "So What?" factor) except that the *We-di-Co Peptomist* is charming and quaint and forgotten, a misplaced shard of existence, as is the forgotten McFadden with his "lustrous" hair and the photographs of him taken 30 years apart showing a man in skin-tight unitard, the earlier photo surprisingly daring in the asslessness of his unitard.

14.  Is part of the essay's job to dip back into the dust heap of forms and people gone by, locating survivors in the wreckage of an imploded building, as it were, grasp them by the hand, and say, "Rise up, Bernarr! Rise up, you Peptomists! Live again, if only briefly. Show us your stuff?"

You may use another additional sheets of paper to answer this question.

Note: this essay will not resort to cheap tricks and it will never lie to you because this essay has signed a contract with you and has left it on your kitchen counter for you to sign and fax back. This essay would like to inform you that the contract works both ways, something that people sometimes miss. But this essay will not lie to you, and you know you can believe what this essay says because it has said it and isn't that proof enough?

This essay does not need to impress you with a litany of dubious facts gathered via a web search and then presented to you as though it has spent weeks in the musty stacks of The University of Iowa Library, bringing book after book to its study carrel where it pores over ancient tomes to find exactly the right bit of information. The library is in fact emptying itself of books and few people seem to notice or care. If, for instance, you are on an errand to locate a copy of Xavier de Maistre's eighteenth-century classic, *Journey Around My Room,* you will be on a fool's errand, as the electronic catalogue will inform you that one copy of said text exists on the fifth floor, call number HN17655.175a. But no such text can be found on the fifth floor, which is itself a ghost library—rows upon rows of metal shelving with nary a book to be seen and the lights turned low as though in some local shop in the final throes of a going-out-of-business sale and the creditors knocking when only the fixtures remain. What we are witnessing here is a great migration of thought, an upheaval, much like the brutal aftermath of the partition of India and Pakistan, but instead of people displaced and done away with in violent fashion, forms and thoughts and ways of presenting thoughts are being tossed around.

15. How can this essay make a callous analogy to such a tragic upheaval
     as the partition of India and Pakistan in 1947 and the borderlines of
     verbal expression? Someone is sure to be offended, and this essay aims
     never to cause discomfort or offense.

If the essay is making all this up, by the way, then kudos to it because it has
a better imagination than most people, and so shouldn't we give it props for
that? Not that this essay feels comfortable with that word "props." "Props"
is not a word this essay would normally use, though it is curious about the
word's etymology. But it is not about to do a web search to find out the
etymology of the word "props" as it is used colloquially in the twenty-first
century.

It will not resort to that trick, so in vogue, of gathering up a list of factoids
and presenting them as a litany as though the simple recitation of random
facts abutting one another has some literary merit.

But this essay has a hunch, and if that hunch is correct then the word
"props" was first used in its colloquial form in an early draft of the Moncrieff
translation of *Swann's Way* by Marcel Proust in which the narrator praises
Eulalie for the masterful way in which she humors the hypochondriacal
Aunt Leonie of the narrator, when he writes:

> My aunt might say to her twenty times in a minute for the way in which
> she humored Aunt: "The end is come at last, my poor Eulalie!", twenty
> times Eulalie would retort: "Knowing your illness as you do, Mme
> Octave, you will live to be a hundred as Mme. Sazerin said to me only
> yesterday." Although Eulalie persisted in referring to Mme. Sazerat as
> Mme. Sazerin, I believe that my poor aunt still gave her props for never
> faltering once in the role in which she was cast in the daily passion play
> whose repeat performances were the only theater I knew for a time,
> peering at this scene both in memory and as a child, as if through a pair
> of opera glasses turned round the wrong way.[1]

Note: see section 2, paragraph 3 of the contract on your kitchen counter.
You don't need to read it if you don't have time—basically, it's a standard
indemnity clause.

This essay does not want to be thought of as pretentious and effete, although
it wonders if simply making an allusion to the Thought Delivery System

formerly known as a Novel by Marcel Proust will hopelessly brand it as such.

Go ahead and try to interrogate this essay. It will not crack. It will not display recidivist narrative tendencies, or patriarchal linear structures because it eschews linearity, because linearity is not artistic and is goal oriented and this essay is not goal oriented though it is at the same time ambitious. Don't look at this essay the wrong way. It will stick a Journalism Major up your ass. Never call this essay unambitious. It received a prestigious award for its ambition and was nominated for others.

This essay practices Hot Yoga, but it's tired and it's bent out of shape and is blending with other essays and other forms of discourse within its personal space. Please stay out of this essay's personal space because some essays smell when they exercise and some are lecherous and that's why this essay would prefer to work out with essays of its own kind (Read: would management please tell literary journalists to find their own workout space?). This essay does not mind a certain amount of blending, but it prefers subversion to blending. They are not the same, you know.

16. Is it just my imagination or is this essay still driving at something?

17. Is the world spinning faster?

18. Is everything simply a digression?

# Note

1 Based loosely on Marcel Proust, *Remembrance of Things Past, Part I: Swann's Way,* trans. C. K. Scott Moncrieff (New York: Holt, 1922), 92.

# 26

# It Is What It Is

Eula Biss

All living matter, and anything derived from living matter, is organic. In the slightly more specific terms of chemistry, organic compounds are those that contain the element carbon. The word *organic* can also be used to describe a harmonious relationship between parts of a whole.

In some definitions the word *lyric* has something to do with feeling. In others it has something to do with musicality. When used to describe a voice, it means "characterized by a relatively high compass and a light, flexible quality."[1]

As a noun, it means the words of a song or a kind of poem. "The range and variety of lyric verse is immense," writes J. A. Cuddon, "and lyric poetry, which is to be found in most literatures, comprises the bulk of all poetry."[2] And so lyric might, when applied to the essay, seem to mean poetic. But that is an open jaw, meaning we fly into one city and out of another.

Organic can refer to a natural development.

Arthur Rimbaud called his prose poetry "pure prose." James Joyce called his "epiphanies." William Carlos Williams called his "improvisations."

In 1940, the same year that the British agriculturalist Baron Northbourne first used the term *organic* to describe a farming practice, the British botanist and Agricultural Advisor to India Sir Albert Howard proposed that the best new methods for growing food were old methods. He argued that rejecting the current system of scientific agriculture for the traditional techniques of Indian farmers was the only way to "safeguard the land of the Empire from the operations of finance."[3]

Naming something is a way of giving it permission to exist. And this is why the term *lyric essay* was so important to me when I first learned it.

Not long after I stumbled across the *Seneca Review*'s description of the lyric essay, I found myself, by some accident of fate, in a crowded stairwell next to Joyce Carol Oates. To make conversation, she asked me how I would classify the writing I had just read to the people who were penning us into the stairwell with little plastic cups of wine. I told her that until recently I would have called it prose poetry, but that now I was inclined to call it lyric essay. "Oh, good," Joyce Carol Oates said to the laughter of someone who nodded knowingly next to her, "because, really, who wants to read prose poetry?"

When Lord Northbourne used the term *organic farming*, he meant "the farm as organism."[4] Applied to any ecosystem, the metaphor of the organism reveals the danger in allowing the parts to distract from the whole.

My students ask me what the difference is between prose poetry and the lyric essay. I tell them that there isn't always a difference. I hear myself saying "artificial categories" while I try to think through all the problems with the question, and then all the problems with my answer. I suggest that not everything that falls somewhere between prose and poetry is prose poetry, and that the term is associated with a particular tradition that has been developing its own conventions for 150 years. I talk about Bertrand and Baudelaire and I say "lineage," but my heart isn't quite in it.

I suspect that genre, like gender, with which it shares a root, is mostly a collection of lies we have agreed to believe.

In the decades after the atom bomb and *Silent Spring*, when the possibility that we might destroy our own world seemed likely, the question of sustainability defined the organic movement. Any practice that could not be sustained indefinitely—such as the massive cultivation of a single crop that would inevitably become vulnerable to diseases and pests, or the use of fossil fuels to ship produce thousands of miles from where it was grown—was to be avoided. This philosophy was in direct conflict with the conventional thinking of the time. To farm on a small scale was to disregard efficiency, and to sell produce locally was to reject the mass market.

One unintended consequence of calling my writing *essay* instead of calling it *poetry*, I discovered rather quickly, was that it would be much more frequently subjected to the conventional expectations of the essay—it would be expected to operate logically, to be cohesive and thorough, to have a clearly supported argument . . .

Holes in an essay, I tell my students, flaws in the logic, contradictions, unanswered questions, loose associations may all be necessary because of what they ultimately make possible. I believe this, but I also have my doubts. I am suspicious of gaps, of silences, of contradictions because I know how easily they hide unfinished thinking.

*Organic*, to some, is a philosophy. To others it is a product.

The USDA standards for regulating the commercial use of the word *organic* came into full effect in 2002. Like most organic standards, they allow for the limited use of several substances that are toxic to humans, fish, and, in one case, honeybees. And because of fees and paperwork requirements, among other things, the USDA certification process inadvertently favors large-scale producers. Under the USDA standards, Stonyfield Farm, which is majority owned by the French dairy giant Groupe Danone, sells organic yogurt made with strawberries from China, apples from Turkey, blueberries from Canada, and bananas from Ecuador.[5] This global sourcing violates, for many, the spirit of the organic movement. But the USDA is not in the habit of regulating spirit.

Occasionally, I use the word *organic* to explain why I write the way I write—as in, "This form is organic to the way I think."

"An organic farm," writes Wendell Berry, "properly speaking, is not one that uses certain methods and substances and avoids others; it is a farm whose structure is formed in imitation of the structure of a natural system that has the integrity, the independence and the benign dependence of an organism."[6]

"Icons beget iconoclasm," Steven Shapin writes of some recent critiques of the organic industry.[7] And this might explain why I feel the need to resist all the current attention to the surface of the essay, and to the shape of it. Empty essays that throw up formal smoke screens ought not to be celebrated any more than overpriced, mass-produced spinach.

"Consumers like boutique brands," the head of the organic unit at General Mills, which owns two major organic names, Cascadian Farm and Muir Glen, told *Business Week*. "There's a feeling of authenticity."[8]

A lot of euphemism and categorization and shuffling of feet goes into the project of making a clear distinction between the kind of nonfiction that deserves to be regarded as art and the kind that does not. Never mind that such a distinction cannot be made, such a project is destructive to our environment.

*Organic* is commonly used as a synonym for *healthy*. By one account, 90 percent of frequent organic buyers believe they are buying "health and nutrition." But there is very little evidence that organic food is any healthier than other food—organic produce has not been proven to offer superior nutrition, and the pesticide residues on conventional produce have not been proven to be harmful. Several studies, however, have found that organic farming uses considerably less energy and produces less waste than conventional farming.[9] So, some organic food is healthier for us in its production, but as consumers we aren't accustomed to buying process so much as we are to buying product. And we want to buy our own health, not someone else's.

Genre is not at all useful as an evaluative tool, but we seem to be tempted to try to use it that way. And we seem to be tempted to rely on just about anything but our own reading of a text to determine its value.

"How to Avoid a Famine of Quality," was the title of one of Sir Albert Howard's articles. In it he suggests that we think a little bit harder about our food.

The supermarket chain Whole Foods sells produce that is classified as either *organic* or *conventional*. This terminology is misleading, in that many large organic producers now use methods that could best be described as a hybrid of organic and conventional practices. Horizon organic milk, for example, is produced without the use of antibiotics or hormones, but Horizon cows are confined in large metal barns that hold 4,000 cows.[10] The result is less expensive organic milk, and more of it. One of the undeniable advantages of conventional agriculture is that it feeds more people.

There is no reason that a work of prose cannot be both lyric and narrative. As categories, we might like to believe they are distinct, but as qualities, they are not mutually exclusive. This is the point at which my students begin to get frustrated with me. I have failed to adequately explain the difference between any number of kinds of nonfiction by now, I have failed to explain the difference between poetry and nonfiction, and I have even failed to explain the difference between fiction and nonfiction.

*Conventional agriculture* might be better termed *experimental agriculture*, in that it is a radical departure from just about the entire history of agriculture and the outcome of this new approach is still entirely uncertain.

A student asks me what a *lyric essay* is. She is holding her pen above a pad of paper and looking at me expectantly and all I can think is, "It doesn't matter."

*Experimental* once meant "based on experience as opposed to authority."

The fine points of the official standards for organic produce become irrelevant if you know where your food comes from and how it was grown. This was once a slogan of the organic movement: "Know your farmer, know your food." But that's easier said than done.

As the meaning of the term *organic* becomes increasingly complicated, alternative terms are emerging. *Authentic food* is one. "*Authentic*," writes Eliot Coleman, who authored the term, "is meant to be the flexible term *organic* once was."[11]

The word *authentic*, Coleman notes, is derived from the Greek *authentes*: one acting on one's own authority.

Old names beget new names, and genres beget subgenres. But knowing what a thing is called—how it is classified, how it is packaged, how it is marketed—is inevitably a poor substitute for knowing what it is.

# Notes

1  *Webster's New World College Dictionary*, 4th ed., s.v. "Lyric."
2  J. A. Cuddon, ed. *The Penguin Dictionary of Literary Terms and Literary Theory*, 4th ed. (New York: Penguin, 1982), 372.
3  Sir Albert Howard, *An Agricultural Testiment* (Oxford: Oxford University Press, 1943), 15.
4  Lord Northbourne, *Look To The Land* (London: J. M. Dent, 1940), 81, quoted in John Paull, "The Foundational Idea of Organic Agriculture," *Elementals: Journal of Bio-Dynamics Tasmania* 83 (2006): 14–18, http://orgprints.org/10138/1/10138.pdf.
5  Diane Brady, "The Organic Myth," *Business Week*, October 16, 2006, www.businessweek.com/magazine/content/06_42/b4005001.htm.
6  Wendell Berry, *The Gift of Good Land: Further Essays Cultural and Agricultural*, 1st ed. (New York: North Point Press, 1981), 143–4.
7  Steven Shapin, "Paradise Sold," the *New Yorker*, May 15, 2006, www.newyorker.com/archive/2006/05/15/060515crat_atlarge.
8  Bruce Philp, "Reality Bites, No Injuries Reported," Brand Cowboy Blog, October 15, 2006, http://brandcowboy.blogspot.com/2006_10_01_archive.html.
9  Wikipedia contributors, "Organic Food," *Wikipedia: The Free Encyclopedia*, http://en.wikipedia.org/wiki/Wikipedia:Citing_Wikipedia (accessed May 18, 2012).
10  Rebecca Claren, "Land of Milk and Honey," *Salon*, April 13, 2005, www.salon.com/2005/04/13/milk_3/.
11  Eliot Coleman, "Beyond Organic," *Mother Earth News*, December/January 2001, www.motherearthnews.com/Real-Food/2001-12-01/Beyond-Organic.aspx.

# 27

# The Inclusiveness of Metaphor

Nicole Walker

One strict criterion for creative nonfiction is that one must exclude the lie, but that seems, like the Arizona Education budget cuts, a little draconian and severe. Nonfiction shouldn't be an exclusive sport like professional football where only the strong facts can play. Nonfiction should be inclusive, like PE in fourth grade where even I was allowed on the dodge ball team, although I dropped to the ground as if a grenade had been tossed anytime that red ball came within 40 feet of me. Which meant I spent most of the class period on the ground. But, like the taste of hyper-waxed gym floor on that weak, fearful girl's tongue, a metaphor provides flavor if not exactly accuracy.

Stephen Colbert, renowned literary critic and poetry scholar, when interviewing Elizabeth Alexander on his show after she read her inauguration commemoration poem, asked her, "What's the difference between a metaphor and a lie?" He said, "I am the sun, you are the moon, that's not true."[1]

She responded the two aren't mutually exclusive. Metaphor is a way to make a comparison to let people understand something as it relates to something else and that's how we use the language to increase meaning.

Why not just say what you mean? Colbert asks.

Because sometimes a writer wants to cast a wide net. Because a writer wants to mean two things at once. Even a nonfiction writer wants to include rather than exclude. That impulse to increase meaning might be one way to think of lying—if I tell a lie and know the truth—two things exist. If I tell you that you're the compass, my sail, and my map, I may have mixed metaphors and I may have lied to you, but at least you know about me that I'm lost at sea and you could be helpful if you'd spend a little more time with me. I've now expanded possibility. I made something exist in the universe that hadn't been there before—a ridiculously shaped person with a sail for a head, a hand for a compass, and a heart for a map, but you got me here, didn't you? A metaphor applies that same lying impulse to the possibility for two things to exist simultaneously. Even straightforward, narrative memoir can't quit the metaphor; the desire to increase and multiply is too strong even for those who resist making stuff up.

The stuff of metaphor is the stuff of pure make-believe. Even the moral essayists lied to make their point. Death metaphors tie terrestrial to ether. Those are obviously lies, or at least speculation, but necessary, because how else can we describe the other side but in comparison?

Seneca about death: "I ask you, wouldn't you say that anyone who took the view that a lamp was worse off when it was put out than it was before it was lit was an utter idiot? We, too, are lit and put out."[2] Seneca's lie is life is a lamp.

Plutarch on death and souls receiving support from a robust body: "A great part of sorrow is blunted and relaxed, like a wave under a clear sky, when the body enjoys tranquil sailing."[3]

Kenko on immortality: "If man were never to fade away like the dews of Adahino, never to vanish like the smoke over Toribeyama, but lingered on forever in the world, how things would lose their power to move us."[4]

Death is always fleeing somewhere, busy in its evaporation, but some metaphors tie things to earth.

For instance food is of the earth. Terroir. Food is metaphorical. From the time your dad buzzed an airplane-spoon full of applesauce into your hanger-mouth, food had to be translated in. And food metaphor makes equivalences of taste. For instance, Adelsheim Vineyard, a winery in Oregon, lists paragraphs about their reserve series wines. The 2005 Elizabeth's Reserve Pinot Noir offers aromas of candied cherry, sage, lavender, clove spice, and hints of smoke and rustic cedar. On the palate, there is well-balanced focus and intensity in the cherry flavors, creamy tannins, and mouth coating finish. The 2006 Chardonnay shows lemons, figs, and apricots—as well as spice and hazelnuts—on the nose. The lies here suggest that you don't ever have to eat again—just drink wine and all the nutritive value will flow through the aromas of fruit and nuts.

One imagines that metaphors might be the provenance of fiction and poetry and just an occasional flourish in nonfiction, but really, nonfiction traffics mainly in metaphor. It is only in the suggestion that my life, in memoir, is relevant to yours in the most parallel and associative ways.

How my life signifies in any way upon yours makes itself known only in metaphorical comparison. I get myself to you through the vehicle of my story. Its tenor coats you like, well, a warm coat, or a 2005 Pinot Noir. You and I, in the memoir, move in together in the coat. We drink the Pinot. Remember that time we lay in our bed spinning after we drank too much of that wine. Remember? Or at least I reminded you well enough about the time you spun. In the way I wrote about the popcorn on the ceiling and that popcorn spiraling me right off the bed into a buttery morning mess. You still with me in this coat of mine?

Metaphor signals a different kind of nonfiction ethic than the truth and nothing but the truth. This alternate ethics suggests that inclusiveness creates a bigger net into which more readers can tumble. Through metaphorical connections readers find entry points and invite themselves right in.

Edward Hoagland is inclusive in his essay "The Courage of Turtles."[5] He includes mechanics who know about carburetors and their governing. He brings in lawyers and diners who are etiquette-challenged. He brings in the penguin and the lion, linking animal with animal, creating a kind of ecology. One metaphor leads to the next, drawing a map of connectedness that returns to the turtle and the turtle is always put in relation to the human. The turtle is known not through its essence, but through its resemblance and similarity to other members of the animal kingdom, including humans. It's this similarity that makes the turtle significant—it has invited us into this planet of connectedness.

Turtles figure for everything and everyone.

- "Turtles are a kind of bird with the governor turned low."
- "They're Personable Beasts. They see the same colors we do and they seem to see just as well, as one discovers in trying to sneak up on them."

Then he contrasts them with snakes and alligators, bringing them into the field even though they're not exactly like turtles:

- "Snakes, by contrast, are dryly silent and priapic. They are smooth movers, legalistic, unblinking and they afford the humor which the humorless do."
- "Alligators are sticklers too: they're like war horses, or German shepherds, and with their bar-shaped, vertical pupils adding emphasis, they have the *idée fixe* of eating, eating, even when they choose to refuse all food and stubbornly die."

And then he brings humans, not just lawyers, into the field:

- "Turtles cough, burp, whistle, grunt and hiss and produce social judgments."

And then far-distant members of the animal kingdom are included:

- "They can stretch out their necks like a giraffe, or loom underwater like an apocryphal hippo."
- "They browse on lettuce thrown on the water like a cow moose which is partly submerged."
- "They have a penguin's alertness, combined with a build like a brontosaurus when they rise up on tiptoe."
- "Then they hunch and ponderously lunge like a grizzly going forward."

He even connects turtles to plants:

- "They're as decorative as pansy petals," he writes.

And to toys:

- "But they're also self-directed building blocks."

And then he returns to animals:

- "If one gets a bit arrogant he will push the others off the rock and afterwards climb down into the water and cling to the back of one of those he has bullied, tickling him with his hind feet until he bucks like a bronco."
- "On the other hand, when this same milder-mannered fellow isn't exerting himself, he will stare right into the face of the sun for hours. What could be more lionlike?"

And then he returns to humans again:

- "And he's at home in or out of the water and does lots of metaphysical tilting. He sinks and rises, with an infinity of levels to choose from; or, elongating himself, he climbs out on the land again to perambulate, sits boxed in his box, and finally slides back in the water, submerging into dreams."

Turtles are humanlike, giraffelike, hippo-like and pansy-like. Hoagland's metaphors make a dramatic ecosystem. Everything's interconnected. Like the ecosystem that once existed in Hoagland's childhood backyard, this larger ecosystem is also threatened. But Hoagland doesn't decry or exclaim or say, where's my land, where are my turtles? Instead, he makes a larger, metaphorical case that suggests if we don't see that interconnectedness, we too could end up metaphorically burying ourselves in the sand.

Or, to continue the metaphor of the boat, if you exclude the turtle, you're excluding yourself. It's like throwing yourself overboard, as Hoagland implies when he's trying to save a salt-water turtle from captivity, but when he throws it over the Morton Street Pier on the Hudson River, he writes:

> He was very surprised when I tossed him in; for the first time in our association, I think he was afraid. He looked afraid as he bobbed about on top of the water, looking up at me from ten feet below. Though we were both accustomed to his resistance and rigidity, seeing him still pitiful, I recognized that I must have done the wrong thing. At least the river was salty, but it was also bottomless; the waves were too rough for him, and the tide was coming in, bumping him against the pilings underneath the pier. Too late, I realized that he wouldn't be able to swim to a peaceful inlet in New Jersey, even if he could figure out which way to swim. But since, short of diving in after him, there was nothing I could do, I walked away.[6]

Hoagland never makes plain the case that what we do to the turtle we do to ourselves. But at the end, in the pathetic creature of the turtle, we see ourselves.

Perhaps the most lyrical essays seem to rely on metaphor, but even practical essays can find the use in them. For instance, if you were at a conference about climate change and your topic was the ecology of metaphor, you could provide metaphorical models for carbon sequestering—"carbon sink" is a common phrase for climate scientists, but imagine the inroads they could make if they could extend that sinking metaphor. Flush the particulates down the drain. Grow mycelia to pipe carbon underground. Trees as lungs. Ferns as carbon doctors. Antarctic ice shelf dismemberment. The emphysamitic planet. The planet with a tracheotomy and we intubating the planet by sticking a tube down its soily, sunken, wormhole. If only we'd sequestered oxygen instead, we could be smoking the ground. The failure to alert people to the calamity of climate change is a failure of the imagination to make good enough metaphors.

So lie to me. Make me good enough. Tell me I'm a saxophone, a tuba, a minor, plastic recorder—tell me how the sound blows through me like so much hot air. Tell me in your Catullus-like ways that I'm a monarch butterfly felled by insistent, righter rain. Tell me I'm a Pinocchio. A Parmigianino. A Cheerio.

*Or lie to me better.* Tell me I'm an oak of fresh air, or a dam in the stream of militant nonfiction talk. Tell me I'm a turtle. Make me feel better. Tell me carbon is a sink full of dirty dishes. Scrub the pan once, leave it alone, scrub again, the little baked-on grease comes away in the trap of your sponge. Sink the sponge. Tie it to the bottom of the ocean like the Exxon Valdez. Turn sponge into coral, make now-clean pan into your turtle home. We are all in the same boat, the earth is the ark and it's sinking.

But you're supposed to be making me feel better with these metaphors. So lie to me some more. Tell me drought is like goose liver: the particles and particulates worry you like veins and gavage but the paradigm shift from forced feeding to cherry-sauce means you can change parched mouth from dry-pity to seemly drool. Tell me, like birds, that words don't just fly, they land. Tell me that time I ate banana splits in France that you ate banana splits in France. That the time I walked in the front door and also thought you were standing in the mirror that you came out on the front porch, smoked a cigarette and remembered the time that you too broke the derailleur on your bicycle and you too and I too drove gear-free down the big hill and leapt off the road together and into something, or someone, else.

## Notes

1  *The Colbert Report,* Season 5, episode 11, directed by Jim Hosiken. Written by Stephen Colbert and Rob Dahm. January 21, 2009.
2  Seneca, "Asthma," in *The Art of the Personal Essay,* ed. Phillip Lopate (New York: Random House, 1995), 9.
3  Plutarch, "Consolation to His Wife," in Lopate, 19.
4  Kenko, "Essays in Idleness," in Lopate, 31.
5  Edward Hoagland, "The Courage of Turtles," in Lopate, 657–61. All subsequent quotations are from this text.
6  Ibid., 662.

# Bibliography

Aarseth, Espen J. *Cybertext: Perspectives on Ergodic Literature*. Baltimore: Johns Hopkins University Press, 1997.

Ali, Kazim. *Bright Felon: Autobiography and Cities*. Middletown, CT: Wesleyan University Press, 2009.

— *The Disappearance of Seth*. Wilkes-Barre, PA: Etruscan Press, 2009.

Als, Hilton. *The Women*. New York: Farrar, Straus, and Giroux, 1998.

Amis, Martin. *Money*. 1984. Reprint, New York: Penguin, 1986.

Anderson, Chris, ed. *Literary Nonfiction: Theory, Criticism, and Pedagogy*. Carbondale: Southern Illinois University Press, 1998.

Anderson, Margaret C. "A Real Magazine," *The Little Review* III, no. 5, August 1916.

Anzaldúa, Gloria. *Borderlands: La Frontera*. 2nd ed. San Francisco: Aunt Lute Books, 1999.

Atwood, Margaret. "Happy Endings." In *Murder in the Dark*. Toronto: Coach House Press, 1983.

Auster, Paul. *The Invention of Solitude*. Revised ed. New York: Penguin, 2007.

Barth, John. *Lost In The Funhouse*. 2nd ed. New York: Anchor, 1988.

Barthes, Roland. *A Lover's Discourse: Fragments*. Translated by Richard Howard. New York: Hill and Wang, 1979.

— *The Pleasure of the Text*. Translated by Richard Miller. New York: Farrar, Straus and Giroux, 1975.

— *Roland Barthes*. Translated by Richard Howard. New York: Farrar, Straus, and Giroux, 1977.

— *Sade/Fourier/Loyola*. Translated by Richard Miller. 1976. Reprint, Berkeley: University of California Press, 1989.

Bashō, Matsuo. *Narrow Roads to the Deep North and Other Travel Sketches*. Translated by Nobuyuki Yuasa. London: Penguin, 1966.

Baxter, Charles, ed. *The Business of Memory: The Art of Remembering in an Age of Forgetting*. St. Paul: Graywolf Press, 1999.

Benjamin, Walter. "On The Image of Proust." In *Walter Benjamin: Selected Writings, Vol. 2: Part I: 1927–1930*, edited by Michael W. Jennings, Howard Eiland, and Gary Smith, 237–47. Boston: Belknap Press, 2006.

Bensmaïa, Réda. *The Barthes Effect: The Essay as Reflective Text*. Minneapolis: University of Minnesota Press, 1987.

Bergvall, Caroline, Laynie Browne, Teresa Carmody, and Vanessa Place, eds. *I'll Drown My Book: Conceptual Writing by Women*. Los Angeles: Les Figues Press, 2012.

Berry, Wendell. *The Gift of Good Land: Further Essays Cultural and Agricultural*. 1st ed. New York: North Point Press, 1981.

Blake, William. *The Marriage of Heaven and Hell*. 1795. Reprint, New York: Dover, 1994.

Borich, Barrie Jean. *Body Geographic*. Lincoln, NE: University of Nebraska Press, 2013.

Borusk, Amaranth and Brad Bouse. *Between Page and Screen*. Los Angeles: Siglio Press, 2012.

Boully, Jenny. *The Body: An Essay*. Ithaca: Essay Press, 2007.

— *The Book of Beginnings and Endings*. Louisville: Sarabande, 2007.

Brady, Diane. "The Organic Myth." *Business Week*. October 16, 2006. www. businessweek.com/magazine/content/06_42/b4005001.htm.

Browne, Laynie. "A Conceptual Assemblage: An Introduction." In *I'll Drown My Book: Conceptual Writing by Women*, edited by Caroline Bergvall, Laynie Browne, Teresa Carmody, and Vanessa Place, 14–17. Los Angeles: Les Figues Press, 2012.

Bryant, Tisa, Miranda F. Mellis, and Kate Schatz, eds. *Encyclopedia. Vol. 1, A-E*. Providence, RI: Enclomedia, 2006.

Butler, Judith. "Critically Queer." *GLQ: A Journal of Gay and Lesbian Studies* 1, no. 1 (1993): 17–32.

Calvino, Italo. *If On a Winter's Night a Traveler*. 1979. Translated by William Weaver. New York: Harcourt Brace Jovanovich, 1982.

Capote, Truman. *In Cold Blood*. 1965. Reprint, New York: Vintage, 1994.

— Interview by George Plimpton. "The Story Behind a Nonfiction Novel." The *New York Times*. January 16, 1966. www.nytimes.com/books/97/12/28/ home/capote-interview.html.

Cappello, Mary. "The Trees are Aflame (A Two-Part Invention in Prose)." *American Letters & Commentary* (2004): 98–107.

Cather, Willa. *Death Comes for the Archbishop*. New York: Knopf, 1927.

— *My Ántonia*. Boston: Houghton-Mifflin, 1918.

— *O Pioneers!* Boston: Houghton-Mifflin, 1913.

Cha, Theresa Hak Kyung. *Dictée*. 1982. Reprint. Berkeley: Third Woman, 1995.

Christman, Jill. "The Sloth." *Brevity*, no. 26, Winter 2008. www. creativenonfiction.org/brevity/past%20issues/brev26hotcold/christman_ sloth.html.

Claren, Rebecca. "Land of Milk and Honey." *Salon*. April 13, 2005. www.salon. com/2005/04/13/milk_3/.

Cohen, Leonard. "Anthem." *The Future*. Columbia studio album, 1992.

The Colbert Report. Season 5, Episode 1. Directed by Jim Hosiken. Written by Stephen Colbert and Rob Dahm. January 21, 2009.

Coleman, Eliot. "Beyond Organic." *Mother Earth News*. December/ January 2001. www.motherearthnews.com/Real-Food/2001-12-01/ Beyond-Organic.aspx.

Coleridge, Samuel Taylor. *Essays and Lectures on Shakespeare*. New York: Dutton, 1937.

Cook, David. *The History of Narrative Film*. 2nd ed. New York: Norton, 1990.

Cooper, Bernard. "Marketing Memory." In *The Business of Memory: The Art of Remembering in the Age of Forgetting*, edited by Charles Baxter, 106–15. St. Paul: Graywolf Press, 1999.

— "Truth Serum." In *Truth Serum*. New York: Mariner Books, 2007.

Coover, Robert. "The Babysitter." In *Pricksongs and Descants*. New York: Grove, 1969.

Cortázar, Julio. *Hopscotch*. New York: Pantheon, 1966.

Cuddon, J. A., ed. *The Penguin Dictionary of Literary Terms and Literary Theory*. 4th ed. New York: Penguin, 1982.

Culler, Jonathan. *Structuralist Poetics*. Ithaca: Cornell University Press, 1975.

Cunningham, Michael. *The Hours*. New York: Picador, 1988.

D'Agata, John. *About A Mountain*. New York: Norton, 2010.

— ed. *The Next American Essay*. St. Paul: Graywolf Press, 2003.

Danielewski, Mark Z. *House of Leaves*. New York: Pantheon, 2000.

— *Only Revolutions*. New York: Pantheon, 2006.

Dante Alighieri. *La Vita Nuova*. Translated by Barbara Reynolds. London: Penguin, 1969.

Darwish, Mahmoud. *In the Presence of Absence*. Translated by Sinan Antoon. Brooklyn: Archipelago Books, 2011.

— *Journal of an Ordinary Grief*. Translated by Ibrahim Muhawi. Brooklyn: Archipelago Books, 2010.

— *Memory for Forgetfulness*. Translated by Ibrahim Muhawi. Berkeley: University of California Press, 1995.

Davenport, Guy. *Objects on a Table: Harmonious Disarray in Art and Literature*. Berkeley: Counterpoint, 1998.

Delaney, Samuel. *Longer Views: Extended Essays*. Middletown, CT: Wesleyan University Press, 1996.

— *Times Square Red, Times Square Blue*. New York: New York University Press, 2001.

Denton, Sally and Roger Morris. "Big Deal in Vegas and How the Local Press Missed It." *Columbia Journalism Review*. November/December 2000.

Derrida, Jacques. "Des Tours de Babel." In *A Derrida Reader: Between the Blinds*, edited by Peggy Kamuf. New York: Columbia University Press, 1991.

— "The Law of Genre." Translated by Avital Ronell. *Critical Inquiry* 7 (Autumn 1980): 55–81.

Dickinson, Emily. "If Ever the Lid Gets Off My Head." In *The Poems of Emily Dickinson*, edited by Ralph William Franklin, 264. Cambridge, MA: Harvard University Press, 1999.

Dillard, Annie. *Living By Fiction*. New York: Harper & Row, 1982.

Dostoevsky, Fyodor. *A Writer's Diary*. Vol. 1, 1873–1876. Translated by Kenneth Lanks. Chicago: Northwestern University Press, 1997.

Doty, Mark. *Still Life with Oysters and Lemon*. Boston: Beacon Press, 2002.

Duras, Marguerite. *L'Amour*. Translated by Kazim Ali and Libby Murphy. Rochester, New York: Open Letter, 2013.

— *The Lover*. 1984. Translated by Barbara Bray. New York: Pantheon, 1998.

— *The Malady of Death*. Translated by Barbara Bray. Reprint. New York: Grove Press, 1994.

— *The North China Lover*. Translated by Leigh Hafrey. New York: The New Press, 2008.

— *The Ravishing of Lol Stein*. Translated by Richard Seaver. New York: Grove Press, 1966.

— *The Vice-Consul*. Translated by Eileen Ellenbogen. 1st ed. New York: Pantheon, 1987.

DuPlessis, Rachel Blau. "*f* words: An Essay on the Essay." *American Literature* 68, no. 1 (March 1996): 15–45. www.jstor.org/pss/2927538.

Egan, Timothy. "After the Deluge." *New York Times*. August 13, 2009. www. nytimes.com/2009/08/16/books/review/Egan-t.html?pagewanted=all.

Eggers, David. Interview by Sara Corbett. "Lost and Found." *Salon*. November 13, 2006. www.salon.com/2006/11/13/eggers_38/singleton/.

— *What Is The What: The Autobiography of Valentino Achak Deng*. San Francisco: McSweeney's, 2006.

— *Zeitoun*. New York: Vintage, 2009.

Elbaz, Gilad. Quoted in Quentin Hardy. "Just the Facts. Yes, All of Them." *New York Times*. March 24, 2012. www.nytimes.com/2012/03/25/business/ factuals-gil-elbaz-wants-to-gather-the-data-universe.html?pagewanted=all.

Elbow, Peter. *Everyone Can Write: Essays Toward a Hopeful Theory of Writing and Teaching Writing*. New York: Oxford University Press, 2000.

Emerson, Ralph Waldo. *The Topical Notebooks of Ralph Waldo Emerson*. Vol. 2. Edited by Ronald A. Bosco. Columbia, MO: University of Missouri Press, 1993.

Epstein, Mikhail. *Emory Improvisations Home Page*. Emory University. www. emory.edu/INTELNET/impro_home.html.

Felman, Shoshana and Dori Laub, M. D. *Testimony: Crises of Witnessing in Literature, Psychoanalysis, and History*. New York: Routledge, 1992.

Foucault, Michel. "Friendship as a Way of Life." In *Foucault Live: Collected Interviews, 1961–1984*, edited by Sylvère Lotringer, 308–12. New York: Semiotext(e), 1996.

— *The History of Sexuality*. Vol. 3, *The Care of the Self*. Translated by Robert Hurley. New York: Vintage, 1986.

Frey, James. *A Million Little Pieces*. New York: Doubleday, 2003.

Frow, John. *Genre, The New Critical Idiom*. Abingdon: Routledge, 2005.

Gass, William H. "The Art of Self: Autobiography in an Age of Narcissism." *Harper's*, May 1994, 43–52.

Genette, Gérard. *The Architext*. Translated by Jane E. Lewin. Berkeley: U. C. Berkeley, 1992.

Gilb, Dagoberto. *Gritos: Essays*. New York: Grove Press, 2004.

Gilmore, Leigh. *The Limits of Autobiography: Trauma and Testimony*. Ithaca: Cornell University Press, 2001.

Gilmore, Mikal. "Family Album." In *The Granta Book of the Family*, edited by Bill Buford, 301–36. New York: Granta Books, 1997.

Gladstone, Brooke. "The Art of Self-Surveillance." *On the Media*, NPR, November 11, 2011.

Goldsmith, Kenneth. *Uncreative Writing: Managing Language in the Digital Age*. New York: Columbia University Press, 2011.

Gordon, Mary. *Seeing Through Places*. New York: Touchstone, 2000.

Gregerson, Linda. "Rhetorical Contract in the Erotic Poem." In *Radiant Lyre: Essays on Lyric Poetry*, edited by David Baker and Ann Townsend, 39–112. St. Paul: Graywolf Press, 2007.

Gutkind, Lee. *The Art of Creative Nonfiction: Writing and Selling the Literature of Reality*. New York: John Wiley & Sons, 1997.

— ed. *The Best Creative Nonfiction*. Vol. 1. New York: Norton, 2007.

— *Keep It Real: Everything You Need to Know About Researching and Writing Creative Nonfiction*. New York: Norton, 2008.

Hammond, C. S. and Company. *Hammond's New Supreme World Atlas*. Garden City, NY: Garden City Books, 1954.

Hann, Michael and Matthew Taylor. "Assad's iTunes Emails Show Music Taste from Chris Brown to Right Said Fred." *The Guardian*. March 14, 2012. www.guardian.co.uk/world/2012/mar/14/assad-itunes-emails-chris-brown.

Harrison, Kathryn. *The Kiss*. New York: Random House, 1997.

Heijinian, Lyn. *My Life*. 1987. Reprint, Los Angeles: Green Integer, 2002.

Hellmann, John. *Fables of Fact: The New Journalism as New Fiction*. Champaign: University of Illinois Press, 1981.

Herman, Judith, M. D. *Trauma and Recovery*. New York: Basic Books, 1997.

Hersey, John. "The Legend on the License." *Yale Review* 70 (Autumn 1980): 1–25.

Herzog, Tobey. "Tim O'Brien's 'True Lies' (?)." *MFS: Modern Fiction Studies* 46, no. 4 (2000): 893–916.

Hesse, Douglas. "Stories in Essays." In *Literary Nonfiction: Theory, Criticism, and Pedagogy*, edited by Chris Anderson, 176–96. Carbondale: Southern Illinois University Press, 1998.

Heyne, Eric. "Toward a Theory of Literary Nonfiction." *Modern Fiction Studies* 33, no. 3 (1987), 479–90.

Hoagland, Edward. "The Courage of Turtles." In *The Art of the Personal Essay*, edited by Phillip Lopate, 657–61. New York: Random House, 1995.

Holladay, April. "Why Do Rivers Follow Lazy Loops and Bends?" *Happy News*. August 25, 2007. www.happynews.com/news/8252007/why-rivers-follow-lazy-loops-bends.htm.

Howard, Sir Albert. *An Agricultural Testiment*. Oxford: Oxford University Press, 1943.

Hurston, Zora Neale. *Tell My Horse: Voodoo and Life in Haiti and Jamaica*. New York: Harper & Row, 1938 and 1966.

James, Henry. "The Art of Fiction." *Longman's Magazine*, September 1884. In *Henry James: Literary Criticism*. Vol. 1. New York: Library of America, 1984: 44–65.

— *The Selected Letters of Henry James*, edited by Leon Edel. New York: Farrar, Straus and Giroux, 1955.

James, Ken. Introduction to *Longer Views: Extended Essays*, by Samuel R. Delaney. Middletown, CT: Wesleyan University Press, 1996.

Johnson, B. S. *The Unfortunates*. 1969. Reprint, New York: New Directions, 2007.

Junger, Sebastian. *The Perfect Storm*. New York: Norton, 1997.

Keen, Suzanne. *Narrative Form*. New York: Palgrave MacMillan, 2003.

Kenko. "Essays in Idleness." In *The Art of the Personal Essay*, edited by Phillip Lopate, 30–7. New York: Random House, 1995.

King, Amy. "The *What Else* of Queer Poetry." *Free Verse: A Journal of Contemporary Poetry and Poetics* (Winter 2009): <http://english.chass.ncsu.edu/freeverse/Archives/Winter_2009/prose/A_King.html>

Kroll-Zaidi, Rafil. "Findings." *Harper's*, December 2011. www.harpers.org/archive/2012/05/0083912

Lamb, Charles. "New Year's Eve." In *Elia and the Last Essays of Elia*, edited by E. V. Lucas. London: Methuen & Co, 1903.

Lopate, Philip, ed. *The Art of the Personal Essay*. New York: Random House, 1995.

Lounsberry, Barbara. *The Art of Fact: Contemporary Artists of Nonfiction*. Westport, CT: Greenwood Press, 1990.

McCloud, Scott. *Understanding Comics: The Invisible Art*. Northampton, MA: Tundra Publishing, 1993.

McEwan, Ian. *Atonement*. 2001. Reprint, New York: Nan A Talese/Doubleday, 2003.

McGlynn, David. *A Door in the Ocean*. Berkeley: Counterpoint, 2012.

McPhee, John. Quoted in Introduction to *Literary Journalism*, edited by Norman Sims, 13. New York: Ballantine, 1984.

— "The Search For Marvin Gardens." In *The Next American Essay*, edited by John D'Agata, 7–20. St. Paul: Graywolf Press, 2003.

McPherson, James Alan. "El Camino Real." In *The Business of Memory: The Art of Remembering in an Age of Forgetting*, edited by Charles Baxter, 62–78. St. Paul: Graywolf Press, 1999.

Mairs, Nancy. "Essaying the Feminine: From Montaigne to Kristeva." In *Voice Lessons: On Becoming a (Woman) Writer*, 71–87. Boston: Beacon Press, 1997.

Mallarmé, Stephane. Interview with Jules Huret, 1891. In Jules Huret, *L'enquête sur l'évolution littéraire*, 55–65. Paris: Fasquelle, 1913.

Mandeville, John. *The Travels of Sir John Mandeville*. Translated by C. W. R. D. Mosely. New York: Penguin, 1984.

Marcus, Ben. "The Genre Artist." *The Believer*, July 2003. www.believermag.com/issues/200307/?read=article_marcus.

Martin, Lee. "All Those Fathers That Night." *Gulf Coast* 22, no. 2 (2010): 33–42.

Martone, Michael. *Michael Martone: Fictions*. Tuscaloosa, AL: Fiction Collective Two, 2005.

Maso, Carole. *Aureole: An Erotic Sequence*. San Francisco: City Lights, 2003.

— *Ava*. Normal, IL: Dalkey Archive Press, 1993.

— *Beauty is Convulsive: The Passion of Frida Kahlo*. Berkeley: Counterpoint, 2002.

— *Break Every Rule*. Berkeley: Counterpoint, 2000.

Medina, Jennifer. "Doctor is Guilty in Michael Jackson's Death." *New York Times*. 8 November 18, 2011, A1.

Miller, Brenda and Suzanne Paola. *Tell It Slant: Writing and Shaping Creative Nonfiction*. New York: McGraw-Hill, 2004.

Minot, Stephen. *Literary Nonfiction: The Fourth Genre*. Upper Saddle River, NY: Pearson Education, 2003.

Molinaro, Ursule. *Power Dreamers: The Jocasta Complex*. Kingston, NY: McPherson, 1994.

Monson, Ander. *Neck Deep and Other Predicaments*. St. Paul: Graywolf Press, 2007.

Montaigne, Michel de. "On Some Verses of Virgil." In *The Essays of Michael Lord of Montaigne*, 1580, 1897. Translated by John Florio, 1603. World's Classics edition. Vol. 3. London: Frowde, 1904.

Moriarty, Laura. *A Tonalist*. Callicoon, NY: Nightboat Books, 2010.

Myles, Eileen. In Tisa Bryant, Miranda F. Mellis, and Kate Schatz, eds, *Encyclopedia*. Vol. 1, A-E. Providence, RI: Encyclomedia, 2006.

Mullen, Harryette. *Sleeping With the Dictionary*. Berkeley: University of California Press, 2002.

Nabokov, Vladimir. *Speak, Memory*. 1947. Reprint, New York: Vintage, 1989.

Nelson, Maggie. *Bluets*. Seattle and New York: Wave Books, 2009.

Nichols, Beverley. *Garden Open Today*. New York: Dutton, 1963.

Northbourne, Lord. *Look To The Land*. London: J. M. Dent, 1940. Quoted in John Paull. "The Foundational Idea of Organic Agriculture." *Elementals: Journal of Bio-Dynamics Tasmania* 83 (2006). http://orgprints.org/10138/1/10138.pdf.

O'Brien, Tim. *The Things They Carried*. New York: Broadway, 1990.

Oliver, Mary. "Wild Geese." In *Dream Work*, 14. Boston: Atlantic Monthly Press, 1986.

Orlean, Susan. *The Orchid Thief*. New York: Ballantine, 1998.

Oz, Amos. Quoted in David Remnick. "The Spirit Level." *New Yorker*. November 8, 2004. www.newyorker.com/archive/2004/11/08/041108fa_fact.

Perl, Sondra and Mimi Schwartz. *Writing True: The Art and Craft of Creative Nonfiction*. Boston: Houghton Mifflin, 2006.

Philp, Bruce. "Reality Bites, No Injuries Reported." Brand Cowboy Blog. October 15, 2006. http://brandcowboy.blogspot.com/2006_10_01_archive.html.

Phillips, Tom. *A Humument: A Treated Victorian Novel*. 5th ed. London: Thames and Hudson, 2012.

Plante, David. *Difficult Women: A Memoir of Three*. New York: Plume, 1996.

Plutarch. "Consolation to His Wife." In *The Art of the Personal Essay*, edited by Phillip Lopate, 17–23. New York: Random House, 1995.

Pollack, Eileen. "The Interplay of Form and Content in Creative Nonfiction." *Writer's Chronicle* 39, no. 5, March/April 2007. http://elink.awpwriter. org/m/awpChron/articles/epollack02.lasso.

Pound, Ezra. "Exile's Letter." In *Personae: Collected Shorter Poems*. New York: New Directions, 1971.

— "A Few Don'ts by an Imagiste." *Poetry* I, no. 6, March 1913.

— "Hugh Selwyn Mauberly." In *Selected Poems, 61–66*. New York: New Directions, 1956.

— "I Gather the Limbs of Osiris." In *Selected Prose*, edited by William Cookson, 19–44. New York: New Directions, 1973.

— *A Memoir of Gaudier-Brzeska*. London and New York: John Lane, 1916.

Proust, Marcel. *Remembrance of Things Past. Part I: Swann's Way*. Translated by C. K. Scott Moncrieff. New York: Holt, 1922.

Purcell, Rosamond. *Special Cases: Natural Anomalies and Historical Monsters*. New York: Chronicle Books, 1997.

Rankine, Claudia. *Don't Let Me Be Lonely: An American Lyric*. St. Paul: Graywolf Press, 2004.

Rilke, Rainer Maria. *The Notebooks of Malte Laurids Brigge*. Translated by Stephen Mitchell. New York: Vintage, 1990.

Robbe-Grillet, Alain. *Jealousy*. Translated by Richard Howard. Boston: Grove/ Atlantic, 1978.

Ryan, Michael. "Tell Me a Story." In *The Business of Memory: The Art of Remembering in an Age of Forgetting*, edited by Charles Baxter, 132–40. St. Paul: Graywolf Press, 1999.

Saramago, José. *The Gospel According to Jesus Christ*. Translated by Giovanni Pontiero. New York: Harcourt, 1991.

Schalansky, Judith. *An Atlas of Remote Islands: Fifty Islands I Have Not Visited and Never Will*. New York: Penguin Books, 2010.

Scholes, Robert E. *Elements of Fiction*. Oxford: Oxford University Press, 1968.

Scholes, Robert E., Carl H. Klaus, Nancy R. Comley, and Michael Silverman, eds. *Elements of Literature*. 4th ed. New York: Oxford University Press, 1991.

Seneca. "Asthma." In *The Art of the Personal Essay*, edited by Phillip Lopate, 8–9. New York: Random House, 1995.

Shapin, Steven. "Paradise Sold." *The New Yorker*. May 15, 2006. www. newyorker.com/archive/2006/05/15/060515crat_atlarge.

Shields, David. *Reality Hunger: A Manifesto*. New York: Knopf, 2010.

Sikélianòs, Eleni. *The California Poem*. Minneapolis: Coffee House Press, 2004.

Silko, Leslie Marmon. *Storyteller*. New York: Seaver Books, 1981.

Simpson, Sherry. "Fidelity." In *The Accidental Explorer: Wayfinding in Alaska*. Seattle: Sasquatch Books, 2008.

Sims, Norman, ed. *Literary Journalism*. New York: Ballentine, 1984.

Skloot, Rebecca. *The Immortal Life of Henrietta Lacks*. New York: Crown-Random House, 2006.

Slater, Lauren. *Lying: A Metaphorical Memoir*. New York: Penguin, 2001.

Soldán, Edmundo Paz. *The Matter of Desire*. Translated by Lisa Carter. New York: Mariner Books, 2003.

Solnit, Rebecca. *Infinite City: A San Francisco Atlas*. Berkeley: University of California Press, 2010.

Spahr, Juliana. *Everybody's Autonomy: Connective Reading and Collective Identity*. Tuscaloosa: University of Alabama Press, 2001.

Stein, Gertrude. *Three Lives*. New York: Vintage, 1958.

Stephens, Nathalie. *Je Nathanaël*. Toronto: BookThug, 2006.

Stoker, Bram. *Dracula*. London: Archibald Constable, 1897.

Sutin, Lawrence. *A Postcard Memoir*. St. Paul: Graywolf Press, 2000.

Tall, Deborah. "Terrible Perfection: In the Face of Tradition." In *Where We Stand: Women Poets on Literary Tradition*, edited by Sharon Bryan, 184–94. New York: Norton, 1993.

Thucydides. *A History of the Peloponnesian War*. Translated by Rex Warner. London: Penguin Books, 1954.

Todorov, Tsvetan. "The Origins of Genres." *New Literary History* 8, no. 1 (Autumn 1976): 159–70.

Walker, Alice. *In Search of Our Mothers' Gardens*. New York: Houghton Mifflin Harcourt, 2004.

Wilchins, Riki. "A Certain Kind of Freedom: Power and the Truth of Bodies— our Essays on Gender." In *Genderqueer: Voices from Beyond the Sexual Binary*, edited by Joan Nestle, Riki Wilchins, and Clare Howell, 23–66. New York: Alyson Books, 2002.

Wolfe, Tom. Introduction to *The Secret Life of Our Times*, edited by Gordon Lish. New York: Doubleday, 1973.

Woolf, Virginia. *Mrs. Dalloway*. London: Hogarth Press, 1925.

— *Orlando: A Biography*. New York: Harcourt, 1928 and 1956.

— *A Room of One's Own*. New York: Harcourt, 1929.

Wordsworth, William. "It Is a Beauteous Evening, Calm and Free." In *William Wordsworth: The Major Works*, edited by Stephen Gill, 281. Oxford: Oxford University Press, 1984.

Young, Kevin. *The Grey Album: On the Blackness of Blackness*. St. Paul: Graywolf Press, 2012.

# Contributors

Kazim Ali is the author of several books of genre-queer writing, including *Bright Felon: Autobiography and Cities* (called by some a book of poetry, by others a memoir), *Fasting for Ramadan: Notes from a Spiritual Practice* (called a book of nonfiction) and *The Disappearance of Seth* and *Quinn's Passage* (called novels). He has also published two other books of poetry, a collection of essays and several volumes of translation. An associate professor of comparative literature and creative writing at Oberlin College, he teaches also in the Stonecoast MFA program and is founding editor of Nightboat Books.

Eula Biss is the author of *The Balloonists* and *Notes from No Man's Land*. Her work has been recognized by a Pushcart Prize, a National Book Critics Circle Award, a Guggenheim Fellowship, a Howard Foundation Fellowship, and a NEA Literature Fellowship. Her essays have recently appeared in *The Best American Nonrequired Reading* and *The Best Creative Nonfiction*, as well as in *The Believer, Gulf Coast*, the *Iowa Review*, and *Harper's*.

Barrie Jean Borich is the author of *Body Geographic*, published in the American Lives Series of the University of Nebraska Press. Her previous book, *My Lesbian Husband*, won the American Library Association Stonewall Book Award, and she was the first nonfiction editor of *Water~Stone Review*. She teaches at Chicago's DePaul University in the MA in Writing and Publishing Program.

Jenny Boully is the author of *The Body: An Essay, The Book of Beginnings and Endings*, [one love affair]*, and most recently *not merely because of the unknown that was stalking toward them*. Her book of verse and prose poems, *of the mismatched teacups, of the single serving spoon*, is forthcoming from Coconut Books.

Karen Brennan is the author of six books of various creative genres, including the forthcoming poetry collection, *little dark*. Her fiction, poetry, and nonfiction have appeared in anthologies from Norton, University of Georgia Press, Graywolf, Michigan, Longman and Penguin, among others. She is a Professor Emerita from the University of Utah and has served as faculty at the Warren Wilson MFA Program for Writers since 1992.

Mary Cappello is the author of four award-winning books, most recently, *Swallow*, based on the Chevalier Jackson Foreign Body Collection in Philadelphia's Mütter Museum. With recent essays in *The Georgia Review*, *Salmagundi*, and *Cabinet Magazine*, and features in the *New York Times*, *Salon.com*, the *Huffington Post*, on NPR and MSNBC, she is the recipient of The Bechtel Prize for Educating the Imagination, the Dorothea Lange-Paul Taylor Prize, and a Guggenheim Fellowship.

Steve Fellner has published a memoir, *All Screwed Up*, as well as two collections of poetry: *Blind Date with Cavafy* and *The Weary World Rejoices*. He teaches at SUNY Brockport.

T Clutch Fleischmann's *Syzygy, Beauty* is available from Sarabande Books. A Nonfiction Editor at *DIAGRAM*, they live in rural Tennessee.

Kevin Haworth's most recent book is *Famous Drownings in Literary History*, a collection of hybrid essays. He is also the author of the novel *The Discontinuity of Small Things* and the essay chapbook *Far Out All My Life*, and editor of *Lit From Within: Contemporary Masters on the Art and Craft of Writing*. He teaches at Ohio University and at Tel Aviv University, and serves as Executive Editor of Ohio University Press/Swallow Press.

Robin Hemley is a professor of English at the University of Iowa and director of the Nonfiction Writing Program. He is author or editor of eight books, including *Do-Over!* and *Turning Life into Fiction* and is editor of the magazine *Defunct*.

Wayne Koestenbaum has published 15 books of poetry, criticism, and fiction, including *Humiliation*, *The Anatomy of Harpo Marx*, *Blue Stranger with Mosaic Background*, *Hotel Theory*, *Best-Selling Jewish Porn Films*, and *The Queen's Throat*, which was nominated for a National Book Critics Circle Award. He is a Distinguished Professor of English at the CUNY Graduate Center.

David Lazar is the author of six books: *The Body of Brooklyn*, *Truth in Nonfiction*, *Powder Town*, *Michael Powell: Interviews*, *Occasional Desire*, *Conversations with M.F.K. Fisher*, and *Essaying the Essay*. Seven of his essays have been "Notable Essays" according to *Best American Essays*. He created the undergraduate and PhD programs in Nonfiction Writing at Ohio University, and directed the creation of the undergraduate and MFA programs in Nonfiction Writing at Columbia College Chicago. He is the founding editor of the literary magazine *Hotel Amerika*, now in its thirteenth year.

Dave Madden is the author of *The Authentic Animal: Inside the Odd and Obsessive World of Taxidermy*. He teaches in the MFA program at the University of Alabama and coedits *The Cupboard*, a quarterly pamphlet of creative prose.

Lee Martin is the author of the memoirs *From Our House, Turning Bones*, and *Such a Life*, as well as four novels, including *The Bright Forever*, which was a finalist for the Pulitzer Prize in 2006. He teaches in the creative writing program at The Ohio State University.

Michael Martone was born in Fort Wayne, Indiana, and is the author of several books of short fiction including *Four for a Quarter, Michael Martone*, and *The Blue Guide to Indiana*. He has taught at Iowa State University, Harvard University, Syracuse University, and currently, the University of Alabama. He is very happy that, now, his computer actually counts the number of words allotted (he has been given 100 words) to tell his life story, like robotic Fates, measuring out the length of the line, there, in the bottom frame of the window, cutting him off at the exact

David McGlynn's books include a memoir, *A Door in the Ocean*, and a story collection, *The End of the Straight and Narrow*, which won the 2008 Utah Book Award for Fiction. His stories and essays have appeared in *Men's Health, Best American Sports Writing, Creative Nonfiction*, and other publications. He teaches at Lawrence University in Wisconsin.

Brenda Miller is the author of three essay collections: *Listening Against the Stone, Blessing of the Animals*, and *Season of the Body*. She is also coauthor of *Tell it Slant: Creating, Refining and Publishing Creative Nonfiction* and *The Pen and the Bell: Mindful Writing in a Busy World*. She is a Professor of English at Western Washington University and serves as Editor-in-Chief of the *Bellingham Review*.

Ander Monson is a maker of paraphernalia including a decoder wheel, several chapbooks and limited edition letterpress collaborations, a website http://otherelectricities.com, and five books, most recently *The Available World* (poetry) and *Vanishing Point: Not a Memoir* (nonfiction). He lives and teaches in Tucson, Arizona, where he edits the magazine *DIAGRAM* (thediagram.com) and the New Michigan Press.

Dinty W. Moore is author of *The Mindful Writer: Noble Truths of the Writing Life*, as well as the memoir *Between Panic & Desire*, winner of the Grub Street Nonfiction Book Prize in 2009. He worked briefly as a police reporter, a documentary filmmaker, a modern dancer, a zookeeper, and a Greenwich Village waiter, before deciding he was lousy at all of those jobs and really wanted to write memoir and short stories.

Lia Purpura's most recent collection of essays is *Rough Likeness*. Her awards include a 2012 Guggenheim Foundation Fellowship, NEA and Fulbright Fellowships, three Pushcart prizes and finalist for the National Book Critics Circle Award. Her poems and essays appear in *The New Yorker*, *The New Republic*, *Orion*, *The Paris Review*, *Field* and elsewhere; she lives in Baltimore, MD.

David Shields is the author of 14 books, including *How Literature Saved My Life*; *Reality Hunger* (named one of 2010's best books by 30 publications); *The Thing About Life Is That One Day You'll Be Dead* (*New York Times* bestseller); *Black Planet* (finalist for the National Book Critics Circle Award); and *Remote* (winner of the PEN/Revson Award). The recipient of a Guggenheim fellowship and two NEA fellowships, Shields has published essays and stories in the *New York Times Magazine*, *Harper's*, *Yale Review*, and dozens of other journals. His work has been translated into 15 languages.

Margot Singer (coeditor) is the author of the story collection, *The Pale of Settlement*, winner of the Flannery O'Connor Prize for Short Fiction. She has received the Carter Prize for the Essay, the Glasgow Prize for Emerging Writers, the Reform Judaism Prize, and a grant from the National Endowment for the Arts. Her recent fiction and nonfiction have appeared in *The Normal School*, *Ninth Letter*, *The Kenyon Review*, and elsewhere. She teaches at Denison University in Granville, Ohio.

Lawrence Sutin teaches creative writing at Hamline University and the Vermont College of Fine Arts. He has published two memoirs (*A Postcard Memoir*; *Jack and Rochelle: A Holocaust Story of Love and Resistance*); two biographies (on Philip K. Dick and Aleister Crowley), one historical work (on Buddhism and the West) and, most recently, a novel (*When to Go Into the Water*).

Nicole Walker (coeditor) is the author of the nonfiction book, *Quench Your Thirst with Salt*, winner of the 2011 Zone 3 nonfiction prize, as well as a collection of poems, *This Noisy Egg*. She teaches for Northern Arizona University's MFA program.

# Index